# Otherworlds

ALSO AVAILABLE FROM BLOOMSBURY

*Technic and Magic*, Federico Campagna
*Prophetic Culture*, Federico Campagna
*Hypnosis Between Science and Magic*, Isabelle Stengers
*The Stuff of Life*, Timothy Morton

# Otherworlds

*Mediterranean Lessons on Escaping History*

*Federico Campagna*

BLOOMSBURY ACADEMIC
LONDON · NEW YORK · OXFORD · NEW DELHI · SYDNEY

BLOOMSBURY ACADEMIC

Bloomsbury Publishing Plc, 50 Bedford Square, London, WC1B 3DP, UK
Bloomsbury Publishing Inc, 1359 Broadway, 12th Floor, New York, NY 10018, USA
Bloomsbury Publishing Ireland, 29 Earlsfort Terrace, Dublin 2, D02 AY28, Ireland

BLOOMSBURY, BLOOMSBURY ACADEMIC and the Diana logo are trademarks of
Bloomsbury Publishing Plc

First published in Great Britain 2025
Reprinted 2026

Copyright © Federico Campagna, 2025

Federico Campagna has asserted his right under the Copyright, Designs and
Patents Act, 1988, to be identified as Author of this work.

For legal purposes the Acknowledgements on p. viii constitute an extension of this
copyright page.

Cover design by Federico Antonini
Cover image: Limestone plaque with two eyes. Cypriot. 480–310 BCE.
The Cesnola Collection, Purchased by subscription, 1874–76
© The Metropolitan Museum of Art
Map image © Rain Wu

All rights reserved. No part of this publication may be: i) reproduced or transmitted
in any form, electronic or mechanical, including photocopying, recording or by
means of any information storage or retrieval system without prior permission in
writing from the publishers; or ii) used or reproduced in any way for the training,
development or operation of artificial intelligence (AI) technologies, including
generative AI technologies. The rights holders expressly reserve this publication
from the text and data mining exception as per Article 4(3) of the Digital Single
Market Directive (EU) 2019/790.

Bloomsbury Publishing Plc does not have any control over, or responsibility for, any
third-party websites referred to or in this book. All internet addresses given in this
book were correct at the time of going to press. The author and publisher regret
any inconvenience caused if addresses have changed or sites have ceased to exist,
but can accept no responsibility for any such changes.

A catalogue record for this book is available from the British Library.

A catalog record for this book is available from the Library of Congress.

ISBN: HB: 978-1-3505-3639-5
PB: 978-1-3505-3638-8
ePDF: 978-1-3505-3640-1
eBook: 978-1-3505-3641-8

Typeset Deanta Global Publishing Services, Chennai, India
Printed and bound in Great Britain

For product safety related questions contact productsafety@bloomsbury.com.

To find out more about our authors and books visit www.bloomsbury.com and
sign up for our newsletters.

Per Arturo e Rain,
il mio arcipelago.

History isn't
the devastating bulldozer they say it is.
It leaves underpasses, crypts, holes
and hiding places.[1]

# Contents

*Acknowledgements* viii

Introduction: Seasons 1

1 Mortals: The Bronze Age 13
  Meanwhile in the Mediterranean . . . : Second millennium BC to fourth century BC 67

2 Foreigners: Hellenism 69
  Meanwhile in the Mediterranean . . . : Fourth century BC to sixth century AD 119

3 Cosmonauts: Late Antiquity 121
  Meanwhile in the Mediterranean . . . : Sixth century to fifteenth century 177

4 Translators: The Middle Ages 179
  Meanwhile in the Mediterranean . . . : Fifteenth century to seventeenth century 231

5 Traitors: Modernity 233
  Meanwhile in the Mediterranean . . . : Seventeenth century to twentieth century 283

6 Migrants: The contemporary age 285

*Notes* 327
*Bibliography and Further Reading* 343
*Index* 367

# *Acknowledgements*

The writing of this book has been a long journey, one that wouldn't have been possible without the help of many people and institutions.

The Warburg Institute, School of Advanced Study, in London, supported the research for Chapters 1 and 4 through a Frances Yates Fellowship, promoted by Prof Bill Sherman and Prof John Tresch, and under the supervision of Prof Charles Burnett.

Castello di Rivoli, Museo di Arte Contemporanea, in Turin, funded the research for Chapters 2 and 3 through a residency, promoted by Carolyn Christov-Bakargiev.

LUMA Foundation, in Arles, funded the research for Chapters 5 and 6 through a residency, promoted by Maja Hoffmann and Vassilis Oikonomopoulos.

My wonderful editor at Bloomsbury, Liza Thompson, championed this project from the start and helped me improve it throughout (also thanks to the assistance of Hannah Wilks), and my friend Leo Hollis from Verso offered his invaluable assistance while I developed the publishing proposal. Judith Gurewich from Other Press offered precious advice to improve my initial draft.

I would like to thank my dear friends: Manlio Poltronieri for helping me refine the last section of the book, and Andrea Bellini, Franco 'Bifo' Berardi and Corrado Melluso for their unwavering encouragement.

Thank you to my family, Elisabetta, Luciano and Nellina, who have always been a beacon of light throughout the years in which I have been writing this book.

Finally, thank you to my beloved son, Arturo, who, among many other things, taught me how to tell a story and to my wife, Rain Wu, who is my horizon and my anchor. This book is dedicated to them.

# A Synchronic Map of the Places Mentioned in this Book

# Introduction

## *Seasons*

The burnt yellow of the cereal fields around Prizzi, my father's village in the Sicilian inland, was at its peak. Under the limestone cliffs, resplendent in the sun, the black marks of the plough were eating away the slopes and valleys. In the high valley at the foot of the mountain, the cluster of peasant cottages was abuzz with a special commotion. A ceaseless chitchat poured through the curtains onto the clearing with the tractors and the manure, breaking the calm of a late August morning. Just a few weeks ago, the emigrants had returned from Germany. Now they were cramming the trunks of their cars with boxes of tomato passata, cans of oil, bundles of oregano. Whenever I chased a mis-kicked ball out of the stone arch of our house, I would see another group of elderly relatives lined along the potholed street. The emigrants did not tire of kissing and embracing them, one by one. The father entered the car, then the kids and lastly the mother. They waved their hands out of the windows, as if to disperse something invisible in the air. Every morning, one of those vessels with foreign licence plates and dashboards lined in synthetic fur started its engine and set sail. The relatives stood on the pavement until the car had disappeared around the bend of the highway. Then the women returned home, and the men walked slowly to tend to the cows. Another year would pass; who knew who would be missing at the next reunion.

It was during those late Augusts of my childhood that I first realized how the time of migrants differs from that marked on calendars. For a migrant, time unfolds along two parallel lines: the suspended instant of their lost homeland, and the rhythm of work in a distant land. To neither time they are completely present, in neither place they are truly at home. The border between these dimensions opens on specific dates, sad celebrations without a name. Even today, these thresholds mark my own time; as if, at the end of every August, I still had to get in the car with my family, take the road to the port and return up North, to Milan, where my own parents had migrated.

But to those who have never migrated, all this remains hidden – not only the seams between nameless seasons, but also other mysterious distortions of reality. They might ignore, for example, that every land exists in more than one dimension. In one of them, it is made up of buildings, trees, soil and water; it can be photographed by satellites; it can be reached by car or by plane. It is open to the return of those who wandered away, but only temporarily and never fully. In its second dimension, however, the same land does not correspond to any geographical location. While invisible to everyone else, it is always at hand for those who once called it home – they only need to search within their memories, fantasies and dislocated hopes. If both these dimensions are real, it is only the latter that the migrant experiences as their reality.

From their distant lives, strangers in a foreign land, migrants do not let a day pass without returning to their imagined homeland. Without formal training in metaphysics, they know how to unlock the doors between the different strata of reality, travelling distances that would seem insurmountable to others.

The Sicilian summers of my childhood, and the seasons my parents and I spent in Milan for work and study, fostered in me an early interest in the imaginary aspect of world-building. I knew by experience that the intuition of migrants – like the gaze with which only a lover can see the unfathomable depths of their beloved – revealed an authentic feature of reality. How little is within the grasp of maps, satellites and travel agencies! Infinite expanses stretch out beyond the material and measurable aspects of existence, perceptible only through the imagination and nonetheless entirely real.

Such awareness often dawns in the wake of a profound loss, whether of one's homeland or a loved one: suddenly one realizes, with a clarity that is no longer merely conceptual, that the material disappearance of an object does not imply its total annihilation. Even though it has become invisible and indetectable even to machines, some of its parts have remained intact. Materiality is only one of the dimensions through which reality reveals itself, and our ability to measure it with apparent precision has given us an exaggerated sense of its importance. The existence of an object – any object, be it a person, a land or the whole world – includes all the aspects that we can perceive through our imagination, stretching even beyond the field of the imaginable. The persistence of an object in our mind, after it has materially disappeared, and the life that it continues to lead within our imagination, engaged in an endless series of metamorphoses, reveal glimpses of its existence in dimensions that lie outside the realm governed by space and time. Indeed, it already existed in those dimensions while it was still materially visible; but its true extent remained obfuscated until loss finally unveiled it. Like the organs of physical perception, the imagination also discloses to us something authentic about the infinite wealth of reality.

What might sound like a fantasy born out of grief is in fact a philosophical intuition shared by thinkers from antiquity to the present age. Reality, considered in itself and as a whole, is a *chaos* so deep and immense that it exceeds any possibility of being understood or experienced. Even something as small as a pebble, if we consider it to the full extent of its existence, becomes a mystery beyond comprehension. We can detect only a fragment of this *chaos*, as filtered by our perceptive apparatus and cognitive limits. Through our imagination, based on our personal inclinations and on the cosmological assumptions of our society, we mould this remaining piece into one of the infinite forms that reality can take. This activity of the imagination provides us with a *cosmos*, a 'world': a place where we can develop those structures of sense that shelter us from the trauma of having been thrown unprepared into a mortal life. Then, spurred by the force of habit and by a desire for comfort, we become progressively convinced that the world we have constructed is an accurate picture of 'nature', and that reality coincides with the metaphysical consensus of a particular society at a certain moment in human history. We tend to forget the imaginary essence of the 'world' that we see around ourselves, and we start drawing hard distinctions between what we deem as 'truly existing' and what we set aside as 'mere fantasy'.

Over the years, this philosophical enquiry merged with a personal sense of longing for my own fantasy of a lost

Mediterranean homeland, leading me to undertake extensive research into the many ways in which, over the millennia, the people of the Mediterranean have filtered and reinvented their experience of reality. Towards them, who lived and died in societies rather different from my own, I felt more familiarity than distance. Studying the remnants of their literature and their artefacts, I recognized how multitudes of common people – not counting the philosophers and the theologians, who specialize in this sort of speculations – lived suspended between 'here' and 'there': the time and space imagined by their society, where they could be disciplined and punished, and another plane, where their surroundings were the product of their own imagination.

This is not a unique feature of the Mediterranean. But in the Mediterranean, this imaginary practice has developed a range of characteristics that render it worthy of special attention.

The Mediterranean has known moments of astonishing splendour, such as the civilizations of the ancient Egyptians, Greeks and Romans, of the Arabs and the Ottomans, whose impact on global history and culture cannot be overestimated. Each of these peaks, however, was followed by an apocalyptic catastrophe. Every great Mediterranean civilization eventually crumbled and collapsed, dragging the people who assumed its cultural values as their own through something which could justly be described as the 'end of the world'. The fall of a civilization does not only consist in the fraying of its social fabric, together with its political, economic and technological infrastructures, but also in the disintegration of its common sense of the nature of the world, which used to stand as the imaginary foundation of a meaningful life. When these fundamental values falter, and then eventually fall, *chaos* begins to seep through the cracks of the *cosmos*.

The peoples of the Mediterranean had to face a long series of such traumatizing events, accompanied by material disasters like wars, famines and plagues. In response to these cyclical apocalypses, they devised a range of radical strategies of survival. Whenever historical upheavals laid waste to their material and immaterial world, many of them decided to migrate in search of an elsewhere that would allow their life to flourish once more. They moved through space, like the economic migrants of which my family and I are also examples, but most importantly, they also moved beyond space and time, outside the confines of History. Instead of clinging to the values of a vanishing world or embracing those of the new rising powers, they dared to migrate to the ground zero of the imagination, where ideas and values can be extracted anew from the infinite virtuality of the possible.

These deserters from History had to face the hostility both of those who remained attached to the old world and of those heralding the triumph of a new order. Their quest to invent a different reality was often a solitary adventure, and even when they managed to congregate in groups, most of their sailings ended in shipwreck. History showed little mercy to communities such as the last Pagans of antiquity, the Manicheans, or the mystic Jews of the Italian Renaissance. They were systematically ground to dust, and their visions failed to prevail as a new common sense about the nature of the world. But despite their defeat, their invention of new *cosmoi* endured as a testament to how a person's vision of the world can be untangled from the dominant social forces, and the *chaos* of reality can be reclothed within narratives that arise from an individual's suffering and desire for life.

These otherworldly migrants and their poetic inventions have been my silent companions for years, until I finally committed to writing a book to retell their defeats, their achievements and their lessons. Unlike other histories of the Mediterranean, this volume does not aim to provide a comprehensive account of the events that occurred in the region, and even less it is a summary of its greatest moments. The pages that follow focus on the periods of crisis, during which the people of the Mediterranean were racked by cataclysmic transformations that they could neither reverse nor resist, except by migrating to an imaginary elsewhere.

Our journey through the Mediterranean imagination will begin in Mesopotamia and Egypt, in the company of gods and heroes, amidst the clamour of the comic battles that set in motion the creation of the universe. We will listen to the voice of the myths, searching for the earliest stories with which humans tried to make sense of the absurdity of being alive and to redeem the inevitability of their mortal condition (Chapter 1).

Next, we will travel East, towards Persia and beyond, along the path marked by Alexander the Great during, but especially after, his brief lifetime. Guided by the tales of the storytellers, we shall witness the chain of reincarnations of the great conqueror as the folk hero of multiple cultures and as a model for transcending any fixed form of identity (Chapter 2).

Our third stop will take us to Late Antiquity, during the tumultuous centuries that saw the collapse of the Western Roman Empire. We will penetrate the secret teachings of some of the most visionary sects of the time, such as the god-hating Gnostics, the ecstatic Hermeticists and the worshippers of the One, walking through the passages that they carved through the shrinking walls of their age, in search of other worlds beyond the universe (Chapter 3).

Then, we will range widely across the Medieval Mashriq, Mahgreb, Iberia and Italy, dragged by the dangerous currents of inter-religious war. From the rise of Islam, through the Crusades and the Christian 'reconquest' of Spain, we will follow the generations of translators who tried to bridge the gap between cultures at war with each other. Looking at their lives and work, we will learn the challenges and the unique powers that come with being 'citizens of nowhere' (Chapter 4).

The fifth stop will take us to the open sea, tossed by the waves that saw the adventures of thousands of pirates and slaves in early Modernity. The stories of those who became 'renegades', changing faith and country to begin a new life in a new world, will show us the life-saving virtues of treason and the imaginative horizons that can be disclosed by the practice of desertion (Chapter 5).

Our journey will end in our own time, from the catastrophe of the two world wars to the ongoing tragedy of the migrant shipwrecks in the Mediterranean Sea. We will reach port in the company of the writers, artists, philosophers and publishers who resisted the call to arms of the twentieth century, searching instead for a secret world that lies beneath the battlefields. The migrants of today, who challenge the established order with the sheer force of their bodies, will take us to the edge of tomorrow, in view of the new imaginations that are shaping the Mediterranean of the future (Chapter 6).

In each chapter, we shall discover an arsenal of stories – mostly taken from the extant historical, philosophical and mythological literatures, though with a diversion into fiction at the very end of the book – whose ability to revolutionize our own understanding of reality remains undiminished. Particularly in our own time, in which long-established ideas about 'nature' and 'facts' are giving way to a new regime of post-natural thinking and post-truth politics, the imaginary experiments recounted in this book resound as urgent invitations to begin anew the process of world-building, starting from the existential anguish at the heart of each individual.

But there is another quality that renders the stories of the Mediterranean imagination exceptionally important for our own era. Whenever the following pages present us with a new school of thought or a heterodox community, these will be hybrids that cannot be assigned to any specific culture, ethnicity or location. Due to the continuous catastrophes and the string of mutual conquests that have befallen this crossroads 'between the lands', the people of the Mediterranean have never been set apart by firm borders. Their cultures, ethnicities and religions have always overlapped, merging sets of ideas, customs and values at war with each other into an indistinguishable, syncretic mesh.

While contemporary politics insists on interpreting the challenges posed by a multipolar world in terms of hard distinctions – the warring rhetoric of the clash of civilizations, the zero-sum cultural game of integration, the mosaic of neatly separate identities imagined by multiculturalism – the Mediterranean suggests syncretism as an alternative method of turning the encounter of different imaginations into a moment of creation. Alongside the thread of poetic world-building in times of catastrophe, that of syncretism also runs throughout this book. During our exploration of the Mediterranean imagination, we shall travel along the fuzzy traces of intertwined cosmogonies (Chapter 1), cultures (Chapter 2) and religions (Chapter 3), assuming a perspective from which there are no firm borders between civilizations (Chapter 4), ethnic groups (Chapter 5) or nations (Chapter 6).

These initial remarks should not lead the reader to believe they are about to embark on a book of strictly philosophical analyses. To the people who inhabited the creations of the Mediterranean imagination as their own world, their power resided less in the impeccability of their conceptual structure than in the charm of their narrative. Even the most sophisticated theory remains sterile if it lacks the immersive quality of literature. Unless it stands as a story that can be experienced from within, like a game of role-play or a theatre piece, it fails to provide a convincing illusion of meaning and thus it is not accepted as a viable human 'world'.

This, too, is a timely lesson: if rational languages, such as philosophy and science, aim to offer a structure of sense for human life, they must recognize themselves, at least in part, as forms of literature. If they want to make their hard logical kernel inhabitable by living creatures, they should not overlook the need to translate it into the soft substance of narrative.

Since the infinite *chaos* of reality will always exceed the limits of any conceptual system, we should recognize that all our attempts at reducing it to a meaningful *cosmos* are merely 'likely stories' – like the *eikos mythos* of Plato's *Timaeus* – at once plagued by, and endowed with, the porous quality of literature. Every conceptual world' that we might devise is ultimately a story for us to live by, and the better ones are not those that reach closer to an absolute truth beyond our grasp, but those that are spacious and flexible enough to offer an imaginary home where a dignified life for all becomes possible.

Hence, instead of a linear history, this book will be a long arabesque of stories, intertwined and nestled into one another. Lurking in the gaps between these cosmic fictions, we will find the disquieting presence of *chaos*: the darkness out of which all worlds are born.

It will be a long journey, in the company of a cast of characters from every part of the Mediterranean – and beyond. The protagonists of our stories will be individuals without a stable home or identity, foreigners in a foreign land. Whether ancient or modern, they will struggle to find a resolution to the trauma of feeling radically displaced, thrown into a world that doesn't recognize them and which they do not recognize as their own. In different ways, each of them will use their imagination to create a bridge over this abyssal feeling of uprootedness – a reminder that the fortunes of humans are built on tenuous, fantastical foundations. Even when we witness their downfall, their story will be crowned by a happy ending. For the brief span of an instant or of a generation, in the narrow space of a written line or in the sudden vision of a different cosmos, they will have succeeded in projecting around themselves a world made anew, in which the need for roots no longer feels as urgent and dire, since everywhere has become home.

I hope that I will be able to give a sense of the Mediterranean imagination as an endless dance of summers and winters, where the steps of *cosmos* and *chaos* are interlaced and at times indistinguishable. The same dancing steps that I witnessed as a child, during a memorable Christmas holiday that we spent back in Palermo. When we landed at Punta Raisi airport, low clouds were shrouding the palm trees around the car park under a strange, ominous atmosphere. Our relatives had come to receive us bundled up in heavy coats, and in the evening, at dinner, instead of ice cream, they brought to the table the sticky sweetness of a marzipan *cassata*, the winter dessert. Then, one day, looking out from the balcony in my grandmother's flat, I saw the clouds break over the beige expanse of apartment blocks, and a wonderful sun appeared above the city. We rushed to the car and drove through the outskirts to the beach of Mondello. The street sellers seemed to have suddenly sprouted from the ground itself, their carts overflowing with fruit and vegetables. Beyond the metal fence bordering the pavement, still wet with rain, the beach teemed with people in swimming outfits. Enveloped by the noise of the swimmers and a faint smell of sunscreen, I pointed my nose up towards the azure of that impossible summer. The seasons had turned into one another so rapidly, in the space of a single day, that I could not believe they had ever been truly separate. With a shiver, I told myself that out there, in infinite space, there were no such things as summers or winters. Out there, in the night that surrounds our world, there was only a desert without time. But here, in our world, we celebrated every moment of summer, however short or implausible. Then, sudden as that day's sunlight, an ice-cream cone appeared from my grandmother's hands. I grabbed it, and all my speculations were swept away by the miracle of a summer day that had broken through the winter.

# 1

# *Mortals*

# *The Bronze Age*

### 1.

Before the flood, the Mediterranean was an iridescent land. Luminous towers of pink and white salt soared from the canyons splitting the arid plains. The milky waters of the lakes, evaporating in the sunlight, dotted the landscape with opalescent mirrors for the clouds. Herds of antelopes grazed the sparse vegetation that grew over the plains of red clay, while rodents scurried among the pristine deposits of grey flint. Along the lush paths traced by the riverbanks, elephants and hippopotami roamed freely between Africa and Europe.

To the West, an uninterrupted mountain range from Iberia to Morocco stood as a cyclopean dyke between the Atlantic Ocean and the Mediterranean depression. To the North, the East and the South, the land of three continents surrounded it. From above, in a sky yet uninhabited by gods, the sun of the Messinian Age watched over the imperceptible movement of the tectonic plates.

For over 600,000 years, the dry Mediterranean held its equilibrium, save for the occasional eruption, the erosion caused by the winds and the evaporation of the inner lakes. Generations of plants and animals followed each other as regularly as their movements across the vastness of the land. Then, something began to change. With every passing year, the waves of the Atlantic were breaking more violently along the frontier of the Western mountains. The sandy beaches were disappearing, swallowed by the ocean, and salty swamps were spreading inland, climbing even over the feet of the mountains. The sound of boulders crashing into the water reverberated through the air, while the rising tides eroded the aura of eternity that once surrounded the coastal cliffs. The Ocean and the Land, it seemed, had ceased to sit quietly next to each other and had begun to fight.

There was a moment, unrecorded in any history, when the mountain dyke stood for the last time. The waves were roaring close to its peaks, as the birds, flying over, had become accustomed to seeing them lately. Another wave pounded the rocks. From deep within the mountain came a rumble. Then, an explosion filled the sky, as if every rock had suddenly shattered, and an apocalyptic tumult erased all sounds for miles around. The head of the mountain collapsed on itself, and the rest crumbled down towards the eastern valley. Flocks of birds sprang out of the foliage, while an indistinct tangle of animal fur, tree trunks, soil and stones vanished in a cloud of dust. Then, with an immense roar, the waves of the Atlantic pushed their way through the narrow passage that had opened. It was a horizontal waterfall, an explosive river like no other. The waters of every ocean seemed to be rushing there, as if each drop wanted to be the first to reconquer the land that had once belonged to the primeval ocean of Tethys.

The water took less than a year to fill the Mediterranean basin from Gibraltar to Sicily. It rested a little against a second mountain chain, between Libya and Italy; then it broke through and flooded the lowlands to the edges of the Middle East. The arid valleys, the iridescent salt mounds, the lush riverbeds, the birds' nests hidden among the trees, the canyons, the hills – everything was obliterated. Only the highest plateaus were spared by the catastrophe.

The creatures that had survived the flood found themselves cut off from their usual migration routes. Some walked for miles along the coast of newly formed peninsulas, looking for a way out. Others had been imprisoned on enchanted islands, where predators were few and the new humid climate promised an endless abundance of foliage. The stranded elephants of Sicily and the hippopotami of Cyprus, unencumbered by the harshness of their past environment, began to shrink in size. Flies and insects, confused by the changing boundaries of the landscape, formed new groups and branched off in ever-increasing differentiation.

A new world had started, which was to last for millions of years. It was in this new world that the bands of early humans coming from Africa and Asia first encountered the Mediterranean Sea.[1]

What did they think, as they first walked along its beaches? How did they imagine the nature and essence of that newly discovered sea? Did they have any notion of the flood that had preceded their arrival?

Indeed, it would be tempting to delve into their thoughts and imaginations. But our knowledge of those early humans is no greater than our knowledge of past geological eras. The only evidence we have for their existence is the faint trace left by their dwellings, paintings, tools and bones, as discovered by archaeologists. Nothing remains that might grant us access to their mind. Even when a finding lends itself to a possible interpretation, it is impossible for us to deduce from it anything certain about the narratives that unfolded in their inner world.

The problem, of course, is the lack of written records. Without texts, any hypothesis regarding their belief systems or their social organization can only be largely arbitrary. Comparisons with the few groups living today in 'palaeolithic' conditions are of little help. There is little in common between the context of today's San people (or Bushmen), barely surviving in scraps of land in Southern Africa, and that of the first Mediterranean people who had entire continents at their disposal. Without written records, archaeologists and ethno-anthropologists can only speculate about the mental narratives of prehistoric people or project onto them their own imaginations.[2]

It is only with the advent of writing, in the fourth millennium BC, that we can begin to trace the earliest development of the Mediterranean imagination. To find the first stories used by the Mediterranean people to make sense of their world, our journey must now take a long leap across the eras, far beyond the time of the Palaeolithic tribes and the Neolithic villages. Compressing millennia in the space of a few lines, we shall travel to the days of the flourishing civilizations of Mesopotamia and Egypt, following the trail of written tablets and wall paintings that have emerged from the dry soil of North-Eastern Africa and Iraq. Through the fragments that have survived from that time, we shall listen to the earliest myths about the dawn of creation, the forces fighting for supremacy over the universe, and the place reserved in the cosmos for those wretched creatures: the humans.

## 2.

Myths are better listened to than read. They flowed from mouth to ear for centuries, generation to generation, before settling into a written form. As they were narrated, the listener could close their eyes, forget their surroundings and watch the story projected in the twilight of their inner theatre. Gods and goddesses, heroes and monsters, walked over the mental stage where each person, at every instant, creates a meaningful story for their life in the world. Only with mythology, this process lost its habitual discretion. While everyday thoughts about the 'good', or a person's identity, or the rules of 'nature', maintain a low enough profile as to pass for the limpid stream of rational thinking, myths took over our inner scene with riotous clamour. Their wildness and brutality were not meant to shock but to strip the human imagination of the cloak that usually keeps its workings invisible. If mythological figures appeared implausible while at the same time demanding to be believed, it was to remind their listeners that the same contradiction befell the mundane thoughts with which they furnished their own world.

Let us consider, for example, the basic concepts that underpin our own experience of everyday life. How can we believe ourselves to be unique individuals, with a name and a character of our own, when we know very well that our living body is the ever-changing product of countless microscopic organisms living in symbiosis with the environment? How can we pretend to be surrounded by a world made of distinct objects, when we are aware that all elements of space are seamlessly conjoined and sustained by the same ineffable spark of existence? How can we sustain the notion of linear time, if a moment of panic or a period of grief suffices to collapse past, present and future into an instant without duration?

Yet we must keep hold of these fictions. We must believe that each person is an individual, that each object stands by itself and that yesterday is different from tomorrow. Were we to renounce the possibility of making sense of reality through them, the world around us would melt into a chaotic expanse, and we would no longer be able to sustain the absurdity of our lives.

Here rests the need for mythology, in antiquity as in modernity. When we listen to the incredible stories of gods and heroes, we rehearse the motions through which we too, every day, endow ourselves with the possibility of being someone, going somewhere, chasing something. Myths are windows opening onto the backstage of our imagination, where the scenography of the world reveals its scaffolding. They unsettle and reassure us at the same time. They show us that the ideas upon which we establish our life are fictions, but that fictions can help us bear our condition as mortal creatures thrown into an infinite universe. They turn our anxious floating through *chaos* into the feeling of walking over a bridge, and they teach us how to look at the abyss through a lens that diminishes its darkness. They show us that dreams and dogmas, make-believes and laws, are made of the same substance, and that the narratives that dominate societies are not sustained by any 'natural' legitimacy. They hearten those who have been made homeless by their fellow people in the name of an invented story, showing how they, too, can use stories to create a nest for themselves.

Above all, myths teach us that we, too, are stories, and that, like all stories, we existed before our beginning and will survive our end.

## 3.

In the beginning was the flood. A dark expanse so ancient and vast that it had had no beginning. The water covered the whole world, and it was the world. An infinite world. It was divine, original, female. *Nun* was the name the Egyptians gave her. Nothing surrounded Nun but her own darkness. In the deepest abysses of her watery body floated two minuscule beings, inert like seeds. Nun's unborn children were the two principles of good and evil, presence and destruction: Apophis, the devourer of worlds, and Amun, the hidden god. They had been sleeping inside Nun since before the creation of time. Then, at a moment without date, a mysterious object began rising from Nun's infinite depths. It surfaced from her water in the form of a blue lotus flower. When its leaves rested on the dark surface, its blue petals opened. A naked, androgynous child sat in silence at their centre. The child opened their eyes, parted their lips and from their mouth an immense cry rose through the darkness.

In that same instant, an imperceptible movement stirred the water of the abyss beneath the child. Apophis, the agent of destruction, swayed his serpentine spires for the first time.

So, time came into being. And the reality which it measured was made up of only three elements: Nun the water, Amun the child and Apophis the snake. But gazing upon the infinite desolation before them, Amun felt growing within themselves an overwhelming sense of loneliness. To counter this emptiness, Amun transformed their hand into a goddess and took on the male gender. Through his hand-goddess, he masturbated, collected his semen and put it in his mouth. Then he sneezed and spat. From his nostrils was born Shu, the god of air, and from his mouth came Tefnut, the goddess of moisture and rain. Having become a parent, Amun changed his name to Atum, 'the finisher'.

That was how, for the Egyptians, the world started to be populated. The waters disclosed their secret, this secret became good and evil, Amun and Apophis, then the force of emotion did the rest. The cosmos came out of sadness and loneliness. And the act of creation transformed the creator.

The feeling of disquiet that buzzes beneath each person's existence was also, in the beginning, the force that created the universe. The transformation that invests a parent at the birth of their child, an artist in the act of creation, a thinker who is traversed by an idea, also befell reality when it first became manifest. The same foundations sustain the person and the universe, the same forces agitate them both, the same fragile destiny binds them.

## 4.

The Mesopotamians had a different view of the origin of the world. Tiamat – as they called the primal waters – was indeed the source of everything. But Tiamat had a husband, Apsu, and a son, Mummu, with whom she shared her dominion over reality. From her, without desire or sorrow, a host of other gods sprang forth.

> When above the heaven had not (yet) been named,
> (and) below the earth had not yet been called by a name;
> (When) Apsu, their begetter,
> Mummu, (and) Tiamat, she who gave birth to them all,
> (still) mingled their waters together,
> And no pasture land had been formed (and) not (even) a reed marsh was to be seen;
> When none of the (other) gods had been brought into being,
> (when) they had not (yet) been called by (their) names (and) their destinies had not (yet) been fixed,
> (at that time) were the gods created within them.[3]

The new generation of gods produced its own offspring, until reality was populated by a crowd of divinities. Each god or goddess was endowed with special powers. And where there is power, there also grows the ambition to use it. A desire to reduce the primal *chaos* to order agitated the young generations. They gathered, plotted and set themselves about designing a new cosmos. But they did not have the time to realize their plans. Their noisy discussions alerted their progenitors, Tiamat, Apsu and Mummu, who decided to restore peace by swiftly destroying all their descendants. The historical tendency of an older generation to school their children by waging war against them finds its origin at the very beginning of the universe.

When news of the impending attack broke among the young gods, 'they hastened about; [then] they took to silence, they sat quietly'[4]. Who would dare to face the wrath of the progenitors? Ea, the god of wisdom, stepped forward. He took his magic arsenal, sneaked behind enemy lines and, through his incantations, he made Apsu and Mummu fall asleep. He slew

Apsu and enslaved Mummu, dragging him along by a nose rope like an ox.

The war was over before it had even begun. Tiamat was spared out of respect for her divine motherhood. But she did not accept defeat. She created a new god, Kingu, and took him as her new husband. Then she gave birth to a host of monsters, organized as an army.

> She set up the viper, the dragon, and the *lahamu*,
> The great lion, the mad dog, and the scorpion-man,
> Driving storm demons, the dragonfly, and the bis[on],
> Bearing unsparing weapons, unafraid of ba[ttle].
> Powerful were her decrees, irresistible were they.[5]

Led by Kingu, the forces of *chaos* descended onto the agents of order. And the young gods trembled with fear.

## 5.

The idea of an ongoing cosmic conflict recurs in Mediterranean cosmologies. A natural rift of enmity stood in particular between a father and his firstborn son. In Greek mythology, Uranus, the original god of the sky, was deposed by his son Chronos, who castrated him and dropped his testicles in the sea. Chronos, in turn, was overthrown by his son Zeus. With each cosmic war, the original chaos progressively diminished. But greater order did not produce an improvement in the condition of the world. From the Golden Age of Chronos, which knew no hunger, no poverty, no old age nor death, where monsters, humans and gods lived together in harmony, the world slid into the Age of Silver, then into that of Bronze and finally sunk in the rotten Age of Iron, where human history currently unfolds. Mediterranean imagination has never championed the idea of historical 'progress', nor has it ever been unconditionally in favour of order. There can be such a thing as too much order: the harder reality is pressed inside a grid of identities and differences, like a river constricted by a system of dams, the closer draws the moment when *chaos* will erupt and consume everything once more.

From an archaic perspective, this progression towards order, and thus towards catastrophe, was an irresistible cosmic tendency. However, the responsibility for its implementation did not always lie with the younger generations. At times, it was the older gods who fought against their children to ensure that everything would fall into its right place, on the path to self-destruction.

This happened, for example, in the family of Atum, the creator god of the Egyptians. As soon as his children Shu and Tefnut were born, they left their father's home to explore the universe. Atum detached from his head his own Eye – itself a goddess – and sent her to pursue his two unruly kids until they were discovered and brought back home. Alone together, having no one else with whom to mate, Shu and Tefnut united with each other and produced two children: Geb, god of the Earth, and Nut, goddess of the Sky. While Shu and Tefnut had left home in search of adventure, Geb and Nut had no desire to go anywhere. Their ruling emotion was love – a love so passionate that when they united with each other their contours vanished, and they started merging into one. For a moment, it seemed that the new generation was going to reverse the cosmic descent towards order, bringing reality back to its original, chaotic unity.

Worried about the consequences of their fusion, their parents decided to break their embrace. Their father Shu, god of the air, slipped between them and stretched his arms upwards, lifting the body of Nut. As he pushed down with his feet, his son Geb remained in a supine position, a solitary erection aimed towards his sister, his eyes glaring angrily at his father.

Thus, Shu created the atmosphere: a space of air between sky and earth where life could flourish and the sun had room enough to rise. It was the 'Perfect Moment', the golden and pink light of the first-ever sunrise. Shu's upstretched arms remained the symbol of life, immortalized in the hieroglyphic image for the *ka*, the life-force that animates body and soul.

## 6.

Meanwhile, in Mesopotamia, the war between generations was at its climax. Tiamat's army of monsters, headed by her new husband Kingu, was about to storm the camp of the young gods and crush their plan for a new cosmic order. Ea, the god of wisdom, whose magic had won the first war, was sent forward to stop their advance. But the sight of Tiamat's army assembled in the plain shook his heart, and he ran away. Another god was dispatched to the frontline, Anu, 'the mighty hero'.[6] As with Ea, the sight of the enemy melted his courage, and Anu also turned back. The young gods were at a loss. Lacking the troops to oppose Tiamat's host, they needed a champion who could win the war in single combat. As a last resort, they turned to a divinity outside their circle, hence below their rank, whose warrior fame had reached their ears: 'the valiant Marduk!'[7]

As when, in the *Iliad*, the Greek war council sent wily Odysseus to persuade Achilles to return to battle, so the gods sent wise Ea to speak to Marduk. But like Achilles, Marduk did not feel duty-bound to fight. As Achilles demanded that his honour be publicly acknowledged before he would return to the battlefield, so Marduk asked for a formal position of power in return for his help against Tiamat.

> If I am indeed to be your avenger,
> To vanquish Tiamat and to keep you alive,
> Convene the assembly and proclaim my lot supreme.
> When you are joyfully seated together in the Court of Assembly,
> May I through the utterance of my mouth determine the destinies, instead of you.[8]

As unpleasant as it sounded to the upper echelons, Marduk's proposal could not be turned down. Either they permitted a lower class of gods access to the levels of power, or the forces of *chaos* would soon overwhelm them.

Before accepting the newcomer as their leader, however, the younger gods demanded proof of his divinity. They summoned Marduk to the Court of Assembly and placed a garment in front of him. 'By the word of thy mouth', they told him, '[command that] the garment be destroyed. [Then] command again, and let the garment be whole!'[9]

Marduk obliged. He spoke, and the power of his word destroyed the garment. Then, through his word, he made it whole again. Like the *logos* (discourse) of the Greeks, the *hu* (naming) of the Egyptians and the *verbum* (word) of the

Christians, the Mesopotamian language was a force capable of performing miracles.

The Court of Assembly rejoiced. They had their hero. Marduk prepared for battle.

## 7.

'War', said the Greek philosopher Heraclitus, 'is the father of all and king of all'.[10] Ancient Mediterranean mythologies agreed on this point: conflict was one of the processes through which the world had come to be. And since all the forces fighting for cosmic supremacy had been born from the same universe, their war had the character of fratricide.

For the Egyptian imagination, fratricide became a key aspect of the latter part of their mythology, dealing with what happened to the second generation of the gods. Once Geb and Nut had been separated by their parents, the fruits of their union came to light. Out of Nut emerged their children Osiris, Seth, Isis and Nephtys. Two sons and two daughters, to ensure the possibility of reproduction. Unlike their parents, however, this new generation was not driven exclusively by love. Indeed, two of them, Osiris and his sister Isis, were so enamoured with each other that they had started copulating even before they were born. But other emotions agitated their siblings. Envy and hatred connected Seth and Nephthys, spouses and siblings, to the rest of their family. Fate had not been kind to them. While Osiris and Isis had been assigned to rule over the kingdom of Egypt (which already existed!), Seth and Nephthys had been relegated to the harsh wilderness of the Libyan desert. Instead of enjoying the lushness of the Nile riverbanks, they had to endure the infinite repetition of the sand.

One day, Seth went with some of his followers to a royal banquet held by Osiris in his palace. They arrived bearing a gift, which they ceremoniously deposited in the middle of the hall. It was a large wooden box, open and empty, beautifully decorated inside and outside. Its long, rectangular shape had never been seen before. The gift, they said, was for the person whose body would match exactly the space inside it. Osiris, excited like a child, insisted on being the first to try. He slid inside the box and, to his delight, found that the tip of his feet and the top of his head rested comfortably within that wonderful object. He could not get enough of looking at the brilliantly coloured paintings that decorated the interior of its wooden walls. A moment later, darkness descended upon him. Seth and his followers had jumped on the box and had sealed it with a lid. Trapped inside, Osiris felt a sudden jolt as his kidnappers lifted the sarcophagus. They brought it out of the palace, carried it to the seashore and dumped it in the waves. In the Mediterranean Sea, whose waters so closely resembled those of Nun, Osiris drowned and found his death.

Having just returned to the palace, Isis looked everywhere for her brother and husband. She searched the cities, the desert, the riverbanks. She travelled far and wide, beyond the borders of Egypt and all over the sea. Years of searching brought her to Lebanon, the land of the cedar trees, and there, encased inside a sweet-smelling trunk, she found the sarcophagus containing Osiris. Weeping, she carried him all the way back to Egypt, to the palace that had seen their happy days together.

The curse of mortality was not unknown to the Egyptian gods. Their long lives were not without end, and they too, like all common mortals, aspired for the immortality that could be granted only by burial rites. Thus, while Isis was preparing the funerary rites, Seth sent his followers into the palace to steal his brother's body. They butchered it into fourteen pieces and scattered them all over Egypt.

Once again, Isis found herself alone. Again, she took to the road.

## 8.

Let us make a brief pause, leaving Tiamat and Marduk, Isis and Osiris frozen mid-movement on the stage of our inner theatre.

Before immersing ourselves in the Egyptian and Mesopotamian cosmogonies, we set out on our journey in search of the ways in which Mediterranean people tackled their feeling of radical displacement and attempted to navigate their experiences of catastrophe. We met the first catastrophe as soon as we approached mythology: not the end, but the beginning of the world. Nothing is more disquieting, and more displacing, than being born in a universe of which we know very little, least of all why it exists and why we exist inside it. Aside from our own joy and suffering, and from the horizon of death that encircles our mortal existence, no part of reality is ever fully revealed to us. The myths on the origin of the universe respond to this perplexity: they unfold a layer of meaning where we might lie down and rest a little, gazing around ourselves without fear of being swallowed by the infinite universe. They do not resolve the riddle of reality, but they manage to bind it within the magic knots formed by the interlacing of their stories.

But then, as soon as the universe was formed, the myths took a different route. It was the time of family dramas, jealousy, ambition and wars raging between divine factions. What to do with all that? How can those stories soothe anyone's feeling of metaphysical displacement or save them from a catastrophe?

After the trauma of being born, the second displacement immediately follows: the discovery of other people, who appear to us just as impenetrable as the infinite universe. We cannot be sure whether they are real beings or mere hallucinations. Even if they were real, we do not know to what extent they resemble us: if they are possessed by the same feelings, if words resound with the same meaning in their minds as in our own.

We know, however, that their existence harbours a mystery as deep and unfathomable as the *chaos* that gurgles beneath the crust of the world. What is more, a gaze stares back at us from the face of another person, piercing us with an energy that is almost divine. Who are all these others that surround us? How are we to behave towards them? What do they want from us, what should we give them? In the myths, we saw the gods behaving towards each other in a way that transcends all notions of good and evil. Their behaviour resembled more the random changes of the weather than the predictable outcome of an ethical agent.

The gods, who live in the dark soil where reality sinks its roots, are not bound by ethical imperatives, and although they must obey a greater Destiny – the cosmic law of *tuche*, as the Greeks called it – this is by no means a moral law. The gods do not ground their code of conduct on abstract concepts, but on the immediacy of their actions. Their behaviour moulds reality, defining fields of friendship and enmity, of attraction and repulsion, in the same way that, a little earlier, it created the original structures of the world. The gods love without having to refer to an idea of 'love', they fight without claiming a moral justification for their wars. Through their very immorality, they reveal the hollow core of all ideas about good and evil.

As the world is the poetic product of our imagination, so too is ethics founded poetically by our actions; by the immediate, decisive gesture with which one accepts the pain of others as one's own or imposes one's own suffering over the desires of others. This is the (im)moral lesson of the myths: it is action, not abstraction, that founds our ethical choices.

But let us not dwell too long on such speculations. Let us close our eyes again, to regain a vision of the inner theatre where we left suspended the mythical characters of our story. Let us return to the midst of their dramas and struggles, where the fabric of the world is being woven.

## 9.

While the Egyptian divine family was being torn apart by subterfuges and treacheries, the war between the generations of the Mesopotamian gods exploded on the open battlefield.

Walking away from the assembly of the gods, Marduk equipped himself with weapons of his own production. A red talisman between his lips, an antidote against poison in one hand, a club in the other, bow and quiver hanging from his side. Behind him, in reserve, he kept the seven winds, the hurricane, the cyclone and the rain flood. The sheer vision of his might sent the young gods into a frenzy.

> Then the gods run about him, the gods run about him;
> The gods run about him; the gods run about him.[11]

He mounted his storm chariot and left for Tiamat's camp. Not only did he not tremble at the sight of her army, but his arrival spread panic among her monstrous troops, melting the courage even of her general and husband, Kingu. Marduk drove straight towards Tiamat. He cried to the venerable and terrible mother of all gods:

> 'Come thou forth (alone), and let us, me and thee, do single combat!'
> When Tiamat heard this
> She became like one in a frenzy (and) lost her reason.
> Tiamat cried our loud (and) furiously.[12]

Tiamat opened her mouth to devour her impudent descendant, and in that moment Marduk sent the winds into her jaws to keep them outstretched. He took the bow from his side, nocked an arrow and shot it into the opening, piercing her insides and reaching her heart. Then, he turned to Kingu. He subdued him and cast him in fetters. While the young gods moved in to surround the rest of army of monsters, he returned to Tiamat's corpse, lying on the ground. There it was, the immense body of the primal waters, empty of life and reduced to pure matter. 'The abortion', Marduk called it disparagingly. 'He split her open like a mussel and divided it into two (parts); / half of her he set in place and formed the sky as a roof.' He ordered the winds to keep

Tiamat's water up there and to not let it escape. With the other half of her body, he made the Earth, so that the world resembled a canopy.

Thus, the Sky and the Earth were created: out of war, matricide and dismemberment. A house whose foundations were soaked in blood and whose roof was weighed down by the dark waters of chaos.

## 10.

Meanwhile, Isis was walking across the vast land of Egypt, looking for the scattered remains of the body of her brother and husband, Osiris. She found thirteen pieces, with only his penis still missing. Back in her palace, she set to work to recompose her macabre load. She tore a long strip of linen to bandage together the severed parts, and through her magical arts, she connected them. She took some gold and used it to fashion a new penis. Then, turning into a hawk, she hovered over Osiris' mummy. As she flapped her wings, the air entered his nostrils and infused him with a new breath of life. He had barely opened his eyes when Isis returned to her womanly form and united herself with his golden phallus. She became instantly pregnant with Horus, their son and avenger.

The months of pregnancy felt bitterly lonely. The revived Osiris was no longer the cheerful god with whom she had shared the years of her youth. His body was wrapped in bandages, lest it fall apart, his golden phallus remained detached, and his skin had turned to the deep green of an ivy leaf. He had become 'the tired god': though alive, he was not really living. It was not long before Osiris bade farewell and left her, to join his kind at the threshold between life and death. He became the Lord of the Underworld, the fearsome but merciful judge of the souls on their final journey to the afterlife.

Meanwhile, their son Horus had grown into a boy. Isis had tried her best to protect him, both from his uncle Seth and from the rage that she could sense burning inside him. But even her magic arts could not steer his destiny off its course. The falcon-headed Horus, confident in his youthful vigour, had no intention of hiding from Seth. He went out looking for his uncle, determined to resolve once and for all the feud that had poisoned his family.

The two gods met at the edge of the desert, on the border between Seth's realm and the lush kingdom of Horus. The battle raged with unprecedented fury. Seth was stronger and more experienced, and had no difficulty wounding Horus, ripping out one of his eyes. At one point, he overpowered his nephew and raped him. But Horus had the energy of youth, fuelled by an inexhaustible rage. They continued fighting for days, years, decades. At last, with a powerful strike, Horus felled his uncle and cut off his testicles. In an ecstasy of blood, he prepared to deal him the final blow. He had just raised his weapon when Isis rushed onto the battlefield. She yelled at him to stop. Seth was family, and it was not appropriate for the gods to kill each other. Horus, incandescent with fury, stood paralysed by his mother's magic. Isis allowed Seth to return to his desert, wounded and defeated. As soon as he could move, Horus turned to his mother, and with the same weapon that he had not been allowed to sink into his uncle, he decapitated her.

Isis could revive any body, including her own, so she did not die. Nor did she lose her love for her son. But the same malign star of war, matricide and dismemberment that had shone over the origin of the Mesopotamian world also cast its light over the beginning of Horus' kingdom.

## 11.

Marduk was outraged to see that his victory against Tiamat had resulted in the enslavement of her defeated army. It was not compassion that moved him, but a sense of solidarity within his own social class. Tiamat's monsters were at least as divine as he was. Children of the progenitor, their blood was perhaps even more connected to the original source than his own. The younger gods had taken advantage of his victory to vent their own frustration. Having agreed to submit to Marduk, they now demanded that their defeated enemies, in turn, serve as their slaves. What remained of Tiamat's army was sent to till the fields of the Earth, to gather the crops and to burn them in sacrifice for the younger gods and their leader Marduk.

But Marduk did not take delight in savouring the smoke rising from the altars, or in beholding the beautiful order of the newly dug canals. The degradation of work befitted a machine, he thought, not a divine progeny.

Thus, Marduk decided to create the perfect working machine, to whom all services required by the gods could be assigned. It had to be a living machine, with flesh and blood, endowed with just enough intelligence to perform its tasks and with a lifespan long enough to ensure decades of faithful service. To this machine, he gave the name *lullu*, 'human'.

He communicated his plan to his peers: with the creation of humans and the liberation of all divinities from work, the new order of the universe was to find its final form. The prisoners from Tiamat's army enthusiastically welcomed his project of cosmic reform. Full automation by intelligent machines would grant them freedom and return them to their rightful status. In exchange, however, Marduk demanded their general Kingu as a sacrificial victim so that his blood could instil the spark of life into *lullu*, the human. The exchange was unhesitantly accepted. They seized Kingu, bound him in fetters and 'punishment they inflicted upon him by cutting (the arteries) of his blood'. Then, with the assistance of Ea, the god of wisdom, 'with his blood they created mankind'.[13]

Thus, humans came to be. Like the planet where they were to reside and the universe that contained it, they came out of blood, suffering and treachery. Their destiny was to be working appliances inside the great pavilion of Heaven and Earth. They were to work for the gods and obey their every demand, while remaining ignorant of the true meaning of their actions. Even though they were learning machines, capable of perfecting their arts over time, they would always remain machines. *Lullu*: the by-product of a defeated general sacrificed by his own comrades, the ransom paid for the freedom of an army of monsters.

## 12.

A dark view of human destiny was shared across the Mediterranean.

At the beginning of the Hebrew Bible, in the book of *Genesis* – probably composed after the Jews' exile in Mesopotamia – the arrival of humans into the world is presented as the fall from a leisurely paradise to a gruelling condition of work, suffering and death.

For the ancient Greeks, the human condition was a curse. One of their myths recounts how, during a hunting trip, Midas, king of Phrygia, came across Silenus, a semi-divine creature of the forest. Midas captured the creature and then, in exchange for his freedom, asked him to reveal what was the best thing to which a human being could aspire. Reluctantly, Silenus complied:

> Why do you force me to tell you what it is better not to know? A life lived in ignorance of your most intimate griefs is the least painful. But for humans it is not possible to have the best thing of all ... since the best thing for all men and women is not to be born. But the second-best thing after this and the first available to mortals, is to die as soon as possible after being born.[14]

According to the ancient Egyptians, too, humanity was marked by grief since its creation. In their myths, humans did not come from the blood of a sacrificed god, like the Mesopotamian *lullu*, but from the tears of a divinity. Their first appearance dated to a time before Isis, Osiris, Seth and Nephtys, when the creator Atum was still dealing with his unruly children Shu and Tefnut.

Let us return to that moment when we saw Shu and Tefnut leaving their father's home to explore the universe. Atum sent his Eye after them, and the Eye brought them back. But when she returned to her usual place inside Atum's head, the Eye discovered that during her absence, the creator god had temporarily replaced her. Blinded by jealousy, the Eye burst out with unfathomable violence. She stormed off and flew all over the universe, unleashing the power of her solar rays and destroying everything in her path. It took Atum a great deal of persuasion to salvage his creation from her fury.

Before storming off, the Eye had wept bitter tears. The first humans were born out of those tears, without any apparent reason for their existence. Children of divine anguish, they were bound to the destiny and the tribulations of the gods.

When Isis travelled through the Mediterranean in search of Osiris, they wept with her and assisted her. When Horus triumphed over Seth, they rejoiced together with him. Humans were also there, a minuscule presence in the background, when the creator Atum, having already outgrown his first name Amun, went through his second metamorphosis.

Atum changed his name to Ra, the god of the Sun. He took his place in the Sky, and from there he bestowed his rays and blessings upon his creation. His rule, however, was not unchallenged, since his children and grandchildren harboured the ambition of taking over his position as world-ruler. A rebellion started brewing inside the divine family. Humans, too, joined the forces of rebellion. And when the rebellion failed, the weight of the repression fell entirely upon them, as often happens to the lowest ranks of an insurrection. To set an example for all future rebels and to remark the boundaries of the cosmic hierarchy, Ra again detached his Eye and tasked her with destroying humanity down to the last person. The Eye flew off and glided down to Earth, letting her rays shine to the full extent of their heat. Wherever she flew, she left a trail of burnt cities and devastated bodies. No one could escape her. At the end of the first day, when she returned to rest inside the head of Ra, the largest part of humanity had already been destroyed.

## 13.

An accidental by-product of divine rage for the Egyptians, a mechanical work-tool for the Mesopotamians, an ornamental addition to the world in the myths of the Greeks, humans found a nobler origin only among the Jews, whose God created them in his own image.

Their general insignificance, however, could not protect humans from the wrath of the gods. In all mythological accounts, humanity hung in a precarious balance – literally, depending on their *preces* (prayers). The smallest sin was enough to imperil the survival of their entire species.

Inevitably, the time came when humans committed such a sin. What they had done was of little importance. Their original sin, perhaps, was being creatures of the world, bound to its cycle of birth, old age and destruction. Extinction, like death, was the natural horizon of their existence.

Thus, one day, the Mesopotamian gods looked down to Earth and felt displeased by the constant proliferation of human beings. Their growing number, their arrogance and the decreasing quality of their service persuaded them that the first generation of the *lullu* machine should be withdrawn. They decided to send down an immense flood, such that 'no man was meant to survive the destruction'.[15]

But the plans of the gods are seldom fully realized. The wise Ea, who had looked after the actual crafting of the first humans, sneaked out of the gods' assembly and descended to Earth to inform one of his creatures of the impending catastrophe. He chose Utnapishtim, who lived with his family on the banks of the river Euphrates.

O man (...) demolish the house and build a boat!
Abandon wealth and seek survival!
Spurn property, save life!
Put on board the boat all living things' seed![16]

Utnapishtim complied unquestioningly. He built a large boat and loaded onboard his silver, gold and cattle, his friends, his family, the beasts of the field, those of the wild and experts in every skill and craft. He had just finished his preparations when the rain started falling. It was a flood as swift and devastating as that which created the Mediterranean Sea at the end of the Messinian Age. It raged for days, annihilating everything over the land. Such was its destructiveness that 'even the gods took fright . . . / they left and went up to heaven (. . .), / lying like dogs curled up in the open'.[17]

Seeing the extent of the devastation, the gods suddenly realized what they had done. By slaughtering the humans, devastating the fields and razing the temples, they had extinguished their own supply of offerings. There was no one left to burn incense or to sacrifice tasty meat and beer for them.

The gods wept . . . [longing] for beer in vain.
The great gods sat weeping,
But, like sheep, they could only fill their windpipes (with bleating).
Thirsty as they were, their lips
Discharged only the rime of famine.[18]

Slowly, the flood receded. And a sweet smell of incense unexpectedly soared from the ravaged world towards the Heavens. The gods looked down to the place where Utnapishtim and his people had disembarked. The survivors were honouring with sacrifices those who had attempted to erase their kind. Relieved yet offended, the gods decreed that Utnapishtim deserved to be rewarded for having saved the seeds of life and to be punished for having defied their murderous will. Thus, they turned Utnapishtim and his wife into immortal beings and exiled them from the human community. The couple was sent to a desert island beyond the Waters of Death, outside the world. They would live there forever, cursed by their own immortality. It will be there, one day in the distant future, that the Mesopotamian hero Gilgamesh will learn from them the secret story of the flood.

## 14.

When the Eye went to sleep after a day of slaughtering, the creator Ra looked down to see how she had accomplished her task. The once beautiful cities of Egypt lay in ruins. Scattered survivors were wandering in a state of shock among the piles of charred corpses, looking for something to salvage or someone to bury. Ra instantly regretted what he had done. Another day of slaughter, and nothing would be left of humanity. He thought of calling the Eye off her mission. But the fury of the goddess was as quick to ignite as it was slow to extinguish. She would remain unstoppable until she had seen the fields of Egypt flooded with blood. So, Ra spoke to one of the survivors, a priest from the city of Heliopolis, and told him to have his servants prepare 7,000 jars of beer. As the servants began to work on the barley, a mound of red mineral miraculously appeared in front of them. Ra ordered them to pulverize it and to mix it with the beer. Once the jars were full, Ra ordered them brought out to the fields and emptied on the ground until the crops were covered with the red liquid. The servants worked all night. At dawn, when the Eye glided again on Earth, she saw her own reflection scintillating over the blood-red flood. She drank avidly, as if to swallow her own image. She returned home completely drunk, oblivious of her mission. From that day, the Eye would be known as Hathor, goddess of love and 'Lady of Drunkenness'. Humanity was saved.

But Ra's worries were not over. Like everything that lives, Ra was mortal. And old age was creeping over him. Lately, his mouth had begun to droop and drool like that of an old man. Soon, he would no longer be able to control the rebellions that threatened his rule. It was advisable to abdicate before someone took power away from him by force. That he did: he abdicated in favour of his son Shu, god of the air. But Shu had made an enemy of his own son Geb, god of the Earth, who had never forgiven him for breaking his embrace with his lover and sister Nut, goddess of the sky. Shu was rapidly dethroned by Geb, who, when his time came, passed the throne to his own son Osiris. After Osiris' murder, power over the world went to Horus, the avenger. After that point, the line of divine rulers mixed with that of the human pharaohs. Each new pharaoh took from his predecessor a power that had once belonged to the gods and assumed over himself the responsibility of protecting the world from the forces of destruction. His task was the same as that of Atum-Ra: preserving *maat*, the harmony of the cosmic order.

Up high, in his boat floating above the sky, Ra assisted the pharaoh's efforts. Now that he had freed himself from the duties of world-government, Ra dedicated his energies to fighting his eternal rival, Apophis, the god who had been born together with him from the primeval waters of Nun. Every night, with the arrival of darkness, Apophis' serpentine form appeared on the horizon. Its gaping jaws, as wide as the universe, were ready to swallow everything in existence. Every sunset, Ra fought with Apophis. Every dawn, the destroyer withdrew, and Ra emerged victorious.

Yet, one day, the fight between the two gods will have a different outcome. Ra will be defeated, and there will be no one left to stop Apophis. The Earth, the Sky, the universe will be consumed by the fury of the serpent. Everything will become indistinct again, as it once was in the dark waters of Nun.

## 15.

So far, our Mediterranean journey has gone from darkness to darkness. Stuck between cosmic wars and planetary deluges, reviled as an accidental by-product of creation, humans have emerged from these myths as the lowliest, most unfortunate beings in the universe. If the aim of these stories was to soothe existential suffering, we might start to doubt their efficacy.

We began by looking at creation myths, interpreting their randomness as a concrete example of the free poetry of world-building. We read the brutality of their fratricidal wars as a subtle lesson on ethics and action. But humanity's doomed destiny, upon which all mythologies seem to agree, how can we interpret it as conducive to anything positive? Surely, the feeling of being lost within reality can only be reinforced by the awareness that suffering is the central element of our lot as human beings. But this is not quite so. These myths speak of our suffering as unrelated to our mistakes as ignorant or sinful creatures. Beyond the sorrows that we can inflict upon ourselves, they acknowledge the feeling of a deep, existential misery, whose roots are intertwined, if not fused, with those that sustain our mortal lives. Even if we reformed our lives and our societies in the most equitable and rational ways, a kernel of suffering would still remain at our centre.

If this realization darkens our horizons, it also provides something precious to those who feel displaced in a chaotic universe: it gives a centre, almost an essence, to our being 'humans'. Suffering is the very rare example of something knowable with absolute clarity. We might doubt the reality of our name, of our identity, of the objects around us, of time and space as anything more than conventions – but when suffering manifests itself in all its horror, its presence is beyond doubt. If we wish to anchor our existence to something certain, we need look no further than the rugged cliffs of suffering. A human is that creature which is defined by suffering – so say these myths. To which we can add, as a deduction: a human society, if faithful to its destiny, is a community that is hinged upon the suffering of each of its members.

Between the lines of these Mediterranean stories about the birth of humanity, we can discern the blueprint for a community built, not around the fear of others or the will to dominate them, but an existential experience that resides within, poisons and defines the heart of every individual. This form of suffering is not a problem that can be resolved, or a load that can be aggressively dumped onto others: it was created together with us, out of our same substance. But while it cannot be dispelled, its burden can be made lighter. Just as a weight that would snap a single thread can be borne by a net, so this inescapable suffering can be shared by humans. Imagining that there is such a thing as a shared 'humanity', holding together those who live under a common destiny, is already a way of dispersing individual suffering across a vast net of solidarity. Out of the curse that was cast on our species, we can make an anchor; out of the mythic darkness of our origin, our community can make its flag.

## 16.

Life begins gradually. Shapes and colours surface slowly through the haze of a newborn's eyes. People, faces and names emerge one after the other in the great atlas of the world.

Death, on the contrary, breaks in with sudden clarity. A moment ago, a body was moving. A hit, a fall, the final assault of an illness, and it no longer breathes nor moves nor speaks. Death is the dark magic of becoming, the horrific face of time.

The discovery of death is the archetype of every trauma and the source of all fear and wisdom. For the ancient Mesopotamians, it was also the kernel of their most magnificent literary work, the earliest epic written by humans about their own kind: *Gilgamesh*. Its original title, *He who saw the deep*, taken from the first line of the poem, gives a sense of its cosmic scope and of the emotional power of its narrative. Rather than love, solitude, hatred, envy or ambition, the driving emotion of *Gilgamesh* was the shock of discovering mortality and its immediate afterglow, the fear of death.

This story begins in the city of Uruk, on the eastern bank of the Euphrates River. The young king Gilgamesh ruled it 'like a wild bull',[19] with no regard for his subjects. He exploited, offended and abused them in every imaginable way. Outraged by his behaviour, the gods decided to educate him on the limits of his power. They created a boy, Enkidu, and deposited him in the middle of a forest. Enkidu grew up in the company of wild animals, strong and honest, unaware of the ways of society. When he became a man, the prostitute Shamhat was sent into the wilderness to domesticate him. Her beauty enchanted him. As he approached her, 'she did not recoil, she took in his scent. . . . / His passion caressed and embraced her. / For six days and seven nights Enkidu was erect, as he coupled with Shamhat'.[20] By the time they left each other's arms, Enkidu had been transformed into a new creature. The wild animals no longer recognized him as one of their own. He had become incapable of keeping their pace, '[he] was weakened, could not run as before, / but now he had reason and wide understanding'.[21] Encouraged by Shamhat, Enkidu left the forest and headed for Uruk, ready to take his place among his fellow humans. As he got closer to the city, he heard about the tyrannical ways of Gilgamesh and the abuses he perpetrated on his subjects. He entered the gates of Uruk with a heart full of indignation, eager to punish the king. He roamed the streets until he found Gilgamesh on his way to exert his right of the first night with a newlywed bride. Enkidu stepped into the doorway of the bride's house, refusing to give way. 'The door-jambs shook, the wall did shudder',[22] as the two young men grappled with each other. They fought on, equal in strength, until their thirst for combat was sated. Neither had met before someone who could match them. They stared at each other in amazement. Gilgamesh recalled a dream from a few days earlier, in which he had seen a rock falling from the sky. When he had asked his mother to interpret it, she had told him that 'a mighty comrade will come to you, [a friend], and he will be his friend's saviour'.[23] A friend – that was who was standing in front of him now.

Gilgamesh and Enkidu fell for each other like two lovers. They spent their days together, enjoying the sweetness of youth and planning great deeds. They travelled to the distant Forest of Cedars, where they fought and killed its guardian, the great monster Humbaba, and together they fought the Bull of Heaven, sent against them by the goddess Ishtar. Their joined strength seemed limitless. The future, too, stretched ahead of them like the promise of an endless adventure.

Until, one day, Enkidu fell ill. Gilgamesh rushed to his side, took care of him and tried to console his sorrow. In a feverish dream, Enkidu saw the gods holding an assembly and heard them decreeing his doom. He knew his end was approaching. With his last words to Gilgamesh, he lamented that destiny had robbed him of an honourable death in battle. Although he was in the arms of his friend, he was dying alone. No one, not even Gilgamesh, could join him in his desperate fight for survival.

'Hear me, O young men, hear me! / Hear me, O elders of Uruk, hear me!' Gilgamesh roared, in tears, 'I shall weep for Enkidu, my friend, / like a hired mourner-woman I shall bitterly wail!'[24]

For the first time, Gilgamesh realized the horror of mortality. He too would die, just as his friend had died. Faced with death, he too would be alone. What use would be his power, his might, his wealth, when an invisible hand could take everything away from him? Like the Indian prince Gautama Siddhartha centuries after him, Gilgamesh abandoned his palace, shed his royal robes and started to wander the land, looking for a cure to his own mortality.

## 17.

While Gilgamesh was travelling broken by grief, deep beneath his feet, in the darkness of the Netherworld, the Egyptian god Osiris sat on the throne of the dead. He no longer concerned himself with the woes of the living. The living came to him reduced to their most essential form, enshrined in their soul. Osiris judged those who had died with the compassion of one who had also walked through the gates of death. His faithful assistant Anubis, whose kindness hid beneath the features of a black jackal, weighed their hearts against a feather resting on a scale. Some would sink together with their hearts into pits of horror and pain, where they would know the torments of hell. Others, light as birds rather than as feathers, would fly over towards the land of plenty. However, more perils would burden their journey to the afterlife. At each step, they risked falling and losing their way. But to those who managed to complete the journey, the Fields of Reeds offered the promise of almost-everlasting joy.

Indeed, for the Egyptians, nothing was endowed with permanent stability, not even the afterlife. As the god Ra grew older, and the outcome of his nightly fights with the serpent Apophis became more uncertain, so time itself approached its own destruction. Once Apophis would manage to close its jaws over the cosmos and everything would be dissolved again into the dark waters of Nun, the souls of the dead would also be liquefied – the evil finding their rest, the good concluding their allotted time of happiness. Everything would return to zero, before restarting.

Birth, death, rebirth. And then death again, and another birth. Time was cyclical in its movement and eternal in its return.

Over the centuries, the Egyptian people developed a deeper interest in this eternal aspect of time. Their interest, in turn, set off a chain of consequences whose ripples reached as far as Osiris' kingdom in the Netherworld. Once the age of the gods had given way to the unfolding of history, the once-insignificant desires and actions of humans began affecting the entire order of the cosmos. One of the most profound transformations occurred in the city of Amarna, on the eastern bank of the Nile River, in the fourteenth century BC, when the sovereignty inaugurated by Horus rested in the hands of the pharaoh Akhenaten. Like all royalty, Akhenaten had been educated in the cult of the crowded Egyptian pantheon. More than any other pharaoh, however, he was attuned to the subtlest philosophical vibrations of theology. To his eyes, the host of Egyptian divinities was merely a smokescreen that hid a higher and more unified divine essence. Behind all the manifestations of the divine, he thought, lay one sole supreme principle. He called it 'Aten' and took its name to define himself: Akhenaten, 'instrument of Aten'.

Such radical innovations are rarely favoured by the existing bureaucracy. Having waited in disgruntled silence during Akhenaten's reign, after his death, the Egyptian priests lost no time in persuading his adolescent son, Tutankhamun, to reverse his father's religious reforms. The god Aten was removed from his position as the unifying principle of the cosmos, and the original pantheon was re-established. Mentions of Aten or of Akhenaten were erased from the stelae and the statuary, in case they might have inspired future reformers.

But something of the brief experience of Akhenaten's monotheism remained nestled within the Mediterranean imagination. It survived partly abroad, in the nascent monotheism of the Jewish people (whose prophet Moses, some speculate, might have been a devotee of Aten),[25] and partly in Egypt, where it hid inside an object of direct pertinence to Osiris: the soul.

For the Egyptians, a person's soul was composed of several parts: *khet*, the physical body; *ka*, its vital force and double; *shut*, the shadow; *ren*, the name, together with other elements. To cater to the monotheistic desire that had remained latent after Akhenaten, the Egyptian priests focused their theological creativity on one of these elements: the *ba*. Literally translatable as 'personality', the *ba* is something closer to an essence. It is the unifying principle, at once immanent and transcendent, that makes a soul 'that' particular soul. Thanks to the *ba*, the disparate parts of the soul united to form the *akh*, the soul as it appeared, after death, to the supreme court of Osiris.

The Egyptian priests who brought back polytheism used the *ba* as the concrete metaphor for the divine spirit that animated the world. They insisted that the gods were many and that they were constantly at hand. At the same time, however, they conceded that all gods shared in the same divine spirit, which distinguished them from the things of the world and made them arcane. This divine essence – internal to the world yet hidden from it – was the *ba* of the world. A microscopic reflection of the divine realm lay inside the soul of every person, and each soul, in turn, was reflected on a macroscopic scale in the otherworldly, divine realm. Thus, when Osiris judged the soul of the dead, it was as if he was also judging the very essence of all the gods.

Through this audacious feat of theological creativity, the Egyptian priests used their imagination to reengineer at once the cosmos, the soul and the everyday experience of their people. They created a network of theological bridges between dimensions, connecting the things 'above' to those 'below' in an endless game of correspondences. As we shall see, they had just inaugurated something that would recur for millennia in the history of the Mediterranean imagination.

## 18.

For days on end, Gilgamesh wandered through the wilderness. He dug wells to quench his thirst, he killed game and wore their hides. At night, he rested and dreamt. 'O Gilgamesh, where are you wandering? / The life that you seek you never will find', he heard a god whispering to him. 'When I enter the Netherworld will rest be scarce? / . . . Let my eyes see the sun and be sated with light! / . . . How much light is there left?'[26] Gilgamesh cried in response. He was travelling to the ends of the world in search of the venerable ancestor Utnapishtim, who had saved the seed of humanity from the flood and who led an immortal existence, together with his wife, on an island beyond the Waters of Death. Among the humans, Gilgamesh thought, only the immortal Utnapishtim knew the secret to conquering Death.

He continued to walk eastward until he reached the twin mountains of Mashu, which guarded the rising of the sun. There he met the scorpion-men, who patrolled the passage under the mountains. He begged them to let him in. They stared at that strange man dressed in animal skins, marvelling at his crazy quest. 'Never [before], O Gilgamesh, was there [one like you,] never did anyone travel the path of the mountain.'[27] They urged him to hurry because he must pass the path before the sun starts its daily course, or he would burn. 'Run, Gilgamesh, run through the darkness, until it lasts!'

The scorpion-men opened the gate, and Gilgamesh rushed through the pitch-blackness engulfing the path. He ran for one hour, two, three, four. Five hours passed, six, seven. Gilgamesh kept running until the night entered its eighth hour, and the first glimmers of light began brightening the air. One instant before sunrise, he reached the end of the path. On the other side of the mountain, he stopped to catch his breath. Gardens of jewels and gemstones surrounded him, as far as his eye could see. Truly, he could tell that he had crossed the frontiers of the world.

He continued his journey without knowing where he was going, since the sun and the stars no longer shone above him, until he reached the shores of the great Sea that encircled all dry lands, except one. Only a stretch of water separated him from the island of Utnapishtim. On the seashore, he found Utnapishtim's ferryman and his crew of animated stone rowers resting after their latest journey. Wielding his axe like a fury, he jumped on the stone rowers and smashed them to pieces. Then he overpowered the ferryman and ordered him to take him across the waters. 'In three days, they made a journey of a month and a half, / [until they] came to the Waters of Death. / Said [the ferryman] to Gilgamesh: / . . . Let your hand not touch the Waters of Death, lest you lame it!'[28]

Standing on the cliffs of his island, Utnapishtim watched the boat approaching and the two men disembarking on the quayside. Gilgamesh rushed onshore, bowing in front of Utnapishtim. He addressed Utnapishtim as venerable, pleading for the wisdom of the one who had survived the flood to live an immortal life with his wife.

Utnapishtim knew that immortality was beyond the reach of this man with sunken cheeks and a face burnt by frost and sunshine. He knew that 'when the gods created mankind, death they dispensed to mankind, life they kept for themselves'.[29] But he also knew that his guest would not be satisfied until he had had proof of his limits. 'If you wish to obtain eternal life – he told Gilgamesh – first try to stay awake for a week.' Gilgamesh sat down, preparing himself for the long vigil. The very moment he rested on the floor, sleep overcame him. He slept six days and seven nights, restoring his body from the hardship of the journey. Every day that he slept, Utnapishtim's wife baked a loaf of bread and left it next to him, like a calendar marker. At the beginning of the seventh day, Utnapishtim awakened him. 'I must have rested only a minute', Gilgamesh blurted out apologetically. Utnapishtim nodded towards the seven loaves of bread, at different stages of ageing. A pang of despair pierced Gilgamesh. Even that small test had been too much for him, a human! All his travels and his pains had been in vain.

Looking at his tears, Utnapishtim's wife reproached her husband. How could he be so rude as to let this rare guest leave their island without giving him anything for his troubles? 'There is one thing that I can give him. – Utnapishtim replied – Here on the bottom of the sea, there is a plant that will rejuvenate you if you eat it. Short of the immortality that you will never find, this is the best that you can hope for'. Gilgamesh took off his ragged clothes and dived into the water, tore the magic weed from the seafloor and prepared himself to commence the journey back home. This time, he would not travel alone. The ferryman, repudiated by Utnapishtim for having allowed a human to cross the Waters of Death, would accompany him to the city of Uruk.

The two crossed the water again, passed the edges of the world and traversed the mountains. Gilgamesh trekked through the wilderness, clutching the precious weed of rejuvenation to his chest. It wasn't until he stumbled upon a pool of water that he paused, setting aside the magic herb to indulge in a bath. While he savoured the small pleasures of human life, he did not notice that a snake had emerged from the brambles. As he watched in horror, the snake sank its fangs into the magic weed, shed its old skin and disappeared into the foliage with the only treasure he had gained from his adventures. Gilgamesh broke down in tears, crushed by his destiny. Human, all too human, he was to suffer the fate of all that lives inside the circle of the Waters of Death. Like Enkidu, he would have to face Death alone, with no weapons to fight it and no hope for success.

## 19.

Like every fable, the story of Gilgamesh ends where it began. When he reached sight of his long-lost city of Uruk, he turned towards the ferryman and told him with pride mixed with sadness.

> O [ferryman], climb Uruk's wall and walk back and forth!
> Survey its foundations, examine the brickwork!
> Were its bricks not fired in an oven?[30]

And the oven that fired those bricks, had it not been built by him, the king? How beautiful was Uruk, the city he had fortified, adorned and organized!

> A square mile is city, a square mile date-grove, a square mile is clay-pit, half a square mile the temple of Ishtar: three square miles and a half is Uruk in expanse.[31]

These words conclude the epic of Gilgamesh. What more could have he said? In the public buildings of Uruk and in the work that he had poured into them, Gilgamesh found his only possible immortality.

For the Mesopotamian imagination, the destinies of gods and humans were irreducibly divided. While the gods could only die at each other's hands in a cosmic battle, death was part of the inbuilt obsolescence of *lullu*, the human machine designed to serve the needs of the gods.

What awaited humans after death was not paradisiacal bliss, but a sad, endless and impoverished retirement. Once their bodies had been withdrawn from the labour camp of the world, their spirits survived in the desolate land of the Netherworld, where there was nothing to feed them, to clothe them or to quench their thirst, except for the offerings burnt for them by the living. Those whose surviving family was numerous and rich enough to maintain their cult could get by almost decently, rejoicing in their supplies for as long as their memory lasted. Those who had left behind no children or not enough wealth in the family would spend eternity in wretched misery.

This grim horizon was revealed in a dream to Gilgamesh by the ghost of his friend Enkidu.

'If I am to tell you the way things are ordered in the Netherworld,
O sit you down and weep!'
... 'Ah, woe!' cried [Gilgamesh], and sat down in the dust.[32]

Long after the composition of the *Gilgamesh*, a similar view of the afterlife returned in the epic tales sung by Homer. During his journey through the Netherworld, Odysseus encountered the soul of his friend Achilles, who had died in the siege of Troy. Oh, how Achilles would have preferred to be still on Earth, he lamented, if only as the slave of a poor man, rather than to bask in his glory among the zombified mass of the dead![33] The glory of one's accomplishments, celebrated by poets and artists: that was all a person could hope for in the way of immortality. A memory so vulnerable to the upheavals of history, however, as to be too fragile to sustain the optimism of hope.

Among the Mesopotamians, and later the Greeks, there began to take root that particular strand of the Mediterranean imagination, which saw hopelessness as the correct way to approach the absurd condition of human life and the mystery of death.

But hopelessness did not mean despair. Without a promise of future deliverance, what remained was the here-and-now, that mesh of gods and people, eternity and time, invisibility and visibility, which humans called 'the world'. That was the only time available to live, to love and to create something beautiful. On the stage of the world, humans could play their role in the tragic comedy of life with such perfection as to be worthy of being remembered. If the human trajectory was a downward spiral, to every person remained, at least, the possibility of falling beautifully.

## 20.

The Egyptians were of a different opinion. No condition could ever be permanent, they argued, least of all death. Just as the sun is born and dies every day, so everything that exists will one day disappear to leave room for the dawn of a new cosmos. The afterlife, too, will come to an end. Once the great serpent Apophis has devoured the world, sinking it again into the primeval waters of Nun, all the souls will return to the initial state of pure virtuality. Anything that had been actual will return to being a possibility, ready to be actualized in a new cosmic cycle. The sinners, whose souls failed to pass the judgement of Osiris and were annihilated into nothingness, will have another chance to exist in a new world.

For those who hoped to reach the blissful Fields of Reeds, the prospect of their posthumous joy eventually ending might have sounded ominous. Yet, by that point, they would have already enjoyed an afterlife worthy of the gods. Once their soul had completed the perilous journey to the afterlife, they themselves would have become gods. Provided that the appropriate rituals had been performed and the right spells pronounced, the deserving could hope to overcome the human condition and become Osiris.

Such a privilege had not been easy to obtain for the people of Egypt. At the time of the first pharaonic dynasties, only the monarch – and sometimes his family – could aspire to merge his soul with that of Osiris after death. It was during the period of political crisis between the twelfth and eleventh centuries BC, known to the historians as the First Intermediate Period, that the Egyptian people managed to wrest this privilege from their sovereign. Continuous rebellions had fractured the Old Kingdom, and a plethora of ambitious noblemen threatened the authority of the pharaoh. Having lost his status as the only legitimate heir to Horus, the source of all kingly power, the pharaoh also lost his exclusive connection to Horus' father, Osiris. A 'democratisation' of the afterlife ensued, granting everyone the hope of being worthy to become Osiris after death.[34]

What counted was no longer a person's social status in life, but their contribution to maintaining the cosmic order, *maat*. Even though the world tended towards its disintegration, the coordinated effort of gods and humans, the latter led by the pharaoh, could ensure that the harmony of the cosmos stayed intact a little longer. Although the cyclical course of all things could not be escaped, and the victory of *chaos*, embodied by Apophis, could not be postponed indefinitely, maintaining *maat* nonetheless counted as the greatest moral task in a person's life and as the criterion to judge their worthiness to access the Fields of Reeds after death.

Thus, out of the crisis of the First Intermediate Period, the Egyptians drew a message of hope. Happiness was possible, both in this life and in the next, and the just reward for good actions, as well as the punishment for bad deeds, would not escape the perfect measure of Osiris, Lord of the Netherworld.

# 21.

What is said about families, that 'all happy [ones] resemble one another; each unhappy family is unhappy in its own way',[35] also applies to civilizations. At the nadirs of history, when the world turns into an unliveable wasteland, the genius of each people discovers within itself creative springs of which they had been previously unaware. The imagination often responds to the trauma of a catastrophe by lunging towards a renewed understanding of the meaning of life and the mystery of reality.

To the Mesopotamians, the shock of mortality revealed a new perspective towards life, centred around the notion of hopelessness. On the contrary, the Egyptians emerged from the collapse of the First Intermediate Period with a distinctly hopeful vision, centred on the figure of Osiris.

Split by the axe of catastrophe, the Mediterranean imagination divided into two branches: hope and hopelessness. From these, over the millennia, two different traditions developed, each with its own peculiar ideas and lifestyles.

As seen through the perspective of hope, the influence of superhuman forces and the plague of worldly sorrows could be effectively transcended and a lasting joy could be achieved – if not in this life, certainly in the next. Gods and humans, attuned by their common desire for liberation, shared the same struggle against the cruel determinism of *chaos*. Freedom, not destiny, was the law of the universe – but freedom, like *maat*, could be preserved only through constant effort. Centuries later, this branch of the imagination would sprout some of the central tenets of Mediterranean Christianity, with its emphasis on human freedom, divine grace and universal redemption. The Egyptian trust in magic, too, will be revived by Mediterranean Christians through rituals, like the Eucharist and the confession, that were able to transform a person's destiny and to affect the very order of the universe.

Through their actions, humans could transcend their condition and merge with the nature of the divinity, achieving *theosis*.

A very different horizon appeared from the vantage point of Mesopotamian hopelessness. As seen through this perspective, the cosmos was governed by an eternal order, whose universal laws were not susceptible to modifications. No amount of ritual, prayer or magic could ever allow humans to transcend their condition. Hence the importance, for the Mesopotamians, of developing an astrological science that could read in advance what was inscribed in the heavenly 'Tablet of Destiny'. Knowledge of the inevitable, rather than the pursuit of freedom, was the highest form of wisdom.

For the early Greeks, too, the order of the cosmos was not a blind force that knew no mercy. Behind the epic stories of humans and gods, it was *Ananke*, the force of Necessity, that played the role of true cosmic protagonist.

> The true hero, the true subject, the center of the *Iliad* is force. ... At all times, the human spirit is shown as modified by its relations with force, as swept away, blinded, by the very force it imagined it could handle, as deformed by the weight of the force it submits to. ... To define force – it is that *x* that turns anybody who is subjected to it into a thing.[36]

Not even the gods had the power to modify the laws of *Ananke*. They too were but things under its rule. Thus, in the *Iliad*, when Zeus realizes that his son Sarpedon is to die at the hands of the Greek hero Patroclus, he is powerless to save him. He can only lament the diktats of destiny – his son's and his own.

'My cruel fate . . .
My Sarpedon, the man I love the most, my own son –
Doomed to die'.
And Zeus the father of men and gods . . .
Showered tears of blood that drenched the earth,
Showers in praise of him, his own dear son.[37]

## 22.

However bleak, the perspective of hopelessness was not without defences. Even though it did not aim to modify the inevitable course of events, it was able to respond to misfortunes with something even more effective than the vertigo of freedom. By accepting their tragic destiny, a person expanded their understanding of their own place inside the cosmos, entrenching themselves in a position of dignified nobility that rendered them immune from the offences of time and history. This attitude towards destiny constituted the essence of both nobility and virtue: it was *arete*, an existential medicine against despair, which doubled as a benchmark of moral perfection. The inner achievement of *arete* attuned a person's actions to the secret rhythm of the universe, suffusing them with the aura of beauty.

The music of Homer's verses, the perfection of the Greek statuary and the precision of the Mesopotamian canals were more than feats of technical ingenuity. Nestled inside their artifice, like characters inside a story, humans could assert their own nobility despite the cosmos' pull towards debasement and annihilation. Only the rhythmic harmony of the verse could redeem the destructions narrated in the Greek epics, just as the perfection of the mathematical calculations redeemed the inescapable destiny prophesied by Mesopotamian astrology. Without promises of future deliverance, the beauty born of hopelessness provided a form of redemption that was here-and-now, tragic and heroic, disillusioned and ecstatic.

> Where history showed us only ramparts and frontiers, poetry discovered a mysterious predestination that makes two adversaries, whose meeting is inexorable, worthy of each other. And Homer asks no quarter, save from poetry, which repossesses beauty from death and wrests from it the secret of justice that history cannot fathom. To the darkened world, poetry alone restores pride, eclipsed by the arrogance of the victors and the silence of the vanquished.
>
> Others may blame Zeus and marvel that he permits 'the good to be ranked with the bad'. With Homer there is no marvelling or blaming, and no answer is expected. Who is good in the *Iliad*? Who is bad? Such distinctions do not exist; there are only men suffering, warriors fighting, some winning, some losing.[38]

In the perspective of hopelessness, art took the place of magic. If neither the soul nor the flesh could escape the millstone of time, a mortal existence could still survive inside the images and the stories that preserved its memory. Their beauty did not depict the outward appearance of a person, but the *arete* with which they had accepted the humiliations inflicted by destiny. By submitting to cosmic forces beyond their power, a person could transcend their tragic condition and rise beyond the misery of the world, towards a plane that was typically reserved for the gods.

The belief in a connection between divinity and artistic perfection remained a key feature of Mediterranean imagination long after the time of the Homeric Greeks. At the beginning of the Middle Ages, when the Arabic people were beginning to coalesce around the message of the prophet Muhammad, the new religion of 'submission' (*Islam*, from *aslama*, 'to submit oneself') saw the literary beauty of its revelation as proof of its divine origin. God himself, in the sura *Al-Baqara* (The Cow), challenged disbelievers to imitate the writing style of his Quran.

> If you have doubts about the revelation We have sent down to Our servant, then produce a single sura like it – enlist whatever supporters you have other than God – if you truly [think you can].[39]

Indeed, the beauty of artifice, whether human or divine, is a force unlike any other. It hovers over the dark waters of destiny without looking for a landing place, polishing the surface of the abyss with the touch of its wings. Again and again, each artistic transfiguration of a mortal life smoothens the waves and renders them clearer. Nothing changes in the cosmos, no event is avoided or accomplished – yet, with each passage, something escapes the deadly embrace of the waters. A subtle shadow, the reflection of a light, the most ethereal essence of what constitutes a life twinkles for a moment over the surface of destiny and projects its own form upwards, towards an invisible elsewhere. Out of the darkness of the human condition, the art of hopelessness produces the shining surface of a mirror. Over this mirror, the flames of our mortal lives cast the glimmers that render them immortal.

For those dreamers who considered that force, thanks to progress, would soon be a thing of the past, the *Iliad* could appear as an historical document; for others, whose powers of recognition are more acute and who perceive force, today as yesterday, at the very centre of human history, the *Iliad* is the purest and the loveliest of mirrors.[40]

## 23.

The outlook on life inaugurated by the Mesopotamians enjoyed a long period of success. After the Greeks, it was also adopted by the Romans, whose belief in an inflexible destiny gave rise to a complex and popular science of divination. No consul or general, not even a common person, would dare to act against the signs of fate. The interest in astrology remained alive throughout the Middle Ages and well into the Renaissance, when it became a major trend among the cultured classes. To this day, echoes of the age of hopelessness resound from the tragedies that are still performed inside the mathematical beauty of the ancient theatres.

Yet, in the long run, it was the perspective of hope and freedom that won history's favour. Having brewed for centuries in and around Egypt, with the rise of Christianity, it exploded across the Levant and Europe. In the hands of the Christian church, the belief in human freedom, combined with the hope for salvation after death, became a dogma of faith. Its rejection by the Protestant reformers of the sixteenth century, in favour of the idea of predestination, played a major role in separating Northern European Christianity from the older Mediterranean Church.

The message of hope offered a range of different existential solutions to those who endured poverty and oppression, as to those who struggled to accept their own mortality. As conveyed by the official channels of the Church, it emphasized the posthumous bliss that awaited the just, regardless of what they had suffered in life. Mortality was not a curse but a condition of passage to the true eternal life. It was unnecessary to respond to the injustices of this world through social transformations, since eventually everything would be resolved elsewhere, in another dimension.

But hope also resounded in the sermons of heretical preachers and in the rallies of revolutionary firebrands, who encouraged the oppressed to rebel against injustice. Since hope referred to a real possibility, and destiny was not already written, there was no reason to wait for the afterlife to begin realizing an earthly paradise. What Adam and Eve had lost with their original sin, humans could rebuild with their own hands here in this world. Utopia, the land that existed in 'no place', was an eternal possibility that awaited only a rightful struggle to become reality.

In the same way that hopelessness spoke of a bittersweet mortality, so the message of hope taught a double lesson of acquiescence and rebellion. It was up to each person which attitude they chose as their own existential drive.

More importantly, however, one could also decide to what extent they shared the vision of the cosmos that their society held as 'real'. Not everyone in ancient Greece or in Mesopotamia adopted a hopeless perspective on life or believed in an unchangeable destiny. Many harboured within themselves a secret hope for universal salvation and did not renounce the fight for a more just world. They stepped outside the cosmos of their contemporaries and compatriots to venture into another reality, built around different metaphysical hypotheses. Equally, in the ages and in the lands ruled by the message of hope, many believed in the ancient, hopeless idea of life as a flash in an abyss of nothingness, ruled by an inflexible destiny. Even today, a deep-rooted fatalism pervades the popular music and poetry of 'Christian' lands such as Greece and Sicily. Even more so in Latin America, where Mediterranean Catholicism found a second flourishing, the perspective of hopelessness remains a significant feature of the social imagination.

Whether in the name of hope and freedom, or of hopelessness and fatalism, this uncoupling of an individual's beliefs from the cosmic vision of their society is a powerful response to the catastrophes of history. Holding onto a world separate from that which is hegemonic in one's own time is a feat of the imagination that can be compared to the creation of a new cosmological system. The early mythologists, too, responded to a hostile environment and a difficult condition as mortal creatures by using their creative imagination to invent a new and meaningful *cosmos*, where a joyful life was possible. They, too, escaped the *chaos* of their surroundings by reinventing from the foundations the very possibility of a world. The wide adoption of their stories as 'myths' simply rendered public a process that is always at play in the mind of any individual who dares to reclaim a different vision of reality.

Such cosmogonic inventiveness constitutes one of the main threads in the long story of Mediterranean imagination. Whenever the events of life or history rendered the world uninhabitable, the Mediterranean people extracted from the deepest level of their imagination the necessary resources to project a new environment around themselves.

As we prepare to leave the era of Mesopotamia and Egypt, the creative spirit of its mythologists will guide us forward across the millennia, towards the next stop in our journey. We will soon land in the time of Hellenisms, on the trail of another person who did not believe in his society's idea of the world. His name, Alexander, is more at home among the fabulous heroes of mythologies than in the dry accounts of historians. When he died, his ghost shunned the afterlife to remain among the living, as an instrument through which they could invent new and strange worlds. If his life produced terrible historical crises from Greece to India, his ghost offered instead the solution for individual and collective crises for centuries to come. For many peoples, he was both the flood that erased their world and the land that resurfaced from the waters. He will be our guide in the next chapter.

# *Meanwhile in the Mediterranean...*

## *Second millennium BC to fourth century BC*

18th–12th century BC – The Mycenaean and Minoan civilizations flourish across the Aegean Sea.

13th century BC – Pharaoh Ramses II reigns for sixty-six years over Egypt.

13th–12th century BC – Raids by the mysterious 'Sea People' are reported all over the Eastern Mediterranean coasts.

12th–11th century BC – Around this time, the historical events connected with the epics of the Trojan War take place.

11th century BC – The Mycenaean and Minoan civilizations mysteriously collapse. The Hellenic Middle Ages descend over Greece.

9th–7th century BC – The Neo-Assyrian Empire rules over Mesopotamia, the Levant, Egypt, Anatolia and parts of Persia and Arabia.

8th century BC – At the end of the Hellenic Middle Ages, an author (or many authors?) known as Homer composed the epics of the *Iliad* and the *Odyssey*.

*814 BC – According to tradition, Carthage is founded by the Phoenician Queen Elissa.*

*753 BC – According to tradition, Romulus kills his brother Remus and founds Rome.*

*587 BC – The Babylonian army destroys the temple at Jerusalem and deports the Jews to Babylon.*

*539 BC – Cyrus leads his army to the conquest of Mesopotamia, founding the Persian Empire. The Jews are freed from their captivity and return to Palestine.*

*510 BC – The people of Athens revolt against the ruling aristocracy and install a democratic regime.*

*509 BC – Rome frees itself from the dominion of the Etruscans, abolishing the monarchy and becoming a republic.*

*492–490 BC – The Persian emperor Darius tries to invade Greece with a mighty army but is defeated by a league of Greek cities.*

*480–479 BC – The Greek cities defeat a second Persian invasion, led by Darius' son, Xerxes.*

*461–429 BC – Pericles becomes Archon (ruler) in Athens, igniting an age of cultural splendour.*

*431–404 BC – Sparta defeats Athens in the 'Peloponnesian War', ending its golden age.*

*420s–340s BC – Plato, disciple of Socrates, produces a corpus of philosophical works of unparalleled beauty and influence.*

*356 BC – Alexander 'the Great' is born in Pella, Macedonia.*

# 2

# *Foreigners*

# *Hellenism*

### 1.

Far from the Mediterranean coasts, beyond the Eastern mountains and the deserts, the sun was setting over a long day of celebrations. In the hall of the old palace of government in Maracanda, a group of men lounged on a few beds arranged in an open square. They looked mismatched among the elegant decorations on the walls and the pillars. Their faces sported long scars, their arms looked too strong to be those of courtiers. And they were much drunker than would have been appropriate for an aristocratic gathering. The drunkest among them was the host of the banquet, a short man in his twenties, with a stiff, bullish neck and a cascade of blondish hair. He raised his cup, boasting about his deeds and the adventures through which he had led his friends. He was the greatest king the world had ever seen, nay, he was even greater than his father! The people of every nation would soon bow their heads to his incoming dominion over the lands surrounded by the great Ocean! The guests spilt the wine cheering loudly, especially the youngest, who had started their adult lives under his command. Only one guest remained silent. He pushed a lock of black hair away from his eyes. 'Very well', he said, 'it sounds like our beloved king did everything himself. But was it not his father, whom he so despises, that created the army that has led him to his victories? Was it not his soldiers who fought those battles that now he claims all for himself? And was it not me, Cleitus the Black, who saved his life in battle?' The guests fell silent, while the musicians continued to play in a corner of the room. The king growled 'What did you say?' Cleitus jumped off his bed, stepping forward. 'You heard me, Alexander. You are not worth your father's little finger, and you don't deserve the loyalty of your generals. You are no longer the warrior who left Macedonia with us, you're one of them now, a Persian!' The music stopped, the guards at the doors woke from their torpor. The king stumbled across the hall, crying for someone to arrest the traitor. Cleitus continued shouting insults. All the guests rose from their beds, begging the two men to calm down. It would have looked like a brawl in a tavern, except for the range of weapons lying about the room. Alexander grabbed a spear from one of the guards, and before anyone could stop him, he plunged it into Cleitus' side. Blood gushed out of the wound all over the pavement. Alexander rammed the spear home. Cleitus collapsed, the guests ran towards him, the guards looked at each other, panicking. Alexander stumbled back to his bed, asking for another drink. Cleitus was dying quickly; Alexander knew how to kill with one blow.

Leaning on the bed, his adrenaline ebbing away, Alexander began to realize what had just happened. He had just killed one of his oldest friends, the general who had made possible many of his victories across half the world, the brother of his childhood nurse, the man who had saved his life at the Battle of the Granicus. An invisible clamp tightened around his stomach, leaving him gasping for air. His wailing rose above the death throes of Cleitus, breathing his last on the floor. Alexander tried to plunge himself onto the same spear, but a friend pushed the point away from his chest. While the guards carried the body of Cleitus out of the hall, the generals took him by the arms and led him to the room that had been prepared for him.[1] Beneath the dim light of torches, they placed him upon the lion fur covering the bed. The king who had brought the world to his feet broke down in tears. He asked for more wine, but he found himself alone in the room. His sword and dagger had been taken away, and from beyond the door someone was whispering to keep watch until the morning. Alexander would have protested that no one should dare lock up the king, but all energy had abandoned him. He stretched one arm under the headrest, searching for the only consolation that had never failed him.[2] He extracted a scroll, unrolled it and struggling to focus on the lines, he mumbled:

> So Hector shouted out
> to Deiphobous bearing his white shield – with a ringing shout
> he called for a heavy lance – but the man was nowhere near him,
> vanished – and Hector knew the truth in his heart
> and the fighter cried aloud, 'My time has come!
> At last the gods have called me down to death.
> I thought he was at my side, the hero Deiphobous –

he's safe inside the walls, Athena tricked me blind.
And now death, grim death is looming up beside me,
no longer far away.'[3]

His lips remained agape, his vision blurred. Alexander rubbed away the tears. He wondered if the gods had tricked him like they had done with Hector; if they had obfuscated his mind to make him kill Cleitus, wishing for his ruin. Everyone would now shun him like a dangerous beast, and he would no longer be able to let his guard down. He had become a foreigner among his own people, unsettled on any side in this endless war.

Alone among the living, he wondered if he might have a kindred spirit at least among the dead. Had not Homer been like him? No one knew whether he was truly a Greek or a Trojan; his *Iliad* gave no clues to his allegiance. Homer had been a patriot of no nation, a blind man who could see the past, a poet of war who had never fought a battle. Maybe he was only a voice that hid within itself the voice of many others. With his robe still drenched in Cleitus' blood, Alexander closed his eyes. Filaments of images flew behind his eyelids, bringing back the memories of a long-gone day, on the sunlit battlefield of Issus. It was the second great victory in his expedition, and Cleitus was at his side. In the Persian camp, they discovered that the emperor Darius, upon fleeing, had abandoned a royal treasure so abundant as to make that of Delphi pale in comparison. But the most amazing discovery took place when they entered the royal tent. Darius' mother and wife were standing surrounded by Macedonian soldiers, shaken yet still intact in their dignity. Alexander entered the tent accompanied by Hephaestion, his lover and comrade. Upon seeing that blondish man with a taurine neck next to his beautiful companion, Darius' mother immediately prostrated herself at the feet of Hephaestion, begging him, as the victorious Alexander, to spare their lives. How they laughed at the look on her face when she realized her mistake! 'Do not worry', said Alexander, helping her up on her feet, 'he too is Alexander'.[4]

Those were other times when he was a different man, as Cleitus had said. But one thing had not changed. Like that of Homer, the name 'Alexander' belonged to him only as the stuff of legends. Anyone blessed, or cursed, by the gods could claim it as their own and share its glory. He was only a character, sung to life by the Muses.

## 2.

At the beginning of his expedition, Alexander had ordered his army to march towards the ruins of Troy. In front of the soldiers assembled at the foot of the hill, the king and his closest friends had shed their clothes and raced naked, like the heroes of old, around the tomb of Achilles. Alexander had spoken to the soldiers, celebrating their valour, telling them how they were part of a mythical story in the making and presenting himself as the long-awaited hero who had returned to avenge the wrongs the Greeks had suffered at the hands of the Persians.

Just a few years later, this mythological narrative had collapsed. By the time of Cleitus' murder in Maracanda, Alexander was hardly recognizable as a Greek. His court overflowed with Persian eunuchs, Asian concubines, Zoroastrian diviners and Egyptian advisors. His soldiers spoke dozens of languages, and his army fielded armoured elephants alongside the old Macedonian cavalry. Having defeated the Persian emperor, he had started wearing the same royal robes and behaving like him. He expected his subjects, including his closest friends, to prostrate themselves in front of the throne, kissing the ground as if in the presence of a god.[5] To the Greeks and the Macedonians, Alexander had become a Persian.

To the Persians, however, he had lost none of his foreignness. His name, Sekandar, as they pronounced it, was followed by the epithet *gujastak*, 'the accursed'. In the folktales that were already springing up throughout Central Asia, Alexander was depicted as a blasphemous demon who had come from a mysterious elsewhere to destroy the rightful order of the world.

Among all his subjects, perhaps only the Egyptians had offered him something close to acceptance. Wise and politically shrewd as ever, the Egyptian priests understood the anguish of their conqueror and were quick to cater to his existential needs. They pointed him to the oracle in the oasis of Siwa, far into the Sahara Desert. There, they said, he could obtain the answer to the question that had long tormented him: who was he, really? Alexander leaped at the chance. He suspended military operations, left his army behind and with a small party of cavalrymen, he headed towards the desert. They had been riding across the dunes for days when they realized that they had lost their way. With no wells in sight, their water reserves depleted and the horses nearing collapse, they began despairing of ever coming out of the desert alive, let alone reaching the fabled oracle. Then, a miraculous flight of birds, sent by gods unknown, brought them back on the right path. Once in Siwa, inside a small stone temple that had been standing there among the palm trees since time immemorial, the oracle confirmed to Alexander that he was not of human origin. Neither god nor demon, he was the son of Ammon, the greatest among the gods. Not quite immortal, he nevertheless carried within himself a spark of divinity. He belonged to the same kin as Heracles, and his destiny encompassed superhuman glory and beastly solitude. He was born to be a foreigner to every land, especially among his own people.[6]

## 3.

Alexander the Great is an unlikely character in our story. When we set out to travel through the Mediterranean imagination, we did not aim to find the great figures of history, but the often-obscure legions of thinkers and dreamers who turned their own state of minority into an opportunity to rethink the fabric of reality. Thus, if Alexander is now our guide through the age of Hellenism, it is not because of his 'greatness' but despite it.

The Alexander that will accompany us is quite unlike the one that can be found in the history books. Neither the great conqueror nor the merciless killer, he is instead the archetype of the 'foreigner'. Wherever he went, he stood out as incongruous to his surroundings. Even though he had been raised within Greek culture, his Macedonian heritage and his fascination with the trappings of Persian royalty marked him as a 'barbarian' in the eyes of the Greeks. To the other peoples he conquered, he was an alien invader. He was too young to rank as an experienced commander, yet too successful to be dismissed as a reckless youth. While too emotionally erratic for his power to stabilize and endure, no one could resist the force of his decisions.

Had he lived in the nineteenth century, during the age of Romanticism, such a combination of opposites would have been considered the mark of his 'genius': if he walked on Earth somewhat awkwardly, it was because he stumbled upon his oversized wings, like an albatross.[7] Having been born in the heart of antiquity, however, his contemporaries took his inability to fit pre-established categories as the sign of a more-than-human nature.

This is the Alexander that we follow: not the actual person, but the mythical figure that stuck in the imagination of those affected by his passage. In the mythical sphere, human crimes and torments are not susceptible to condemnation or pity, but they are part of a revelation of a dark and complex reality. The mythical Alexander served as an example and an admonition: he was the 'monster', who showed (Latin: *monstrare*) the existential potential of being a foreigner within the world, while at the same time warning (Latin: *monere*, the other possible etymology of 'monster') of the costs that came with it.

For the people who, for centuries, would continue to reinvent his story, his figure became increasingly detached from the individual who had waged war across Europe, Africa and Asia. He embodied the canniness and charisma of a trickster intent on exploring a world to which he did not belong. His radical foreignness veiled his actions with a sense of melancholia, yet it endowed his figure with the lightness of a fairy, always available to visit the dreams of whoever wished to summon him. He could be a model for a monarch who sought to renew their kingdom as much as for a subject who wished to escape it. His stories could be an opportunity for entertainment or an esoteric teaching about the limits of the world and the ways that lead beyond it. The mythical Alexander especially favoured those who looked with suspicion on the bonds of society: to them, he lent himself as the softest of masks.

## 4.

When Alexander launched his invasion in 334 BC, the Persian Empire was the largest on the planet. Stretching from modern-day Kazakhstan to Bulgaria and from India to Libya, its extensive network of roads connected a multitude of nations, cultures, languages and religions. To its inhabitants, it was simply *Xsaca*, 'The Empire'. Two hundred years after its foundation by Cyrus the Great, the Achaemenid dynasty ruled it according to a wise policy of regional autonomy, ethnic coexistence and religious tolerance. As long as their subjects recognized the authority of the emperor, paid taxes and served in the military, the Achaemenids were content to let them live according to their own customs. The Persian Empire was at the same time an area of borderless exchange and a mosaic of peoples who maintained their own distinct identity.

Only once, the Achaemenids had dared to offend the beliefs of a community in their empire. By order of Cambyses II, the Persian army had desecrated the Egyptian temples, arrested their priests and slaughtered the sacred bull Apis.[8] Even then, however, they had not been motivated by religious or ethnic intolerance. The Egyptian priesthood had been the breeding ground for a string of revolts, and Cambyses II's brutality was meant to show them that their nigh-sacred status did not exempt them from the obedience that all subjects owed to the emperor. Like any form of freedom, also that offered by the Persians came at a price.

The advance of Alexander's army brought this world to an end. In just a few years, the peoples of 'The Empire' witnessed the collapse of its political, economic and social structures. The mythical aura surrounding Alexander, and the apparent invincibility of his army, added a sense of inevitability to the fall of the old order. It seemed as if, not Alexander, but Destiny itself was steering history along a new path.

Once the old world was over, everything seemed possible. The various ethnic groups could have rebelled against the new rule, seeking their own autonomy. Alexander could have established a regime of segregation between the Greek conquerors and their new subjects. Or he could have entirely disregarded the problem of governance, focusing instead on his dream of reaching the final frontiers of the world, leaving behind himself a glorious trail of ruins. Who could have said that he might not have succeeded?

The inhabitants of the old Persian Empire found themselves on the brink of a catastrophe. The shadows of civil war loomed near.

## 5.

If it had been up to Alexander, his expedition would have not stopped before reaching the shores of the great Ocean, which the Greeks believed encircled all dry lands. Undefeated by his enemies, he could not suspect that, in the end, the only army that would vanquish him would be his own. When they reached the Indian river Hyphasis, worn down by months of monsoon rains and decimated by epidemics, his soldiers mustered their courage and mutinied. Alexander could not believe that his men had lost the desire to write their own myth alongside his. He threatened them, begged them, cried, then he sulked in his tent. His army waited outside for days until he finally surrendered to their will. The great adventure was over.[9]

On the furthermost point they had reached, he ordered the erection of a pillar with an inscription and twelve altars to the Olympian gods. He also ordered his engineers to build a huge encampment with monumental barracks furnished with oversized beds – so that posterity would know the titanic nature of those who had been there.[10] When all was done, and the altars had smoked with the burnt flesh of sacrificial victims, he gloomily ordered the return to Persia. Half of his army would go by sea with the admiral Nearchus, with the additional task of exploring as much as possible along the way.[11] The rest would march with him through the harsh Gedrosian desert, in an ordeal of collective atonement.[12]

As it had happened during the journey to the oracle at Siwa, the desert march soon turned into a nightmare. The soldiers were fainting under the sun and dying of exhaustion. Water became scarce, then ran out completely. This time, however, no miraculous birds came to their rescue. When they finally reached the Persian capital, almost a third of his army had perished.[13]

Once in the capital, Alexander could no longer postpone the problem of governing the gigantic territory he had conquered. His approach to policymaking, however, had more of the performer than of the statesman. To express his favour for the mixing of different ethnicities, he presided over the public collective wedding of 10,000 Persian women with as many soldiers in his army. He added to his first wife, the Bactrian princess Roxana, two Persian princesses from Darius' family, and had his own lover Hephaestion marry one of their sisters, so that their children could call each other siblings. Whatever the future of his empire, its lifeblood had to flow as freely as that great Ocean which he still dreamed of reaching.[14]

Hephaestion and Alexander's plan of building a common family, too, was to remain only a dream. One day, while the court was residing in the city of Ecbatana, Hephaestion began to suffer from intense pain in his side. The royal doctor Glaucias, hastily summoned, prescribed him a strict diet. After a few days of abstinence from food and drink, Hephaestion started feeling better. Relieved by this improvement, the doctor decided to reward himself with a night out at the theatre. As soon as he had left, his patient decided to celebrate his returning health with a sumptuous banquet and plenty of drinks. When the doctor returned, he found Hephaestion unconscious. Alexander barely had the time to bid farewell to the love of his life, dying in his arms. The doctor was promptly executed, his ravaged body exposed in front of Hephaestion's lodgings, like the Trojan prisoners whom Achilles had sacrificed on Patroclus' pyre. As in the *Iliad*, Ecbatana resounded for days with spectacular funeral games, while a special envoy galloped to Egypt to petition the oracle of Siwa to grant Hephaestion the status of a divinity. To conclude the funeral, Alexander ordered the destruction of the temple of the god of medicine, Asclepius, who had failed his lover.[15]

From then on, the gods ceased to assist him. Once Hephaestion's ashes had grown cold, Alexander fell in a spiral of alcoholic self-destruction. Eight months later, in the city of Babylon, he met that fatal destiny which had always spared him in battle. On a torrid day in June, after a brief fever, he drank himself to death. He didn't have a chance to see his mother again, or to walk once more on the snow-covered slopes of Macedonia. He was thirty-two years old.[16]

## 6.

Lying on his deathbed, encircled by the nervous crowd of his generals, Alexander whispered that his empire should go 'to the strongest among you'.[17] He left behind no political plans and a difficult legacy: an empire too vast to be governable, and the uncanny mask of a mythological character, 'Alexander' the accursed, the conqueror, the foreigner.

His generals, however, did not have time to ponder the deep meaning of his legacy. Each of them withdrew to a corner of the empire, summoning his own army. After two years of armed truce, bitter fighting erupted across Macedonia, Egypt and Asia Minor. Alexander's former generals turned against each other, and his empire, at one point the largest on Earth, fractured into a mosaic of enemy kingdoms. The war of all against all also ripped the intimacy of the imperial family. Princess Roxane, Alexander's favourite wife, had his two other wives killed, while his mother Olympias swiftly exterminated anyone in the royal family, including children, whom she felt might pose a threat to her safety. Captured by her enemies, she was stoned to death by the relatives of her victims. Six years later, Roxane and her fourteen-year-old son were executed. Alexander's bloodline was utterly extinguished.

One by one, the warring generals fell by each other's blades, with the seemingly invincible Antigonus dying at eighty-one on the field of the first battle he had ever lost. It took decades of war for the partition of Alexander's empire to find a stable form.

As during Alexander's youth, the world kept changing at a reckless speed. Yet, history seemed to have grown tired of change. In the centuries that followed Alexander's death, it seemed as if his ghost, free from his mortal body, had remained firmly in control of the destiny of his subjects.

His former generals, now kings, claimed legitimacy for their rule by presenting themselves as his faithful *diadochoi* (successors), if not as his living avatars. Even their coinage, issued in mints thousands of miles distant from each other, showed them as uncannily similar emanations of their common archetype.[18] They too had realized that 'Alexander' was a mask that belonged to whoever could wear it.

Each of them also imitated Alexander's betrayal of Aristotle's teachings on nation and ethnicity. While Aristotle emphasized the natural superiority of the Greeks and the need to preserve them from Barbarian contaminations, the new 'Alexanders', like the original, promoted the mongrelization of nations, cultures and religions. Through his reincarnations, Alexander continued fuelling that syncretic process, which, in centuries to come, will assign Apollo's face to Christ, will fill the Platonic Academy with Indian voices and will insert Zoroastrian symbolism into the philosophy of Islam.

## 7.

To intervene in worldly affairs from the afterlife, Alexander's ghost could count on an army like no other. Its ranks did not consist of cavalrymen and foot soldiers, but of storytellers from the four corners of his empire. Nestled in their stories, Alexander continued to grow and to undergo transformations, shaping the imagination of millions of people across Africa, Asia and Europe.

In the words of the storytellers, as if in a crucible, the historical figure dissolved and reformed as a legendary character endowed with countless different lives. Some of his posthumous existences faded together with the voice of their narrators. But others survived, scattered and authorless, in the informal corpus of oral folktales. Eventually, a selection was assembled and written down to form a masterwork of Mediterranean literature: *The Alexander Romance*.

Just like its hero, the *Romance* is a wonder and a mystery. It is a mythological tale of adventure, an anthology of letters, the story of a trickster, a travelogue through a fantasy landscape. It features faint elements from history, combined with cliches from popular narratives and fragments from unrelated texts. If it were to be placed within a library, it would sit somewhere between the epic of Gilgamesh, Aesop's fables, the adventures of Sinbad the sailor, a picaresque novel and the four Gospels.

During the Middle Ages, the *Romance* gained such universal renown that it was translated into dozens of languages, including Arabic, Bulgarian, Czech, Farsi, French, Gaelic, German, English, Hebrew, Icelandic, Latin, Pahlavi, Rumanian and Syriac. Each translation transformed the plot, inserted new characters, tweaked the order of events and removed those that no longer seemed relevant. The *Romance* was an authentic folk epic, written and rewritten over centuries by people from different territories, cultures and languages. It was as if Alexander's ghost had been writing its own story, reshuffling its episodes and locations in the same way that memories chaotically surface in a reminiscing mind.

In the many versions of the *Romance* that were produced until the end of the fifteenth century, Alexander lent himself to an endless chain of adventures. He built the iron wall that contained the demonic forces of Gog and Magog, descended into the abysses of the Ocean inside a glass bell and flew above the clouds in a cage carried by magic birds. He fought against giants, survived the desert ants, witnessed rivers of sand turning into water and saw entire forests shrink and vanish at dawn. He became Egyptian and Persian, Christian and Muslim. Like water, he took the colour of the vessel that held him.

## 8.

In our present day and age, the art of storytelling is but one piece of the formidable arsenal of technical and technological artifices deployed by the contemporary system of communications. When we prepare to enjoy a story today, we expect to be overwhelmed by such a tightly packed avalanche of stimuli that there is no empty space left to be filled by our imagination. Coming in with such expectations, we can easily remain underwhelmed by what we find in ancient fables and folktales. Those narratives rarely indulge in the meticulous world-building of modern films and novels. Their stories jump from action to action, leaving characters unexplored, skipping descriptions, barely touching introspection. We might find ourselves at a loss: how is it possible to feel engaged or to identify with the characters of a story that seems to lack all the mechanisms capable of capturing our attention? In front of an ancient tale, we, modern readers, might feel like gods who have not been properly invoked.

The same feeling might hit us upon opening the *Alexander Romance*. The narrative jolts between scenes; the protagonist is a weird creature, whose reasons are often inscrutable; the landscape across which he moves is barely sketched out. Yet, this is precisely how such a story should be told. A folktale like the *Romance* is not meant to be just a means of entertainment, it also contains the instructions for a mysterious, difficult journey that the readers can undergo together with its fictional characters. If its narrative lacks artifice, it is because it is faithful to the actual workings of human life.

When we try to make sense of our own reality, our imagination, too, jolts from image to image, without much regard for the smooth passages of logical reasoning. When we focus our attention on developing the idea that we have of ourselves, our surroundings become increasingly indistinct. We are often unaware of the true reasons behind our actions, and the protagonist of our own existential story, too, is a weird, inscrutable creature.

The scattered narrative of a folktale is, in fact, a sequence of handgrips along which our imagination can climb the impervious path of an existential transformation. This is typical of Mediterranean creations: emerging from a territory that is constantly ravaged by the flux of history, their primary aim is to help their audience resist, or escape, a state of crisis. If political manuals teach readers how to wield their power to shape their surroundings, fables and folktales are instead guides for those whose only power is to transform themselves in the face of overwhelming adversities.

Thus, the true protagonist of the *Romance* is not Alexander, but the reader; the adventures it describes are not those of an ancient conqueror, but the initiatic path of anyone who is a foreigner to their world. The *Romance* does not take place on the page, but behind the eyes of those who enter it.

## 9.

Like frames enclosing liquid colours, the different versions of the *Romance* contain few fixed elements. Only one thing recurs without exception. Every version of the story begins at a time before Alexander, among a people that Greeks and Macedonians would have considered foreign.

The *Romance* confirms Alexander's doubts about his relation to the king of Macedon, Philip II. Indeed, his true father was a king, but not one who reigned over a country of rocks and snowy peaks. His bloodline sprung from a place far to the south of Macedonia, among the temples and palaces of the Nile valley, in the days when Pharaoh Nectanebo defended the kingdom against the attacks of the Persians.[19]

Like every Pharaoh, Nectanebo held the power, and the responsibility, of connecting Earth with the blessings of the Heavens. Unlike his predecessors, however, he was able to complement his semi-divine status with a supreme proficiency in the magical arts. Every army that the Persians sent against

Egypt, he destroyed before they could even reach the border. He could see their image in a pool of water, and it was enough for him to sink it with a finger. Until, one day, the water showed the reflection of the Egyptian Gods marching at the head of the invasion. That time, it was Destiny, rather than history, that had come to challenge him.

Nectanebo stumbled away from the pool. He sent away his servants and shut the doors to his rooms. He took off his royal attire, put on some dirty rags and shaved his head. Then, he sneaked out of the palace into the street. At the port, he embarked on the first ship sailing to Greece. After a few days at sea, while rumours of his disappearance and news of a Persian invasion were spreading among his people, Nectanebo landed on the shores of Greece. He continued his travel by foot, sustaining himself along the way with magic tricks performed for the passers-by.

By the time he reached the gates of Pella, the Macedonian capital, his fame as a magician already preceded him. He had barely settled in the city when a messenger summoned him to the royal palace for an audience with Queen Olympias, the wife of Philip II. Nectanebo fell for her as soon as he saw her. She asked him about her future, and he sat with her to look at her horoscope. He announced the arrival of a god who had come to mix his blood with hers. That same night, he took the form of a large serpent and slipped inside the queen's chamber. Night after night, Olympias expected the arrival of the serpent until she became pregnant with the child of a god, or of a Pharaoh or of a trickster.

In the years that followed, Nectanebo found a way to stay close to his son Alexander without disclosing his secret.

Disguised as a courtier in the queen's palace, he accompanied him to the threshold of puberty. One night, when Alexander was twelve, Nectanebo took him to the hills outside the city to teach him the secrets of the stars. 'You see, my son', he said inadvertently. Alexander jolted, pierced by a pang of doubt. He pushed Nectanebo; the old man slipped, lost his balance and fell tumbling down a ravine. Alexander did not move to help him. He stared down at Nectanebo, bleeding to death, and listened to his confession until he was sure that the man he had killed was his true father.[20]

## 10.

The Alexander of the *Romance* is inhumane and superhuman. He commits atrocities, but never makes mistakes. No sign of regret ever breaks the grin stamped on his face. Only an existential torment still binds him to common humans. Uninterested in gaining immortal glory, he desperately seeks the perfection of eternal youth.

His wish to escape the curse of age and death would trace the course of his adventures. Once he had overcome his own historical achievements, managing to conquer the whole world, the Alexander of the *Romance* continued his journey beyond the limits of geography. His army, this time, did not desert him, but marched with him to the threshold of the Land of Wonders. At the final frontier of the world, they found a long bridge suspended over the abyss that separates what actually exists from the infinite realm of the possible. Alexander told his men to wait while he explored the surroundings. Not far from the bridge, covered by a mass of thorny shrubs, he spotted the profile of a statue. He got off his horse and with his bare hands began clearing it. The inscription on its base read: 'I have reached this point and I had to return. Dare go no further!' Exhilarated by his discovery, Alexander continued clearing the brambles. He stopped suddenly, aghast. The features of the statue's face, although worn by time, were unmistakably his own. And the lines on its base, he realized, had been inscribed by another version of himself, who had already been there. For a moment, the *Romance*'s Alexander and the historical Alexander were meeting each other in an uncanny game of mirrors.

Alexander remounted his horse and galloped back to the army assembled at the bridge. 'Rejoice, my men!' he cried, 'the omens are auspicious! Not far from here I found the statue of a god. The message inscribed on its base said: go further! The gods are with us, let us go!'[21]

Crossing the bridge into the Land of Wonders, they entered a deep-dream landscape, where the norms of the world no longer applied, and the distinctions of reason were suspended. Such was their amazement at the marvels they saw that they did not realize their march was taking them beyond the Land of Wonders. Only a change in the atmosphere signalled that they were about to enter a realm beyond imagination. Darkness descended upon them, permeating men and beasts. Their skin began to darken, until their silhouettes became indistinguishable from the landscape. Alexander raised his hand to stop the march. The soldiers made camp, staggering in the night. In the royal tent, raised in a clearing, Alexander waited for the cook to bring him food. By that point, the best that the supply wagon had to offer was a barrel of salted fish. The cook groped his way in the dark to a nearby stream to wash the salt off the fish. The moment he dipped his hands into the water, however, the fish came back to life and swam away.

The cook rushed back to Alexander, but when he reached the royal tent, he saw that the army was already on the move. A flock of magic birds had just appeared above the camp, crying that they had trespassed into the Land of the Blessed and that they needed to leave at once. Alexander disregarded the rules of humanity, but he did not dare to transgress those of divinity. He had ordered an immediate return to the bridge, and the cook was sent to his marching place among the foot soldiers. He had to wait until they had returned to the actual world before he could tell his king what had happened at the spring of eternal youth, now lost forever.[22]

## 11.

Death spared Alexander the sufferings of old age. When he died in the royal palace of Babylon, at the age of thirty-two, his youth was enshrined for eternity under a veil of legend, and his mortal body was replaced by the ethereal substance of ghosts. His corpse, however, was not without value. Like a holy relic, its possession would guarantee its owner an almost divine legitimacy as the successor to Alexander's throne. Alexander's general Ptolemy, now king of Egypt, was the first to reclaim it. Where else could the king's corpse be entombed, he argued, but in the most magnificent city that he had founded? Doubtlessly, out of the many cities that carried his name scattered across his empire, the one on the Mediterranean coast of Egypt had been his masterpiece.

Alexander had entrusted the construction of the city to Dinocrates of Rhodes, one of the most visionary architects of his time. Dinocrates had entered Alexander's retinue before the beginning of the expedition, winning the king's trust with a proposal well attuned to his megalomania: he had planned to carve an enormous statue of Alexander over the entire length of Mount Athos, to build a city on a terrace held by its right hand, and to channel the mountain streams into an artificial lake in the shape of a cup held by the statue's left hand. Alexander loved the project but could not proceed with its construction due to the lack of sufficient agricultural land in the surroundings to support the necessities of the population. From that day, the king and the architect became very close. Dinocrates accompanied Alexander in his expedition, parting ways only when they reached Egypt: he was to remain to supervise the building works of the new Alexandria while Alexander headed East to defeat the remaining Persian forces.[23]

Before leaving, Alexander took part in the rites that accompanied the foundation of a new city. The Egyptian priests poured flour along the perimeter of the first nucleus of Alexandria-by-Egypt. As soon as they had finished, all kinds of birds glided upon the flour and started devouring it. Disquieted by that celestial portent, Alexander asked his diviners to interpret it. It was a good omen, they reassured him. Like birds come from everywhere and go everywhere, so this city would welcome people of all races and its citizens would travel around the world.[24]

In fact, what had been promised for the new Alexandria already applied to the whole of Egypt, where a multitude of people from Africa, Asia and Europe lived alongside the natives. The Greek community was the most prominent among these resident foreigners: their merchants had travelled its routes for centuries, their mercenaries filled the ranks of the Egyptian army and their scholars flocked to the temples along the Nile to perfect their studies. The Egyptian priests used to mock the visiting philosophers by reminding them that, compared to their own ancient civilization, 'you Greeks are like children'.[25] Indeed, like children, the Greeks reverently looked to Egypt as the ancestral home of all knowledge.

Despite the persistence of its mythical aura, however, the Egypt that had fallen into Alexander's hands was no longer the splendid kingdom of old. Under the Persians, it had been reduced to a peripheral province of the empire. Its constant rebellions had made it suspect in the eyes of the authorities, who had not hesitated to punish and humiliate it. Although the Nile valley continued to gift its bounties and the priests still performed the sacred rites, a deep wound ran through the spirit of the Egyptians. That wound, Ptolemy realized, traced the way to winning the heart of his new subjects.

## 12.

When Ptolemy mounted the throne, he was aware of what was expected of him. Like the Pharaohs of old, the ruler of Egypt incarnated an invisible bridge between Heaven and Earth, channelling the blessings of the gods onto his people. But more importantly, at that time, the Egyptians thirsted for someone who could heal their bruised pride. They were looking for a saviour. And Ptolemy presented himself as such: Ptolemy *Soter*, 'The Saviour'.

He could not count on the magic arts of Nectanebo, nor could he rely on a native bond to the land to entice the favour of the local gods; his connection with the divine realm had to be forged from scratch. Thus, with the confidence of a storyteller who begins a new tale, one day Ptolemy announced that the the light of a new god had started shining in the Heavens: Serapis, the bestower of abundance upon the people of Egypt, an aid in their path to resurrection. In fact, he specified, Serapis had always existed. To the Egyptians of the previous generations, he had appeared in the form of the gods Osiris, Apis and Ammon. To the Greeks, he was known as the triad of Dionysus, Demeter and Zeus. But it was only now, under Ptolemy's rule, that his name had been discovered and his cult properly established.

Ptolemy ordered the construction of a monumental temple to Serapis, the Serapeum, in the centre of Alexandria. From there, the new cult spread throughout the whole Mediterranean and far beyond it, reaching the British Isles and Central Asia.

Serapis' artificial origin did not pose a problem to his worshippers. They were perfectly aware that what humans could see of reality was a product of their imagination, and that the gods, as humans knew them, were the fictional masks through which superhuman forces manifested themselves. The Mediterranean people of the time knew, and their mythologies often reminded them, that the true essence of the gods exceeded human understanding. Their authentic form must remain invisible, lest humans be destroyed by it. Conventional names must cover their authentic ones, which were to remain forever unpronounceable.

A detachment from language, the embrace of fiction and the practice of silence were shared attitude among initiates to the ancient mystery cults. They were also a staple, in a much more practical way, among those who lived in the kingdoms established by Alexander's generals. The Hellenistic monarchs enjoyed absolute power and were careful to identify and repress any dissent. The democratic assemblies of the Greek *poleis* had become a thing of the past; political life outside of the court and its bureaucracy was virtually extinguished. The last glimmers of freedom had withdrawn to the secret rooms where the mysteries were celebrated.

Secrecy itself deserved to have its own mythological mask. The theologians of Alexandria-by-Egypt stepped up to the challenge by creating the divine character of Harpocrates, god of silence and secrets. He was the young son of Serapis and, like his father, he condensed within himself the essence of other gods: the Egyptian Horus the Child and the Greek Eros, the winged son of Aphrodite. The Alexandrian artists fashioned for Harpocrates the body of a young boy, with cheeky eyes and a finger perennially lifted to his chin. From their workshops, a stream of statuettes with his effigy transported the god from Egypt to North Africa, Europe and as far as the Indian border.

But the inventiveness of kings, theologians and artists would not have sufficed to keep Serapis and Harpocrates alive, if the Mediterranean people had not made them their own. Travelling diviners, lowly priests and common worshippers nurtured and carried the new gods across the borders and the centuries, handling them with the same loving carelessness with which the storytellers carried the character of Alexander. Like Alexander, these gods continued to change as they moved through different landscapes, assuming new colours and learning foreign languages along the way. Thanks to their syncretism, their ineffable knowledge became communicable across peoples and cultures.

## 13.

Ptolemy began his life in the mountains of Macedonia and ended it on the coast of Egypt. He entered adulthood as a soldier and closed his eyes as a Pharaoh. He lived in an age when anything could reinvent itself as anything else, if Destiny so allowed. The same familiarity with invention characterizes the monumental project for which he remains best known. In the last years of his reign, he began draughting the plan for an edifice in Alexandria-by-Egypt, where old stories about the world would be preserved and new ones created: the Museum and its Library. Ptolemy's creation would soon become a centre of knowledge for the whole Mediterranean and a favourite home for ancient scientists. The Museion and its Library were much more than just repositories for objects and books: they were a space where scholars engaged in new research, produced new publications and ignited groundbreaking debates on all aspects of knowledge. Many of the greatest splendours of Greek science took place in their rooms, which hosted the mathematician and inventor Archimedes; the early anatomists Herophilus and Erasistratus; the astrologer Aristarchus, who first proposed a heliocentric system; Eratosthenes, the father of scientific geography and chronology; Hero, who invented the first steam engine; Ctesibius, the inventor of the science of pneumatics; among many others.[26]

Together with the scientists, hundreds of scholars in other disciplines lived in the Museion with free room and board, a generous salary provided by the state and full exemption from taxes. Hellenistic Alexandria also imposed itself as a capital of literature, with poets such as Callimachus of Cyrene, Apollonius Rhodius and Theocritus, the progenitor of pastoral poetry, grammarians like Aristophanes of Byzantium, who first introduced accents in the transcription of Greek and thus made possible a written grammar of the language, and literary critics like Aristarchus of Samothrace, to whom we owe the definitive editorial version of the Homeric epics, among countless other writers and thinkers.

The elderly Ptolemy's plan for the creation of the Museion and of its Library came to fruition after his death, through his son Ptolemy II Philadelphus. Although born in the safety of the royal court, Ptolemy II shared his father's curiosity for the adventurous transformations of the grand narratives. His patronage kickstarted one of the most important translation projects of antiquity, which would impact the course of history for millennia to come. Ptolemy II gathered the seventy most prominent Jewish scholars of his time and housed them on the island of Pharos, where they were tasked with producing the first-ever Greek translation of the Hebrew Bible. The *Septuaginta* (from the Greek 'seventy') is still celebrated as a work of truly inspired scholarship, since its authors were believed to have worked under the direct guidance of the divine spirit. Unbeknownst both to Ptolemy II and to his Jewish translators, their work would later play a fundamental role in spreading Christianity across the Greek-speaking world and, from there, to Europe.

Piety and studiousness, however, were not the only traits of culture under the Ptolemaics. A wind of radical ideas and transgressive practices also swept through their kingdom, issuing from the North African city of Cyrene. The founder of this movement, Aristippus the Elder, a former disciple of Socrates, had established his school in the same house where he lived, scandalously, in the company of prostitutes. His philosophy claimed that there were no real foundations for the things and values that people held as 'natural' or 'moral'. The true reality of the world was inaccessible to people's minds, and all that humans could know was the range of their own sensations. When a person looked at a white wall, they should avoid saying that it 'was' white, but rather, more modestly, that the wall 'was whitening' their gaze. The only things that people could hold as real were their own feelings of pain and pleasure, suffering and happiness. Thus, any norm that inflicted suffering had to be discarded, and beliefs in the existence of both 'natural' and 'supernatural' things had to be deemed as superstitions. Aristippus's ideas passed to his daughter Arete, the new head of his school, and then to her son Aristippus the Younger. Before being temporarily erased by history, they culminated with Aristippus the Younger's favourite student, the philosopher Theodorus, known as 'The Atheist'. While the Ptolemaic monarchs, priests and artists were busy replenishing the Heavens with new divinities, the Cyrenaics were intent on emptying them.[27]

## 14.

The Ptolemaic dynasty was to be the longest in Egyptian history. Only the rise of the Roman Empire could extinguish it when the last ruler of Egypt, Queen Cleopatra VII, commited suicide rather than being taken prisoner. In her splendour, both in life and in death, Cleopatra perfectly embodied the spirit of the Graeco-Egyptian world. She was a cosmopolitan polyglot well-versed in the political uses of culture, and a daring innovator who brought together different traditions to produce an atmosphere of dazzling syncretism. Her roots were set so firmly in the world started by Alexander that when she died, it was as if an entire age had died with her.

The very term 'cosmopolitism' dates to the days of Alexander. It was first used by a peculiar character, who was to become Alexander's favourite doppelganger. His name was Diogenes, but to his contemporaries, he was known simply as 'the doglike', that is, the *cynic*. He practised philosophy on the streets of Athens, where he lived inside a tub. His true home, he would rejoin when challenged, was larger than any king's palace. When asked where he belonged, Diogenes would reply with a neologism, saying that he was a 'citizen of the world', a *kosmopolites*. The only true commonwealth, he claimed, is that which is as wide as the universe.[28]

During his long life, Diogenes passed through adventures worthy of a *Romance* of his own. As a young man, he was exiled from his native city for having forged the official coinage. To the judges, he replied that all things should be held in common. While sailing through the Mediterranean, he was captured by pirates and sold into slavery. At the slave market, when asked what job he could do, he replied that he could govern people. Then, pointing to a wealthy man among his prospective buyers, he told the seller, 'Sell me to that man, he needs a master'. When he arrived in Athens, he studied under the philosopher Antisthenes. Diogenes learnt from him to distrust anyone who took pride in belonging to a land or a nation. Those who boasted to have sprung from their native soil, Antisthenes said, were no better born than snails and wingless locusts.[29]

Like the philosophers of Cyrene, Diogenes refused to bow to social conventions. The only true law was that of happiness, which required one to cater only to the simple necessities of human life. Wealth, power and social status were the typical attributes of those who lacked the essentials. The wise wanted for nothing, as long as they had what was strictly necessary to live. The wise were free, because very little, if anything, could be taken away from them.

One day, this 'Socrates gone mad', as people sometimes called him, crossed paths with Alexander the Great – although it would be more accurate to say that the king went out of his way to meet him. Alexander looked for him in Athens and found him stretched out on his usual street corner, basking in the sun. Their brief exchange went down in history. 'I am Alexander, the great king', he said. 'And I am Diogenes, the doglike', was the reply. When the young king asked him what he could offer to such a wise man, Diogenes demanded that he 'Step out of my light'. Alexander walked off, amazed. To his friends, he said, 'If I was not Alexander, I wish I was Diogenes'.[30]

Like a spell, these words did not fail to bring about their effect. On the same day when Alexander breathed his last in his Babylonian palace, the old Diogenes, after eating a raw octopus, died on the streets of Athens. Having no empire to leave to greedy generals, he asked that his body be thrown to the dogs, so that also in death he might be useful to his brethren.

## 15.

Alexander and Diogenes were to meet again under another sky. Their story continued in the pages of the Romance at the time when the great expedition to the East was about to enter the vastness of India. The army was marching through unknown landscapes, among the aerial roots dangling off the banyan trees and the flashing colours of birds as yet unseen by the Greeks. Frightening legends surrounded those regions. Alexander and his generals, who had studied under Aristotle, expected soon to be reaching soon the final frontiers of the world, where the continents plunge beneath the great Ocean. The foot soldiers, drawing from old folktales, were on the lookout for monsters. As they proceeded through the forests, they took each step with a hint of hesitation.

A scout informed Alexander that, not far from there, a community of sages lived among the trees, naked and solitary like the beasts or the gods. The local people revered them like saints, claiming that their leader, in particular, was the wisest man in the world, around whom the other sages gathered like petals on a stem. That was enough information for Alexander. He left his soldiers in the encampment, took a range of splendid gifts from his treasury and mounted his horse. He rode without escort, following a path through the forest. He did not find it unbecoming for the most powerful monarch in the world to venture in search of a common man, like a child on their way to their teacher. At the end of the path, he found a naked man lying on the roots of a massive fig tree as comfortably as on the softest bed. Alexander laid his gifts on the ground. Only a sense of royal dignity held him from bowing. The naked man slowly lifted his gaze to the intruder, then looked at the gifts, then went back to resting. 'Your treasures are of no use to me', he said calmly. Alexander remained silent. He would have liked to reply that he had much more to offer than a handful of gifts. The whole of Asia had bowed to his sword! As if replying, the naked sage continued: 'What use is there in having amassed the largest empire on Earth, when in just a few years you will be devoured by worms or consumed by the fire of a pyre, like the poorest peasant? All that will be left of you is what you have been, not what you have amassed and conquered'.

Under the shade of the trees, thousands of miles from Greece, Alexander felt strangely at home. He could almost hear the marketplace buzzing behind him, and the dogs barking around a philosopher's tub. Why, wasn't it Diogenes in front of him? His words had a different accent, his skin looked darker, but the truthfulness of his discourse, his *logos*, had not changed since those bygone days in Athens.

It was he, Alexander, who had changed. He was no longer the youth who had said to his friends, 'If I was not Alexander, I wish I was Diogenes'. By the time he had reached India, Alexander had become an old man – as old as anyone who is nearing the end of their life. Standing in front of the naked sage, Alexander did not apologize for the way he had spent his life, nor for the suffering he had inflicted. He had lived as his Destiny had willed for him: imprisoned in a life so impoverished that he had everything except himself.

As he remounted, Alexander bade his farewell in a dreamy voice, as if speaking to someone from a distant past.

'Sometimes – he said – I wish I was not Alexander'.[31]

## 16.

The episode of Alexander riding alone through the forest to meet the naked sage has little in common with the facts of history. His conversation with the wise man comes from a literary divertissement by the late-ancient Christian bishop Palladius of Galatia, inserted in the *Romance* by unknown hands. A devout follower of the monks living in the Egyptian desert, Palladius put in the mouth of the Indian Brahmins the typical Christian reproaches against worldly attachments, as if to stress their universality. In good Mediterranean fashion, Palladius and those who copied his text had no qualms about transgressing borders: religious, linguistic, geographic and chronological.[32]

Alexander did indeed meet the Indian sages during his expedition, but when he rode into the forest, he was accompanied by a retinue of writers, scientist and philosophers. Little remains to document the exchange between the Indian *gymnosophoi* (naked sages) and the Greek *pilosophoi*. Of the philosophers who took part in the meeting, only one made it back to Greece to divulge what he had learnt. His name was Pyrrho, native of Elis. Not long before his Indian adventure, he had worked as a painter in a modest workshop until a chance encounter with the teachings of Democritus, the theorist of atomism, directed his life towards the path of philosophy. We do not know what led him to join Alexander's expedition, but we are told that he followed it to the end. Upon his return to Elis, he took to living austerely outside society, like the sages he had met in India. To the growing number of students who gathered around him, he consigned his teachings directly, never resorting to writing.

He taught them that the world does not offer the kind of terrain where absolute truths can grow. Our senses deceive us, our mind is limited, even our logic is a victim to inescapable contradictions. Whatever distinctions we draw between entities, whichever names or values we assign them, the true nature of the world will remain utterly indeterminable. Only the pure principle of existence truly exists, but it lies beyond the short reach of our concepts and language. Thus, he said, we need to suspend our judgement towards the world and withhold any firm assertion about reality. The apparent order of the world, as shaped by the norms and definitions invented by the unwise, is to be abandoned in favour of a wise speechlessness (*aphasia*) towards the existent. Only in silence can we hope to catch a glimpse of things as they are. Then, in silence, we can patiently try to harvest the most precious of treasures: freedom from worry (*ataraxia*).

The Indian roots of Pyrrho's teachings bore fruit long after his death. Through his student Timon, his ideas reached the young philosopher Arcesilaus, who was to become the head of the Platonic Academy in Athens and to impress such a novel form on official Platonism that it acquired a name of its own: *skepsis*, 'inquiry'.

The voice of the Indian sages continued to resound through the *logos* of Pyrrho, Arcesilaus and the sceptics. They chastised the intellectual ambitions of the philosophers, reminding them that during our lifetime, we can aspire to achieve wisdom, not knowledge. They warned that worldly goods cannot deliver happiness, since happiness consists in not being moved by the illusions that we project around ourselves and in not falling for the temptation of believing our own thoughts. They encouraged every person to sabotage their own inner machinery, from which concepts are thrown onto reality like nets vainly cast to catch the sea. They exhorted us to doubt even doubt itself, and to strive for the freedom that comes with complete tranquillity: to live in the world, as it is our destiny, but without ever surrendering to it.

# 17.

While the ideas of the Indian sages were travelling Westward, the Mediterranean world was moving to the East. Following in Alexander's footsteps, a stream of Greek migrants began pouring into Central Asia. The *Yonas* (Ionians), as they were called by the locals, made their home in a land that, not long before, had seemed unreachable to their compatriots.

They settled in the cities founded by Alexander, establishing themselves as the keepers of a commercial and cultural network that connected all regions of Central Asia. To the incoming travellers, their cities felt like a strange combination of exotic and familiar atmospheres. Greek theatres and gymnasia rose among the porticoes, where merchants and travellers exchanged goods and information from every corner of Asia, Europe and North Africa. Altars to the Olympian gods smoked near the Buddhist stupas and the temples dedicated to the Hindu divinities. Their lifestyle and the language which some of them still spoke were Greek – yet they were also Central Asian, or, in the vocabulary of the time, 'Indian'.

When the early generations of Greek migrants died out, the memory of the Mediterranean shores also began to fade. In its stead, the new Indo-Greeks created a Mediterranean of their own, stretched across sand and valleys, with caravanserais as its coasts and camels as its sails. Like the sea of their ancestors, it was a place where tradition survived by never remaining stable, and identities endlessly merged into one another. It was a crucible of the imagination, where the substance of the world was constantly dissolved and coagulated.

Eventually, this dislocated Mediterranean produced its own mythological 'Alexander'. His name, like Alexander's, came in different versions: Menander to his Greek-speaking subjects, Milinda to his Indian admirers. To both groups, he was the rare example of a wise monarch with a true interest in philosophy. According to legend, he expected every scholar who entered his kingdom to present themselves at his palace and expound their doctrine in front of him. Thus, Brahmins, Magi and Greek philosophers flocked to his court to defend their theories. Menander listened to their arguments, tested them and having found them invariably flawed, politely dismissed them. But he continued to search for knowledge, although with ever-decreasing hopes. Until, one day, he was visited by a Buddhist sage called Nagasena. The king welcomed him and proceeded with his usual examination. Their conversation continued throughout the day and after sunset, while the philosopher and the king sparred with questions and answers. When Nagasena finally fell silent, Menander stood up and bowed in front of him. From that day onwards, he would take on the Buddhist *dharma* as his own doctrine.

Menander ordered the construction of stupas dedicated to the Buddha, and on his coinage, he swapped the images of the Greek gods for the Buddhist symbol of the wheel. When old age reached him, he abdicated the throne to move to a hermitage in the wilderness, to prepare himself for the next round of transformations. His legacy, however, lived on in the hearts of his people. His ashes, like those of the Buddha, were divided as relics among his subjects, and the Indo-Greeks did not cease to lend their skills as thinkers, writers and artists in the service of the 'noble eightfold path' of Buddhism.[33] His ghost made its home in the pages of the canonical Buddhist text *Milinda Panha*, where his conversation with the sage Nagasena continues to this day.[34]

## 18.

Long before Menander's reign, another hybrid people inhabited the lands of Central Asia. They lived in hidden valleys high up in the mountains, where Alexander first encountered them. They had blue eyes and spoke Greek, and they welcomed the Macedonians like long-lost relatives. Since Alexander had arrived while they were celebrating a festival in honour of Dionysus, they invited him to take part in their sacrifices. Late at night, over abundant drinks, they confided to him the secret story of their origin: they were the descendants of a much earlier expedition, from a time before history, when the Gods still walked on Earth.[35]

In those days, so the story goes, Dionysus was still intent on actively spreading his own cult all over the world. Since the people of India had refused to offer him sacrifices, the young god mustered two armies and waged war against them. The first army included drummers, flautists, maenads, shamans and soldiers from the Mediterranean coasts; the other, satyrs, centaurs, cyclops, nymphs, panthers, climbing plants and creatures from the underworld. The two armies formed a dancing procession, ready to slaughter anyone who dared to stand in their way. The lakes turned red at their passage with the blood of the fallen. But Dionysus, in his mercy, transformed the stains of war into wine.

After a long and brutal conflict, the Indians eventually succumbed to the assaults of Dionysus' army. As he prepared to head Westward towards Greece, the victorious god left a parting gift to his new subjects. He taught them the art of winemaking, and the slopes of India soon bloomed with the fruit of the vine.[36]

Alexander, too, knew how to mix blood and gifts. Among the ruins of the Indian cities he had conquered, he planted a seed that, like that of the vine, was to bear a fruit of ecstasy. It remained underground for centuries, waiting for the opportune moment to come to light. It sprouted around the time of Menander, during a period when the religious landscape of Asia was undergoing a profound transformation. Buddhism was growing out of its earlier form, focused on the self-liberation of a spiritual elite, into a project of salvation for every sentient being. Its heavens were filling up with *Bodhisattvas*, heroic figures who bestowed their wisdom and compassion upon all creatures. Its preachers were broadcasting the good news that every person, no matter their status or provenance, had in themselves the potential of the 'Buddha nature'. Its philosophers, too, were developing new ideas about reality. They described the world as the flickering of a light, or a gallery of fleeting images, behind which lay the absolute void, invisible and without substance. Buddhism was becoming a 'Great Vehicle' (*Mahayana*) available to anyone who wished to sail beyond the painful illusions of the world.

To propagate this new universal doctrine, the old set of devotional images was no longer sufficient. In the beginning, the Buddha had been represented only through symbols, such as the shape of two footprints, the silhouette of an empty throne, or the foliage of a fig tree. Now, a more powerful visual language was needed, capable of moving hearts and minds across borders.

It was at that point that Alexander's gift finally fructified. From the followers of his Asian expedition, a lineage of painters and sculptors had emerged who still preserved the techniques and aesthetics of their forefathers. The ones in the region of Gandhara, in particular, had developed their skills to an impressive level of syncretic perfection. The Buddhism of the Great Vehicle turned to them to create a style that was at once so familiar and so foreign as to be able to speak to people from every nation.

The result was a visual and religious revolution. For the first time, the Buddha acquired a body. A distinctly foreign body. The halo surrounding his head resembled the solar circle of Apollo; his face had something of a youthful Dionysus; his posture mimicked that of an athlete; the drapery on his dress was unmistakably Greek. Even his hair, with flowing curls tied in a chignon, spoke of a remote elsewhere.

The Gandharan statues of the Buddha and the *Bodhisattvas* portrayed foreigners passing through the world on their way to liberation. Their compassion knew no preference for this or that community. In their eyes, the whole world was the syncretic oneness of all living beings.

## 19.

It is extraordinary how a brutal man such as Alexander could become, after death, a poet of world religions. Thanks to him, the Egyptian pantheon gained new gods, the message of *Mahayana* Buddhism was made visible and the epics of the Greeks acquired a new hero. Only for his earliest enemies, the Persians, was he nothing but a blasphemous demon.[37] What he had done to their religion, on the night of his conquest of the sacred city of Persepolis, had been truly beyond forgiveness.

It had been a drunken night of celebrations. Among the forest of pillars in the main hall of the imperial palace, he and his generals had gathered with the courtiers and the women in their retinue. At daybreak, the alcoholic frenzy reached its peak. An Athenian woman stood up, rallying the party to avenge the honour of the Greeks. A century ago, she cried, the Persians burnt the Acropolis of Athens; now it is the Greeks' turn to burn down the Persian monuments! Torches suddenly appeared in everyone's hands. Flames engulfed the palace. The local Persians stared horrified at the raging blaze. Everything was burning: the symbols of power, the works of art, the treasures of textile, ivory and gold. Most tragically, in the inner chambers of the palace, the only existing copies of the Zoroastrian holy scriptures were being reduced to ashes.[38]

Alexander immediately regretted the arson. He took on Persian habits, started thinking of himself as a Persian emperor, and even gave a royal funeral to his defeated predecessor, Darius. Yet, to the Persians, he remained *Sekandar gujastak*, 'Alexander the accursed', the antithesis to their very spirit.

For once, his crimes seemed to be preventing him from posthumously intervening in the world. But it was not so. To return to Persia, Alexander's ghost had only to wait until the jolts of history would destabilize the imagination of its people once again. He laid in waiting for over a millennium. The sun set over the age of Hellenism, then over the empires of the Parthians and the Sasanians. By the eleventh century, the Persian lands were embroiled in a cataclysmic transformation. The old Zoroastrian faith was on the brink of vanishing, while the new message of Islam was taking hold of popular devotion; hostile Turkish tribes were pushing from the North, and the weak rulers of Persia were struggling to keep them behind the borders.

Alexander chose this fragile moment to stage his comeback. He made his entrance through the verses of a masterpiece of epic poetry, Abul-Qasem Ferdowsi's *Shahnameh*, where the shattered line of Persian history was recomposed as a seamless unity. Among the lineage of the rightful kings of Persia, Ferdowsi reserved a place for Alexander. His extraordinary life was a model for any monarch who wished to create a unified country out of a war-ravaged land. In the *Shahnameh*, Alexander was portrayed as a living coincidence of opposites: he was a Christian who lived by the guidance of his Greek-pagan tutor Aristotle, respected Zoroastrianism and visited the Kaaba in Mecca. He was a wise king, more interested in acquiring wisdom than in conquering new territory. To his enemies, he would say: 'I have no wish to seize your country, nor to fight against you on the plains of war. My aim is to travel round the earth, to see the spacious world in its entirety. I look for justice.'[39]

Such a lofty perspective, however, belonged to Alexander only by virtue of his natural, essential Persianness. To the Greeks who believed he descended from the king of Macedon, and to the Egyptians who wanted him to be the child of a Pharaoh, Ferdowsi responded that Sekandar (Alexander) was, in fact, the secret son of the Persian emperor Dara. His father had repudiated his mother on account of her bad breath and had sent her back to her native Macedonia. He did not know that she was already pregnant with his son. When she arrived back home in Pella, she gave birth to a boy and called him Sekandar, after the herb that had cured her of her bad odour. Under the guidance of Aristotle, Sekandar grew into a powerful warrior and a wise king. Meanwhile, in Persia, his father Dara had raised his arrogant half-brother Darab (Darius) as his own heir. The two siblings would meet on the battlefield, where the correct hierarchy of birthright was to be re-established. Sekandar fought and defeated Darab in what was, in fact, a civil war between Persian kings. To his vanquished brother, he said that they were 'from the same stock, the same root, the same people'.[40] Sekandar had conquered the whole world only because he was a Persian monarch, as a fulfilment of the superior destiny of the Persian people.

To be accepted as a legitimate ruler, Alexander was expected to renounce the radical foreignness that had been the mark of both his life and his afterlife.

## 20.

Even after his redemption, the Persian Alexander retained something of his earlier demonic nature. Two horns bulged on his forehead. He kept them disguised under his crown until, at the opportune moment, he would reveal them to terrify his opponents.

In the tales of the travelling storytellers, Sekandar ceased to be 'the accursed' to become instead *Dhu al-Qarnayn*, 'He of the two-horns'.

These two horns had a noble, even sacred origin. According to Islamic tradition, they played a role also in the establishment of the Muslim faith. During Muhammad's lifetime, his fellow tribesmen had consulted the Jewish sages, asking for their help to assess the truthfulness of his message. The Jewish sages recommended asking Muhammad about a man who had travelled and reached the East and the West of the Earth: if he could speak about these things, he was indeed a prophet. Put to the test, Muhammad told the story of Dhu al-Qarnayn, 'He of the two-horns', the hero who had chased the sun from its deathbed in the West to its cradle in the East. Dhu al-Qarnayn had been a righteous king, who had modelled his life in accord with the law of God. He had also been a valorous warrior, who had imprisoned the hordes of Gog and Magog behind an iron wall, where they will remain until the end time.[41]

'He with the two-horns' is mentioned in the eighteenth Sura of the Quran, and even though his real name is left unspecified, there is little doubt among the commentators that Dhu al-Qarnayn is, in fact, Alexander. Of course, Alexander had lived long before the revelations of Muhammad, but so had also those ancient Jewish prophets who were revered as Allah's early messengers. Alexander was not an Arab, but the same was true of Adam, the first perfect man, and of millions of Muslims beyond the Arab world. And yet, more seriously, Alexander had been a murderer, a brutal conqueror and a man devoured by his thirst for glory. How could these traits, so remote from anything holy, allow him to enter the gallery of Muslim heroes?

The answer, of course, is that there was never just one Alexander. Especially after his death, the historical Alexander had almost entirely vanished, evolving into the character of an endless fable. His new incarnation as a Muslim hero was not sanctioned by the historians or approved by the religious jurists, but it was crafted by the voice of the poets. Not the high poets of the royal court, like Ferdowsi, but the anonymous poets of the popular tradition.

Different versions of Alexander's story emerged in Persia during the Islamic Middle Ages. Their written retelling, the *Iskandarnamah*, played an important role in spreading Islam in once-Zoroastrian lands.[42]

In his new life as a Muslim, Alexander was finally free from the shackles of history. His adventures became entirely uncoupled from their historical geography, growing into a full circumnavigation of the world, from Greece to Andalusia, through the Land of Darkness and the great Western Ocean, to Russia and China. He was made to walk through a new Land of Wonders, even more extraordinary than the one in the *Romance*. He fought the giants and the elephant-eared people, conquered the valiant flying fairies and eventually married their queen. By mixing his own blood with the fairy queen and promoting the marriage of males and females from the two species, he started a hybrid race of human-fairies. He saw the trumpet-carrying angel Israfil standing on top of the world-mountain Qaf, at the point where Heaven touches Earth. He was granted access to a level of reality which is usually reserved only for the prophets.

The Muslim Alexander was no longer obsessed with glory, adventure or knowledge. He was moved instead by a deep faith in the ineffable Divinity residing at the heart of reality and by a burning desire to witness its splendour. This Alexander conquered the world almost by accident, while travelling in pursuit of the invisible God who is known under the name of Allah. He spent his nights in prayer, and everything he did, he accomplished only to fulfil the orders of the angels of God.

## 21.

The Muslim Alexander, too, ventured in search of the spring of eternal youth. News had reached him that the mythical spring flowed in the Land of Darkness, beyond the edge of the world. He set out with his army, and after a long march, they reached a strange community of people who lived without kings, without judges and without doors. They held everything in common, and thus they needed for nothing. Among them, he found an exceptional character: al-Khidr, the holy 'green man', green as the robes of the inhabitants of Heaven and as the couches on which they recline, green as the dome of the Mosque of the Prophet and as his favourite colour. Wherever he sat, he would turn even an arid landscape green with vegetation.[43]

Alexander realized that Khidr had been sent by God to help him find the spring of eternal youth, and promptly placed his own army under his command. With Khidr at their head, they ventured beyond the world, into the Land of Darkness.

Throughout the journey, Khidr stayed with Alexander's army during the marches and disappeared as soon as they would stop to rest. One day, while wandering alone, Khidr came across a rivulet of water emerging from the soil. He drank from it, and it tasted like nothing he had ever savoured. He hurried back to

Alexander to tell him that he had found the mythical spring. The two jumped on their horses, galloped to the exact same spot, but when they arrived, the spring had already vanished. The following day, Khidr, too, was gone.[44]

At this point, the storytellers of the *Iskandarnamah* would look at their audience, gathered in a square or in a house and would lower their voice: 'The King was sick at heart and full of regret; all his efforts had been in vain.' It was inevitable that Alexander would fail where Khidr had succeeded. As recounted in the Quran, even Moses had failed to keep up with Khidr, thus wasting his chance to drink, not from the spring of eternal youth, but from that of divine wisdom.

Back in the early days of Israel, Moses had been sent by God to look for a mysterious teacher, Khidr, who would bring down his arrogance for having been chosen as God's prophet. Moses was told to carry a salted fish and to expect to meet Khidr as soon as the fish would come back to life. As it had been said, so it happened. The fish revived moments before Khidr appeared. Moses implored to be accepted as his disciple, but Khidr had little desire to teach someone who 'would not be able to remain patient with me'. Moses promised complete and unquestioning obedience, until, after much insistence, Khidr agreed to take him as his travelling companion. The two walked to the shore 'at the confluence of the two seas', where they embarked on a boat of friendly mariners. Once the coast had receded in the distance, Khidr began damaging the boat. Moses, bemused, could not help questioning his master. 'Didn't I tell you that you would not be able to remain patient with me?' Khidr replied.

Back on land, Khidr seemed to take pleasure in ever more erratic behaviour. They met a young boy on the road, and Khidr killed him with his staff. Then they entered a village where the locals refused to give them food and hospitality, and Khidr repaired the crumbling wall of one of their houses. Again, Moses could not control his disbelief. 'Why are you doing these things?' he asked. He had disobeyed his master once too often. Khidr revealed to him the secret reasons behind his actions, then turned around and vanished, never to return. As a parting admonition, Khidr only said: 'and all these things, I did not do of my own accord'.[45]

Moses lost the only teacher who could have disclosed to him a truly divine knowledge. He failed to grasp the mystery that animated everything, without distinctions between 'good' and 'evil', 'this' and 'that' and 'native' and 'foreigner'.

## 22.

Without Khidr, Alexander had no defences against his own mortality. His body succumbed to illness and death, while his youth remained only that of a character in a fable. But his adventure with Khidr in the Land of Darkness had not been for nothing. Although Khidr could not save him from his destiny, in the end, it was Alexander who changed the destiny of Khidr.

From then on, the venerable Green Man multiplied his appearances. He continued travelling the world, undertaking each journey disguised as a different character. He presented himself to the Jews as a manifestation of the prophet Elijah or the angel Samael, the divine prosecutor who struggled with Jacob for an entire night. For the Christians of the Levant, he took on the form of Saint George or Saint Sargis the General. For the Zoroastrians, he embodied the spirit of Sraosha, the angel of consciousness. To this day, in the shrine of Beit Jala, near Jerusalem, Muslims, Christians and Jews venerate Khidr together, praising him in a symphony of different names.

The meeting with Alexander also changed Khidr's bearing towards his own followers. His earlier ways as a trickster grew into those of a spiritual commander. In Sufism, the mystical tradition of Islam, Khidr became the archetype of the perfect master. Like him, a Sufi master would demand inexhaustible patience from their students. The master would become a living display of the ineffable complexity of reality, which never comes with its own explanation. The students, in turn, would be expected to follow their master with unquestioning obedience. This would be only the first stage of their travel with Khidr. As the Green Man had done with Moses and Alexander, so the Sufi master brought their students as close as possible to the springs of eternal life and knowledge. At that point, a further transformation was required. The student was bound to fail unless they abandoned the distinctions of language and recognized the grain of evil that stains the good and the goodness that irradiates from the darkest abyss. They had to cease identifying with themselves and acting 'of their own accord', relinquishing all ownership of their own identity. If they wished to succeed where Moses and Alexander had failed, the Sufi student had to grow out of the position of being Khidr's travelling companion to become themselves Khidr.

Then, in the blaze of their old selves, they would find at last what Moses and Alexander could not grasp. From then on, Khidr would live through them. They would find themselves again on the shoreline at the edge of the world, at the confluence of all the seas. Only, this time, they would already know where to go.

We, too, will continue our journey through the Mediterranean imagination along the path of spiritual adventure. As we depart from the age of Alexander, we should prepare ourselves to enter the company of another generation who sought a life outside time and a homeland beyond geography. In the next chapter, we shall walk with them through one of the darkest turns in the history of the Mediterranean. We now take leave from the foreigners of Hellenism, to join the cosmonauts of Late Antiquity.

# Meanwhile in the Mediterranean...

## Fourth century BC to sixth century AD

*338 BC – Rome defeats all its neighbours and gains control over the entire Italian peninsula.*

*264–146 BC – After three major wars, Carthage is destroyed and Rome takes over its territories. In that same year, Rome conquers the Greek peninsula.*

*50 BC – Julius Caesar completes the conquest of Gaul.*

*44 BC – Julius Caesar is assassinated.*

*30 BC – Rome conquers Egypt, and the last Hellenistic Pharaoh, Queen Cleopatra VII, commits suicide rather than fall captive.*

*27 BC – Augustus, great-nephew of Caesar, ends the Republican age of Rome and becomes the first Roman emperor.*

*0 AD – A boy called Jesus is born in a stable in Bethlehem.*

*54–68 AD – The Roman emperor Nero unleashes the first wave of persecutions against the Christians.*

*66–73 AD* – During the First Jewish-Roman war, the Second Temple in Jerusalem is set ablaze and destroyed.

*117 AD* – The Roman Empire reaches its maximum territorial extent, from Scotland, through Germany and Romania, to North Africa and Iraq.

*193 AD* – The 'Year of the Five Emperors' inaugurates a period of bloody civil wars to determine who would succeed to the imperial throne of Rome.

*286 AD* – Diocletian divides the Roman Empire into a Western and an Eastern part.

*313 AD* – The emperors Constantine I and Licinius issue the Edict of Milan, declaring that Christianity is now a tolerated religion within the Roman Empire.

*324 AD* – The emperor Constantine lays the foundations of a new capital: Constantinople.

*378 AD* – In the Battle of Adrianople, an army of Goths defeats the Roman legions and kills the Eastern Roman emperor Valens.

*406 AD* – A major crossing of the Rhine River by barbaric tribes destabilizes Roman control over central Europe.

*410 AD* – The Visigoths, led by the former Roman general Alaric, sack the city of Rome.

*476 AD* – The child emperor Romulus Augustulus is deposed by the Goth general Odoacer, marking the customary date for the end of the Western Roman Empire.

*529 AD* – The emperor Justinian orders the closure of the Academy in Athens.

# 3

# *Cosmonauts*

# *Late Antiquity*

### 1.

A small convoy of carts was passing through the south-eastern gates of Rome one autumn day in 417 AD. The drivers, wrapped in woolly grey cloaks, bounced on their seats to the rhythm of the large stones that paved the road. The morning light cast a soft glow on the surrounding countryside, gilding a metallic sheen on the surface of the funeral monuments that rose like riverbanks along the roadway. From the mute inscriptions, the dead reminded the travellers that their final destination was not at the end of the road, but underground on its sides.

Hey, you, come here. Rest a little. Are you shaking your head? Don't you want to come? All the same, you will have to return here in the end.

You who are reading, think! From nothingness, how rapidly we fall back into nothingness.

> Here lies Leburna, acting teacher. I died many times, but never like this. To you up there, I wish well.
>
> We are the dust of this road.[1]

The servants shivered, perched amidst the stacks of furniture and supplies on the open carts. From the curtains of a large, covered carriage, the sound of chatter was spreading between the hoofbeats of the draught animals. In the half-light inside the carriage, seated upon carpets and cushions, a group of elegantly dressed men were in rapt conversation. They laughed often, prolonging their laughter until it revealed the effort. One of them took a glass from a tray and raised it towards the man sitting at the back of the carriage. 'Recite, Rutilius, once again!' The others joined in the toast, while Rutilius Namatianus, straightening his back as much as the low ceiling allowed, stretched out his arm and hand in the manner of the rhetoricians.

> Listen, O fairest queen of the world, Rome . . . thou mother of men and mother of gods . . . thee do we chant, and shall, while destiny allows, forever chant. None can be safe if forgetful of thee.[2]

His voice faltered mid-sentence, hurriedly clapped for by his friends. Rutilius turned around and drew back the curtains, letting in a stream of autumnal light. It was almost time for the grape harvest, but the vineyards were abandoned. He could see the remains of burnt houses scattered across the fields and the fresh graves of those who had been caught by the fury of the Visigoth troops. From the vegetation that grew luxuriantly, knotted in green and yellow tangles over the sides of the road, he could sense the awakening of a primal power, ready to swallow up the works of men.

Rutilius remained silent while the rewilding countryside passed by. Rome, the city that had welcomed people from all over the world, was now deserted by them all. Rutilius, too, was among the fugitives. News had reached him that the Visigoths had also attacked his native land in southern Gaul, and he felt duty-bound to try and salvage what he could from the land of his ancestors. He would have much preferred to stay. Rome had taken him in as a young man and had given him everything the world had to offer. It had made him a citizen and a member of the senatorial class. It had also made him a poet, and now that everything was lost, only poetry was left to give him some relief.

'Don't stop!' his friends called out to him. Rutilus extended his arm once more, though this time it hung lower, his voice cracking with emotion.

> Oh Rome, wherever there are living things, there are you also. You have united distant nations . . . What was only a world, you have made a city . . . Hear me, O Rome: may misfortune be forgotten; may your wounds close and heal. . . . Surrounded by failure, hope for prosperity; may you be enriched by all your losses. Even the stars must set before they rise again. You know the moon wanes before it waxes.[3]

The splashing sound of waves announced their arrival at the port of Fiumicino. The men dismounted from the covered carriage, stretching their limbs as if rising from a midday sleep. Rutilius looked back towards the road to Rome. He listened to the wind, seeking the distant sound of crowds gathered in the theatres and in the circus. In the sky, among the autumn clouds, he thought he could see a radiant glow opening up over the seven hills of Rome. His friends surrounded him one last time, and Rutilius did not tire of embracing them and bidding them farewell while his slaves transferred the luggage to the boats hired for the journey.

It was not the season for sailing, but the inland roads to Gaul were hardly less dangerous than the stormy sea. Nobody seemed able to put a stop to the raids of the Visigoths anymore. In the countryside, the peasants sought refuge within the walls of their masters' farms. Rome itself was moribund. Its few remaining inhabitants clustered around the stones of the old buildings, like mussels on a rock. The temples were in ruins, their secret chambers pillaged; the walls were breached, the aqueducts obstructed, the fountains dry and covered in weeds. Only the churches remained intact, spared by the fury of the Christianized barbarians. Rutilius looked at his small fleet at the docks and at his nervous crew. What devastations would they find in Gaul, at the heart of the lost war against the barbarians?

## 2.

When Rutilius undertook his voyage, Rome had already ceased to be the capital of the empire. The court had withdrawn to Ravenna, on the Adriatic coast of Italy, hoping that the malaria-ridden swamps would protect them from aggression. After decades of civil war, the Western Roman provinces had virtually no army left to fight off the assaults of Goths, Slavs and Germans. The nadir had been reached a few years earlier, while Rutilius was still in the eternal city. The Roman general Alaric, disappointed with how his Visigoth troops had been treated by the emperors they had served, had crossed the Alps and threatened to invade Italy. The senate had indignantly refused to negotiate, even when Alaric had entered Latium and laid siege to Rome. Thus, in the August of 410 AD, for the first time in eight centuries, Rome had been conquered and sacked.[4]

News of the sack reverberated throughout the Mediterranean. Even the Christians, whose golden age had just dawned, felt the ground crumbling beneath their feet. For Saint Jerome, 'the whole world perished in one city. Who would believe that Rome, the mother of nations, had also become their tomb?'[5] For Saint Augustine, now that the 'city of men' had fallen, history itself had come to an end: the future lay beyond the catastrophes of the world, in the 'city of God'.[6]

Rutilius and his retinue had no interest in swapping this world for some heavenly 'city of God'. Yet, as they sailed northwards, a sense of cosmic death began infecting them also. Having left the ruins of Rome, their journey towards Gaul continued along a trail of ruins. Life seemed to have transferred from the realm of humans to the unruly vegetation that encroached on everything; like that small harbour on the Tyrrhenian coast of Italy, where they disembarked for a day of rest. It used to be a prosperous centre, with a lighthouse gleaming on the shore, porticos rolling to the outer walls and temples smoking with sacrifices.

> Now the monuments of an earlier age can no longer be recognised; devouring time has wasted the mighty battlements away. Traces only remain among the crumbled walls: under a wide stretch of rubble lie the buried homes. Let us not chafe that human frames dissolve: here it is how cities too can die.[7]

Rutilius walked among the ruins of the town. He returned to the ships, impatient to leave. He would try his luck again further along the coast. At another harbour, he left his fleet at anchor to venture inland. The incoming winter was granting a few days of respite; in the fresh sunlight, the sound of chants echoed among the rewilded fields. Rutilius followed it into the deep countryside, the *pagus*. There, in a small village, he found the countryfolk, the 'pagans' as the Christians called them, intent on celebrating a feast in honour of the Egyptian god Osiris. How splendid they looked! It was as if time had not passed, and the Mediterranean gods still shared the Earth and the Sky in harmony. In the *pagus*, Rutilius felt as if the colours of the old world still had a chance to blossom over the frost that covered its ruins.

## 3.

Late autumn clouds shrouded the Mediterranean sun, while Rutilius' fleet moved slowly towards the North. New islands appeared along the way, Capraia and Gorgona. Little islets of rocks and shrubs, barely worthy of mention but for the strangeness of their fauna. In the shade of the caves, a rough breed crawled like nocturnal beasts. They were still few, hiding in their troglodytic abodes, but their numbers grew by the day, and it would not be long before they would overflow their dens and spread to the mainland. Rutilius looked at them from his ship, cutting waves in full sail.

> We passed Capraia, a dreary place, where there are men who shun the light and call themselves 'monks', because they wish

to live with no one. . . . . Then we met the island of Gorgon. We shunned it because its cliffs are monuments to disaster: not long ago a Roman youth met there a living death. For some mad reason, he left the ways of mankind and in superstition came here to hide. He imagined that sacred things are discovered in filthy places. He was crueller to himself than even the offended gods. Surely these beliefs are as powerful as the drugs of Circe: in her day, man's bodies were turned into those of pigs; now it is their minds that are thus changed.[8]

At that time, the Western Roman Empire was disintegrating under the assaults of barbarian peoples and rebellious generals such as Alaric. These formidable enemies, however, shared something of Rome's very lifeblood. Brutal, aggressive, merciless, they embodied a spirit akin to that of Rome in its heyday. Their crimes were motivated by life-affirming reasons: power, booty, a lust for blood. They wanted their share of 'Roman happiness', even at the cost of destroying it.

But what of those Christian monks on the islands of Capraia and Gorgona? They were silent and peaceful, like a mountaintop moments before an avalanche crashes over a village. Most of them were Roman citizens, some even from the upper classes. Yet, to Rutilius, they were more foreign than any barbarian from the Asian steppes. The monks despised their own bodies, treating them like shackles cast over their souls. They hated the world as if it was the site of a demonic ambush. The Christians were blind to the dance of the nymphs of the springs and deaf to the gods who whispered from the crackling fire. They ridiculed the ancient myths and the wisdom of the Pagan prophets as superstitions. In other words, they were thoroughly atheist. How else would you describe those who denied divinity to anything but their own, invisible God? They degraded the gods to demons, humans to animals and animals to bundles of blood and tendons. In an age rife with signs of the end, the Christian monks appeared to Rutilius as the harbingers of the force that would truly bring about the downfall of the world.

## 4.

Just above the horizon, the mountains on the coast of southern Gaul were now visible. Rutilius saluted them with anxious excitement. A new journey inland was about to begin, even more perilous than the previous weeks at sea. As the ships moved closer to the coast, we can imagine Rutilius ordering the sails to be lowered. We can almost hear him murmur to himself that it was not yet time to conclude the first part of his odyssey. Standing on the deck, he turned towards the watery expanse to his South, just as in Fiumicino he had looked one last time at the road that led back to Rome.

Let us grant him his wish. Let us suspend for a moment the last stretch of his navigation. As he would have wished, let us turn back the direction of our travelling – if not in space, at least in time.

Rutilius basked in the last rays of an era. Like the worshippers of Osiris whom he had met in the *pagus*, he was still a Pagan at a time when the empire had officially embraced Christianity. In hindsight, people like him were living anachronisms. History was not going to turn in their favour. But to them, their case did not yet seem hopeless. Just fifty years earlier, a major Pagan revolution had come so close to regaining control of the empire that Rutilius might have reasonably believed that the match against Christianity was not yet over.

The initiator of that revolution was still remembered with reverence in Rutilius' circle, his name mentioned with caution. Unlike most pretenders to the imperial throne, he had not come from the senate or from the army. When he had first arrived in the Western Roman capital of Milan, he was still sporting a beard after the fashion of the philosophical school of Athens. His name was Julian, the orphan son of Julius Constantius and the cousin of the emperor Constantius II, his father's murderer.

Julian and his brother Gallus spent their childhood within the boundaries of a solitary villa in the Anatolian countryside. They lived under strict police surveillance, like prisoners awaiting execution. Day after day, they expected a messenger to announce a lethal swing in the mood of their imperial cousin. Yet, year after year, they continued to live. By order of their cousin, they were raised as good Christians. They took their classes, learnt the doctrine and obeyed orders. But in secret, Julian nurtured a passion for philosophical studies. He read whatever he could find, pondering within himself questions that he could not share with anyone.

As soon as he was given permission to travel, Julian moved to the magnificent city of Pergamon, on the Aegean coast. He applied to the school of the Neoplatonic philosopher Aedesius, humbly reapplied after being rejected and then tried to find his way in with a bribe. But the elderly philosopher had no desire to be associated with someone in such a fragile position as Julian's. To get rid of this pestering youth, he sent as a substitute teacher his own student Maximus, a native of Ephesus, renowned for his eloquence and for his magic arts. In front of a group of rival philosophers, Maximus had demonstrated his theurgic skills by animating a statue of the goddess Hecate. Her lips had curled into a smile, and the stone torches in her hands had magically come alight.[9] Julian threw himself headlong into studying under Maximus, who initiated him into the mysteries of Hecate and Mithra. The years of his adolescence seemed to be about to open up the horizon of a new life, free from his family and his Christian upbringing.

## 5.

While Julian was exploring the Pagan past, his brother Gallus was firmly grounded in the present. He swallowed his resentment towards their cousin, the emperor, and endeavoured to enter his good graces, receiving in return an important position. He established his own micro-court in the Turkish city of Antioch, where he worked relentlessly to consolidate his power. He fought external aggressors, crushed internal rebels, pampered the crowds in the hippodrome, annihilated political opponents and carefully monitored dissent among his subjects. Fertilized with blood and terror, his power grew like a carnivorous plant. But he appeared to have forgotten that the soil where it was rooted did not belong to him. The emperor sent word to Gallus that he wished to see him in his court in Milan. They had to discuss important matters, he said, hinting at a possible promotion to even higher positions. Everything was going splendidly, Gallus must have thought upon leaving Antioch. Along the way, he did not notice that the local garrisons had been substituted by imperial guards. Once he had travelled far enough from his domain, Gallus was arrested, interrogated and beaten. Finally, he was executed for treason. With his death, the last remnant of Julian's childhood was gone. His only remaining family was his cousin, the emperor, the murderer of his father and his brother.

Julian was commanded to go to Milan for a test of his loyalty. In the presence of the emperor, the young philosopher feigned idiocy. 'His neck and shoulders twitched and trembled; his eyes roamed; he was constantly scurrying about, screwing up his face. He laughed noisily and inappropriately; his speech was marred by wheezing and snuffling; his questions were incoherent, and his arguments devoid of logic.'[10] His skit convinced Constantius II, who allowed him to continue his strange but clearly innocuous existence.

Julian hurried away before his cousin could change his mind, reached the Adriatic coast of Italy and embarked on the first boat to Greece. Once in Athens, he looked for a new teacher. He entered the school of the Neoplatonist philosopher Priscus of Thesprotia, devoting himself so completely to his studies that he was rewarded by being initiated to the Eleusinian mysteries. In Athens, Julian felt he had found a home, maybe for the first time in his life. He lived among friends, in a sort of collective pilgrimage to the celestial heights of the mind, where the gods had their abodes.

Until another dispatch arrived from his cousin, he was ordered to return immediately to Milan without any further explanation. The last time his brother had been summoned in such a way, he had not come back alive. Julian bid farewell to his master and his friends, preparing himself to meet death in a manner befitting a philosopher.

What awaited him in Milan was worse than a swift execution. His cousin had decided to promote him to the high-ranking position of *Caesar*, and to dispatch him to the oriental borders of Gaul. He was to become a military commander in charge of the legions facing the barbarians on the frontline of a catastrophic war.

## 6.

Years of privation, violence and constant danger awaited Julian in the frosty encampments along the Rhine River. Such a prospect might have felt unbearable to most people. But Julian was no ordinary man: he was a philosopher. Pagan Neoplatonism had equipped him with an all-encompassing way of life, which rendered him capable of withstanding almost any adversity. He was already used to a stern regime of austerity and self-sacrifice: he barely drank, ate parsimoniously and no gossip surrounded his seemingly absent sexual life. The energies of his youth were entirely channelled into the attempt to perfect himself in order to attune his mind to the invisible perfection that animates the world. Philosophy had transformed him into a polished rock, a mirror for the divine nature of existence.

Once in the legionary encampments, Julian threw himself into military training with the same energy with which he had studied under Maximus and Priscus. He shared the regime of his soldiers, slept and ate as they did and learnt from his subordinates the fine details of military administration. After a few weeks, he was able to keep up with his men. Rumours of the commander-philosopher began spreading, making Julian a favourite of the legions stationed along the oriental frontiers. He had yet to prove his skills on the battlefield, but that kind of opportunity was not in short supply. When summer came, an army of Alamanni headed by King Chnodomar crossed the Rhine River and invaded Roman territory. Numbering around 30,000 warriors, the Alamanni were far from a manageable proposition for Julian's 13,000 legionaries. But they were the only Roman force in the region that could attempt to stop Chnodomar's advance.

Under a bright August sun, Julian led his men against the Alamanni. They took position along the slopes of a hill in the fields near the town of Argentoratum. Julian stood among his soldiers, as Alexander the Great used to do. The Alamanni warriors charged from the bottom of the valley, a wave of iron crashing against the legionaries' shields. The Roman lines grew thinner after each assault, but the legionaries held onto their position; one step back, and everything was lost. Assault by assault, the day declined into evening. After another wave had crashed in vain, the Alamanni began to lose heart. At that point, Julian ordered the wings of his army to move forward. Seeing the legionaries closing around them, the Alamanni turned in panic towards the Rhine River. The Romans chased them, hunted them down, driving them into the water like prey.[11]

Julian's victory had been complete. Now, he just had to inform the emperor of what he had achieved in his name and to send him the prisoners and the spoils taken from the enemy. Julian reluctantly obliged – for the last time. Why fight for the man who had ruined his life? The time had come to pursue something bigger than just training himself to spiritual perfection. Exhilarated by his first victory, Julian resolved to free not only himself but the whole Roman world from the rule of people like his cousin.

## 7.

Julian wrote a letter to his friends in Athens, explaining the reasons for his rebellion.[12] The philosophers were still his peers and the judges of his behaviour. Then, he ordered his troops to march South, towards Constantinople, where his cousin was overseeing the war against the Persians. They were barely halfway there when news reached them that the emperor was dead. Without a battle, without drama, in a single day, Julian had become the most powerful emperor on Earth.

Julian immediately set about reorganizing the imperial machine according to Platonic rationality. By intervening in the details of administration and legislation, he intended to harmonize the workings of the lower sphere of the universe with the higher cosmic orders. He also strove to recreate that complex Mediterranean harmony which the rise of monotheism had threatened to eradicate. In line with the old Roman tradition, he wished to open again the imperial pantheon to the different revelations of the Divine. He reinstated a full tolerance of all religions, including Christianity, and attempted to correct the wrongs caused by previous emperors. To the Jews, he promised to fund the reconstruction of the Temple in Jerusalem, which the Romans had destroyed during the wars of the first century.[13]

Then he set his eyes on a general reform of education. He forbade Christians from working as teachers of the Greek classics, especially the texts that dealt with mythology.[14] How could they teach what they believed to be a superstition? Poetic works such as Homer's were not innocuous pieces of literature but prophetic texts of the Pagan tradition. Poetry was a music attuned to the song of the Muses. Through its beauty, it set the conditions for the spiritual initiation of their listeners: by refining their awareness of the beauty of the world, it set them on the path to developing an awareness of the ineffable essence of reality. Rutilius Namatianus would have agreed on this point: the world retains its beauty even in its darkest hour. Not because it is untouched by evil but because evil has a poetry of its own.

While Julian was busy working on his reforms, the Persians, perennial enemies of the Romans, prepared for war on the Eastern frontiers. Julian had to abandon his desk to organize an expedition into the deserts of Mesopotamia. He led 80,000 Roman soldiers to the south-eastern borders, entering Persian territory without difficulty. They crushed the little resistance they encountered along the way and marched forward into the desert. It was almost too late when Julian realized that they had ventured too far. He ordered the legions to veer back towards the Roman provinces. At that moment, the Persians attacked.

On a torrid day in the summer of 363 AD, a skirmish ensued between the retreating Romans and the Persian vanguard. The Roman lines were dangerously overextended, and Julian was darting up and down to support every section. So rapid were his movements across the battlefield that his attendants could not bring him the armour and shield he had left behind. He was fighting amidst his soldiers when a spear came out of the melee, passing through his belly. He fell from his horse, blood and faeces pouring out of his side. He stood up and climbed back on the saddle, then fainted. He died in his tent while his soldiers were singing to celebrate the victory. His reign had lasted less than two years.

Julian's legacy faded like a comet. His successors halted his projects and overturned his reforms. Less than twenty years after his death, the emperor Theodosius declared Christianity the only legal religion in the empire and outlawed public displays of Paganism. The choir of the Mediterranean imagination, once brimming with a multitude of sacred voices, was to become a solo.

## 8.

It might be clearer now why people like Rutilius thought that the match against Christianity was not yet over. Standing on the deck of his ship, where we left him floating in front of the coast of Southern Gaul, he might have pondered what would have happened if Julian had not died. Even then, the problem was that the barbarians had already been won over by the Christian message. Their energy had been turned to serving a world-hating project; no wonder that their attacks were proving so catastrophic.

We can imagine Rutilius emerging from these kinds of thoughts to shout to his crew to steer towards the coast. Their journey would continue by foot, through the ruined landscape that had once been home to Rutilius' ancestors. We can imagine his crew preparing to disembark, fastening their weapons at their side . . .

Yet, from this point onwards, we can only imagine. Rutilius' manuscript ends here. Centuries of anti-pagan librarians and negligent copyists have spared only an amputated version of his account. We can suppose that he eventually reached his ancestral home, repaired his mansion and fortified it against further assaults. Then, he must have sat down to write his memoir of his voyage in the form of a long poem. We can only wonder to what extent he realized that he was about to produce a masterpiece of late Roman poetry.

While writing, Rutilius might have consulted the scrolls in his travelling library. With a pang of nostalgia, perhaps, he might have returned to a short book, *On the Gods and the World*, penned by one of Julian's closest collaborators soon after the emperor's death. The Neoplatonist philosopher Saturninus Secundus Salutius had intended it like a message cast upon the waves of the future, in the hope that somebody, someday, would discover it and rescue from oblivion the world which it described.

As Rutilius fades away from our story, Salutius will act as a guide for the next leg of our journey through the age of Late Antiquity.

His book starts sharply, tackling two fundamental problems of the Mediterranean imagination: the relationship between truth and fiction, and the right way of relating to mythology. Salutius wanted to respond to those who mocked the Pagans for believing the fantastical and often immoral stories narrated by the myths. Certainly, he conceded, the events recounted in the myths never 'actually' took place – but that is because they are not facts. Instead, they are the kind of events that 'never actually happened; but are always'.[15] Mythic stories belong to an otherworld, beyond space and time, whose reverberations appear here, in our everyday world. Like the light of distant stars, the eternal actions of gods and heroes are visible to us only faintly, and myth is the sole form in which humans can communicate them.

Mythic stories resembled the eternal laws of mathematics: they are always here with us, yet they are irreducible to what we can see of them. They run alongside the flow of time, and when they enter the present, they emerge like messengers from an invisible elsewhere. They penetrate the fabric of the world at every instant, to the extent that the whole world, in its everyday normality, should be considered itself myth. 'For one may call the world a myth, in which bodies and things are visible, but souls and minds hidden'.[16]

For Salutius, Julian, Rutilius and the last Pagans of Late Antiquity, the world was a realm where the visible and the invisible, facts and stories, time and eternity were indissolubly intertwined. Nothing was merely what it seemed, and 'facts' were just fragments of a mythic story as wide and ancient as existence itself.

## 9.

Just as every culture has its own signs to represent the same mathematical numbers, so too it has its unique way of representing the blend of sacred and profane, visible and invisible, that underpins reality. A Greek nymph, an Egyptian god and a Persian angel are just different manifestations of the same infinite essence. Hence the ease with which the Romans welcomed foreign divinities into their own pantheon and combined their mythological discourses.

This intuition, which constitutes the core of the Mediterranean imagination, found a masterful expression in the philosophical system of Neoplatonism. Founded in the third century by the

Egyptian philosopher Plotinus, Neoplatonism treated reality as a complex realm composed of multiple dimensions. Only a fraction of it can be experienced through the senses and classified by human language; beyond this fragment, an infinite dimension yawns, surpassing any sense or concept. This arcane dimension sustains the existence of everything that is manifest in the world, yet humans can refer to it only through imprecise and insufficient terms, such as 'God', 'pure existence' or, in Plotinus' vocabulary, the 'One'. The 'One' is the Being of each being, the Life of anything living, the Presence of anything present. While remaining always the same, it takes on the infinite forms allowed by the world, thus appearing in different guises to different peoples or creatures. Hence the paradoxical nature of the world, which is at the same time one and many: infinitely varied in its appearance, yet one in its essence and in its existence.

To illustrate this vision, let us imagine the world as a glass prism, which is traversed by the light of an eternal realm beyond space and time. Neither the transparent glass nor the colourless light is visible on its own. But as soon as they meet, they bring about an explosion of colours. Each beam of coloured light, like the mythology of each religion, is just one of the countless possible manifestations that result from the encounter between time and eternity, language and ineffability, the profane and the sacred.

According to Salutius, this was precisely what the Christians had failed to understand. The Christians wished to destroy the prism of the world and to retain only the colourless light of their God. The result, however, was the complete obfuscation of reality: they were blind to the colours of the world, yet they were still unable to see the invisible essence of God's light.

Salutius did not hate the Christians. He believed their mistakes stemmed from ignorance rather than malice, echoing Plato's view that 'if someone were to know what is good and bad, then . . . intelligence would be sufficient to save a person'.[17] With his book, he wished to rescue them from their error and to expose them to a wider metaphysical vision. Even though the Christians were a danger to the empire and to themselves, they had to be helped and forgiven. As their Messiah had said, 'they know not what they do'.[18]

## 10.

After Rutilius' generation, the Late Pagan intelligentsia became rapidly extinct. Their books ceased to be copied and the few that survived, like Rutilius' poem, were horribly mutilated. Only the weakest sections of their polemics against Christianity were preserved, inserted inside the treatises that had been written to confute them.

But the disintegration of Pagan culture involved more than the silent fading of manuscripts. Mob violence, fuelled by religious fervour, tore through the streets of once-tolerant cities. Alexandria-by-Egypt, for centuries a beacon of syncretism, became the epicentre of this struggle.

In those difficult times, the Neoplatonic philosopher Hypatia still resided in Alexandria. Since her childhood, 'being endowed with a nobler nature than her father, [the mathematician Theon,] she was not content with the mathematical education her father gave her, but occupied herself with distinction in the other branches of philosophy'.[19] Hypatia was not the first female mathematician to have risen to prominence in Alexandria, having been preceded by Pandrosion, but she had a unique way of combining mathematics with philosophy, and both disciplines with a natural talent for teaching. Even her Christian colleagues had to concede that she was intellectually peerless. According to her contemporary, the Church historian Socrates Scholasticus, 'all persons who were studious about philosophy flocked to her from all parts. . . . She was addressed frequently even to the Magistrates. . . . Nor was she ashamed of appearing in a public assembly of men. For all persons revered and admired her.'[20]

The city where she lived, however, was steeped in an atmosphere of religious war. The Christian community, conscious of being on the winning side of history, sought to remake Alexandria in their image, dictating the rhythm of life for all its inhabitants. They were guided by the bishop Cyrillus, whose intolerance has remained legendary. Stoked by his sermons, anti-pagan violence overflowed into the streets, the marketplaces, the political assemblies. One day in the spring of 415 AD, an ageing Hypatia was riding in her chariot on her way back home. Passing through the familiar streets of the city centre, she paid little attention to a crowd that was gathering in front of her. As she slowed down her horses, the crowd rushed towards the chariot, pulled her out and dragged her inside a nearby church. There, 'they stripped her naked and murdered her with sharp shells. And when they had torn her piece-meal, they carried all her members [through the city] to a place called Cinaron and consumed them with fire'.[21]

The slaying of Hypatia sparked a chorus of indignation. Her biographer, the Neoplatonic philosopher Damascius, presented her as the equivalent of a martyr, whose death announced the impending doom of the entire world of Pagan wisdom. Damascius too, like his heroine, was to experience the brutality of the new age. He had found a haven in the Platonic Academy in Athens, the last stronghold of Pagan philosophy, where he worked as the director, or *scholarch*. He would be the last person to hold this role. In 529 AD, the Eastern Roman emperor Justinian issued an edict forbidding all 'heretics' (including Jews and Pagans) from 'dragging the minds of the simple to their errors'[22] by teaching their doctrines. Nine centuries after its foundation, the Platonic Academy was permanently closed. Damascius abandoned Athens with six other colleagues, crossing the southern borders to seek refuge at the court of the Persian king Khosrow I. They hoped to convert him to the practice of philosophy and, through his patronage, to create elsewhere what could no longer be dreamt of at home. But for Khosrow, as for most monarchs, dabbling with philosophy was nothing more than a fashionable hobby. After a few fruitless months at his court, the seven philosophers decided to return to Greece. One of them, Simplicius, spent his last years scraping a living as a freelance writer. Damascius retired to a quiet and anonymous existence. No records remain of what happened to the other five.[23]

## 11.

The closer one gets to the centre of a world that has grown old, the louder one can hear the convulsive rhythm of its heartbeat.

For the Mediterranean Pagans, the heart of their world was in Egypt, the cradle of humans and gods. All forms of art and culture had sprouted from the banks of the Nile River. They had been the gift of Thoth, the Ibis-headed god of wisdom and expediency. Humans owed to him the inventions of writing, alchemy, astronomy, magic, medicine and every technique through which the world 'below' can look at the heavens 'above'.

Having sparked the birth of human civilization, Thoth also held the secret of its end. Around the third century AD, not long before the final catastrophe of Paganism, Thoth revealed to his worshippers the fate of Egypt, a reflection of that of their whole world.

> A time will come when the [*gods*] will return from earth to heaven, and Egypt will be abandoned . . . O Egypt, Egypt, of your reverent deeds only stories will survive, and they will be incredible to your children! . . . The people of that time will find the world nothing to wonder at or to worship. This all [*i.e. the world*] – a good thing that never had nor will have its better – will be endangered. . . . They will prefer shadows to light, and they will find death more expedient than life. No one will look up to heaven. . . . Such will be the old age of the world.[24]

The vanishing of the Egyptian religion, its hieroglyphic language and its rites announced the storm that was about to hit the entire Mediterranean. Everything was set to change. Thoth himself took on a new role as universal prophet and changed his identity. He shed his animal face to wear the semblance of the Greek god Hermes; from the Jewish God, praised by his angels as 'Holy! Holy! Holy!', he borrowed a triple attribute of greatness; like the ineffable One of the Neoplatonists, he shrouded himself under an aura of mystery. He embodied the conjunction of all opposites, female and male, human and divine, fictional and real. Thoth became *Hermes Trismegistus*, the 'Thrice Great Hermes'.

Hermes Trismegistus offered himself as a raft on which the survivors of a dying world could sail beyond the tragedies of history. To us, too, embarked on this journey through the Mediterranean imagination, he shall offer his guidance as we take another step forward, upwards, towards a glimmer of light at last.

# 12.

Life in Late Antiquity was a precarious affair. War, pestilence and famine weighed on people with unfathomable brutality. Meanwhile, the enslavement of millions of people suggested that a human life was ultimately indistinguishable from the dumb existence of a machine.

The Mediterranean had sunk inside one of history's nightmares. But Hermes Trismegistus came to its rescue, teaching that the nightmares of history were no more than bad dreams. Although they might be frightful, painful, even lethal, their attempts to debase human dignity were destined to fail. No catastrophe other than ignorance could ever rob humans of their divine essence.

> For the human is a godlike living thing. . . . Or better, the one who is really human is above the gods. . . . For none of the heavenly gods will go down to earth . . . yet the human rises up to heaven and takes its measure and knows what is in its heights and its depths . . . and – greater than all of this – he comes to be on high without leaving earth behind. . . . Therefore, we must

dare to say that the human on earth is a mortal god, while that god in heaven is an immortal human.[25]

'A human being is a great wonder, a living thing to be worshipped and honoured',[26] said Hermes Trismegistus. But another great wonder is the whole world, where even a speck of dust reflects the structure of the universe, and each fleeting moment harbours the seed of eternity. The very existence of every being is a miracle, since it transcends its visible presence in the same way that the meaning of a word transcends the sounds and signs that are used to express it.

This all-encompassing existence, the life-force that animates and transcends everything, we can call 'God'.

> For what is God . . . but the being of all things and, of things that are no longer, at least the very substance of their existence. This is God, this is the Father, this is the Good.[27]

God is inside the world. But the world, too, is inside God. The universe, with its planets and stars, exists within the infinite space of the *Nous* (the Mind of God). The visible world and its creatures are divine thoughts, which God makes 'present' by bringing them into its awareness, much as a person brings a memory to mind.

If we may, for a moment, jump forward a few centuries, we could illustrate Hermes Trismegistus' cosmological vision with an example borrowed from our contemporary technology. We could say, then, that the Mind of God resembles the software of a video game running inside a computer, while the physical reality of our universe is equivalent to the flow of images on the screen. The different items and characters that appear on the screen can be considered distinct entities only when they are interpreted within the narrative of the video game. In fact, though, they are all manifestations of the software that produces them – like the objects and the living beings that populate the world are just the outpouring of the Mind of God.

But software also requires hardware: a support that allows the narratives to appear on the screen, while being composed of an entirely different substance from theirs. God's Essence can be compared to such hardware, since it allows for the existence of worldly beings while being irreducible to them. Hence the opacity of reality to our eyes: just as the characters in a videogame cannot fathom the different form of existence of the hardware that allows them to exist, so the creatures of the world cannot understand the true nature of God.

Indeed, most worldly beings don't even realize that they are simply the outcome of a divine Mind. According to Hermes Trismegistus, only one creature is capable of this level of self-reflection: the human. Humans are that part of the cosmic software – God's Mind – which is designed to look back at its own workings and to wonder about the invisible structures of reality.

The similarities with the functioning of computers, however, end here. Unlike a computer's hardware, the essence of reality is not made of perishable materials. God's Essence is eternal, beyond time and space. And it shares its own eternity with anything that exists within its Mind. Even though the creatures of this world appear mortal to each other, this is only due to their limited knowledge of the real nature of the cosmos: in truth, each thing in the universe shares the same eternity of the divine Mind that is dreaming it. Thus, said Hermes Trismegistus, every living thing is immortal.

There is nothing in the cosmos that does not live.... For there never was any dead thing in the cosmos, nor is there, nor will there be.... How can there be dead things in God, in the image of all, in the plenitude of life? . . . Nothing is corruptible or destroyed – terms that disturb human beings. Life is not birth but awareness, and change is forgetting, not death. Since this is so, all are immortal – matter, life, spirit, soul, mind – of which every living thing is constituted.[28]

## 13.

Hermes Trismegistus offers a vertiginous vision. His cosmos is simultaneously multiple and unitary, like a single mind filled with infinite thoughts. The material objects that compose it are both visible in their body and invisible in the mystery of their existence, fleeting in their presence yet made of the eternal substance of God. Nothing that exists can ever die or be destroyed, but it constantly slips in and out of the world, like thoughts that enter and exit the awareness of a mind. All in all, reality resembles a dream, through which God's awareness moves like that of a lucid dreamer. At times, God loses itself in the contemplation of its dream-creatures; other times, it looks back at itself through the eyes of humans.

But here comes a problem. If humans are the equivalent of God's self-consciousness, why is their understanding of reality so cloudy? Why do they fail to penetrate the ineffable mystery of existence?

These philosophical questions might seem less abstract if we apply them to the way in which we understand ourselves. We, too, are only partially visible to ourselves. When we look in a mirror, we see flesh, hair, teeth and nails, while nothing appears of our essence or of our thoughts. If we try to communicate to others the mystery of our own existence, we realize that this exceeds the possibilities of our language. We might say 'me', or 'human', or we might utter our own name – but the idea of having an ego, the hypothesis of belonging to a species, or the convention of having a name, are nothing more than fictions. They are mythological tropes that we use to define ourselves as something rather than as a living nothingness.

In the same way, mythological stories are the means through which God can look back at its own ineffable nature and discover something rather than nothing. Like us humans, God thinks of itself in the form of a narrative and tells itself the endless adventures of its own living Mind in the form of a fiction. Mythology is not a human product but a form of divine autofiction, which God inscribes in every fold of the world.

Hermes Trismegistus, too, was a mythological character. Yet, to his disciples, he was as real as if he had been of flesh and blood, and the possibilities opened by his teachings were also all too real. Mimicking God, he offered his followers not an arsenal of concepts to crack the enigma of reality, but a narrative landscape where their lives might flourish within and around their own mystery.

# 14.

Hermes Trismegistus himself had once been the disciple of a mythic master. He met him one day while resting in a state of dream-like vigil.[29] He looked up, and there it was: an enormous humanoid being, towering over him. The giant presented itself as Poimandres, the manifestation of God's Mind. Then, Poimandres stared Hermes Trismegistus in the eye. It stared so deeply and for so long that Hermes Trismegistus felt his senses coming loose. Sinking into a state of awe and terror, he witnessed an explosion of light soaring to the heights and an ocean of darkness opening below. He heard an inarticulate cry breaking out of the light and saw the darkness coiling around it. In a time without duration, he learnt all the mysteries of reality. And when his consciousness returned to its normal state, he recounted his cosmic visions through a language that could only be mythological.

In the beginning, Hermes Trismegistus told his disciples, the totality of existence was compressed in the form of one androgynous God. It was one God, but it had many aspects. It had a *Nous* (mind), a *Logos* (word) and an ineffable Essence. Through the power of its *Logos*, God created a lower divinity, the Demiurge and charged it with the task of creating the visible world. When the Demiurge had finished its job, the androgynous God gave birth to a new creature: Anthropos (human), the first androgynous human being. As the sibling of the Demiurge, Anthropos asked their androgynous 'Father' for permission to contribute to the creation of the world. God gave its assent, and Anthropos started meddling with the visible world. Looking down into the world, Anthropos saw a beautiful creature, Nature, and the two fell in love. From their sexual union, Anthropos and Nature produced seven androgynous *Anthropoi* (humans) who started to populate the world. For a long time, God's worldly creatures lived undisturbed, until God decided to divide them along lines of gender, male and female, and told them to go and multiply. Before returning to its invisible state, God gave them one piece of fatherly advice. 'Remember that your essence is invisible and that you partake to my same eternity. Remember this, and you will live forever. However, if you become so entangled with the visible world as to forget your divine and immortal nature, then you will suffer the pain of death *as if* you were mortals'.

For the Mediterranean people of Late Antiquity, constantly threatened with death by the political authorities and with damnation by the Christian church, the revelations of Hermes Trismegistus had a revolutionary ring. His teachings offered a method of immediate liberation. The worldly rulers had no power over those who knew themselves to be immortal and not in need of any further salvation. For the followers of Hermes Trismegistus, the world ceased to be a battlefield or a prison, blossoming instead as a dream of supreme beauty.

## 15.

Hermes Trismegistus' teachings offered some respite from a catastrophic age. But most of his contemporaries did not share his optimism. It is easy to philosophize about goodness and immortality, they objected, but what about the reality of life in the world? Humanity is riddled with suffering; its mortal existence is a constant decline into weakness and death, and the horrors of this world cannot be erased with a bunch of abstract notions. The most reasonable explanation for all this gratuitous pain, they thought, is the exact opposite of what Hermes preached: the world is an evil place, and life is a curse.

Rather than sinking them into despair, however, this bleak realization spurred them into action. Surely, this situation could be resolved by intervening in its original cause. And since nobody doubted that the world had a divine origin, the cause of evil must also lie at the level of divinity. Thus, they concluded, if the world created by God is evil, then God must not be good, but evil.

Following this logical deduction, a new breed of thinkers grew within the religions of Late Antiquity. The God-haters: united by outrage at the injustice of having been born to suffer and die, and by a common quest to escape this destiny.

Their intuitions, however, clashed with the sacred texts of the religious denominations to which they belonged. The Bible, for example, spoke about the magnificence of God and the goodness of its creation. This contradiction could be resolved, they responded, if the Bible's message was read obliquely: not between the lines, but by looking through its apparent meaning. The Bible was a piece of propaganda written by the evil God in order to deceive us. It told us the truth about creation, but it lied about the intentions of our creator. To those who read it with a clear mind, the Bible disclosed itself as the record of the crimes of God, who created us in order to torment us.

Christ had been sent precisely to stop this evil God. They all agreed on this. Christ had attempted to save us. He had come from a remote elsewhere, beyond our world, and had descended into our abyss, not by God's order, but as a saboteur of God's work. He had been killed by the order of God, who feared and hated him.

Where had Jesus come from? Where would he have taken us, had he been able to complete his mission? What were people to do now that he was gone? To these questions, the God-haters of Late Antiquity dedicated the full range of their creative energies. In so doing, they produced one of the most daring plans for escaping beyond the world in the history of the Mediterranean imagination.

## 16.

Today, this diverse group of God-haters is collectively known as the 'Gnostics'. In the history books, they are usually relegated to footnotes to the rise of the great monotheistic religions. But in their own time, their pessimistic message reverberated with many, and their ranks were filled with people from all corners of the Mediterranean.

Their doctrines were so popular among the Pagans that the Neoplatonist philosopher Plotinus felt obliged to issue a public confutation to try to stop them from spreading among his students.[30] For the Christian theologians, having to defend the orthodoxy against Gnostic arguments was such a frequent necessity that the anti-Gnostic polemic became a standard exercise of ecclesiastic rhetoric.

At one point, the number of Christian Gnostics swelled to such an extent that they came close to taking control of the official church. The first canon of Christian scriptures, for example, was established by the Anatolian Gnostic Marcion of Sinope. Another Gnostic, the Egyptian theologian Valentinus, had such influence within the church that he was a candidate for the position of Bishop of Rome, the office of Pope. Had Valentinus won the papal election, the history of Christianity would have taken a very different turn. But he narrowly lost and eventually exited the church to establish his own religious community.

Most Gnostics, however, kept their distance from the struggle for theological hegemony, preferring to reserve their energies for their fellow believers, the only ones endowed with *gnosis* (true knowledge). The Gnostic communities welcomed disgruntled Jews, Christians, Pagans and Zoroastrians, and existed separately from each other, in an anarchic harmony of differences. They had no common church and shared no dogmas, and their stories about the nature of the world and the secret of its origin had only a familial resemblance to each other.

Then, over the centuries, religious repression got the best of them, and they disappeared. By the end of Late Antiquity, the cultural legacy of the God-haters was virtually extinct. The Gnostic texts ceased to be copied and their ideas were erased from history, except for what remained in the old polemical works of the Christian heresiologists. Although a Gnostic sentiment resurfaced spontaneously among medieval heretical sects, the experience of the original Gnostics was consigned to oblivion.

Until one morning, in 1945, two Egyptian brothers set out for a day of labour in the fields, searching for fertilizer in the arid countryside near the town of Nag Hammadi. Their shovels struck something unexpected – a large clay jar. A cascade of ancient books tumbled out. The brothers brought their discovery home to show it to their mother. Though she could not understand what they said, she recognized that the books were written in Coptic, the language of Egyptian Christians. Thus, a couple of them ended up immediately in the stove, kindling the fire for the evening soup. She had no desire to hold onto any Christian manuscripts. But the brothers saw the potential to make some money by selling them to antiquarians in the city. Thus began the odyssey of these ancient texts, which passed from hand to hand for years until a few of them ended up with the great Iranologist Henry Corbin, who first realized their significance. It took yet more decades before they were published and translated into modern languages.

The Nag Hammadi papyri, as they became known, brought back the voice of the Late Ancient Gnostics.[31] They spoke of Yaldabaoth, the evil god, of his court of malevolent Archons, who created our faulty human bodies, and of the extra-cosmic realm from which our souls derive their spark. They told the story of our mother Sophia, of her fall and of the Saviour's attempts to rescue her legacy trapped within us. Through them, our Father, the androgynous Alien God, unveiled the long-silenced origin of our condition.

## 17.

The same intuition united all the Gnostic groups: the creation of the world had been a cosmic catastrophe, but humans could play a role in reversing it. At the cost of losing some of the complexity of the various Gnostic accounts, we might cast a panoramic view over the general vision they shared and attempt a single retelling of the amazing cosmogonic tales that compose the Nag Hammadi library.

Our retelling should begin 'in the beginning'. Yet, for the Gnostics, at the beginning of the universe, there was less than nothing. There was only an Abyss. No word, concept or image could convey its nature; no one and nothing could ever comprehend it. In the beginning, the Abyss had a thought without content. The Abyss united itself with it, like a male unites with a female, and the two merged into one perfect, androgynous being.

From this union emerged a cascade of other beings, the Aeons. Each of them personified one of the hidden qualities of the Abyss. Altogether, they constituted the divine Fullness (*Pleroma*) in which the Abyss saw itself manifested. The Aeons were not abstract concepts; they were creatures with a life and character of their own. They were endowed with desires, and thus with their own peculiar weaknesses. Ironically, the Aeon that embodied the faculty of divine Wisdom, Sophia, was the least wise in this divine family. She refused to accept the unfathomable mystery of the Abyss. She desired to look back to her origin and decipher it.

Sophia paid dearly for her ambition. Not only did she fail in her ambition, but she was expelled from her family and cast out of the Pleroma. Her unfulfilled desire did not vanish; instead, it grew within her until it became alive. It condensed into a half-formed dark mass, became sentient, started to move and took on the male gender.

Sophia ripped him out of herself, but he did not die. He grew up alone, with no one to guide his terrible strength. He had the body of a snake, the face of a lion, eyes of flames. Since he could not see anything around himself, he believed he was the only thing that existed in the universe. He built a throne for himself, which he called Heaven, and a footstool, Earth. Then he created seven assistants, whom he called Archons, 'the authorities', and tasked them with administering the world. He also produced a bureaucracy of angels and archangels, 365 in total, to whom he assigned control over time. When all this was done, he gathered his subjects and proclaimed to them: 'I am God, the only one that exists!' Suddenly, a voice thundered from the heights: 'Yaldabaoth, you are not the only god. There is an Abyss above you, and me, from whom you have descended.' Thus spoke Sophia, calling him Yaldabaoth.

Upon hearing his mother's voice, Yaldabaoth cried louder: 'I am the true God, and I am a jealous God! You shall not have another but me.'[32] But Sophia's appearance had shaken Yaldabaoth's kingdom. Everyone had seen the beauty of her form, when her reflection had lit up for a moment the waters of the world.

Yaldabaoth told his court to come closer. He murmured: 'What you saw and heard, that was our enemy, who wishes to destroy our world. We must fight her! Let us create a creature in her image, to discourage her from attacking us, and let us multiply it, so that we will have a multitude of slaves at our disposal.'

Archons, angels and archangels set immediately to work. Each of them created a portion of the human body, and when they had finished, they assembled them together. Yaldabaoth named the result 'Adam' and waited for him to awake. But Adam lay on the ground, like a lifeless puppet.

Looking down from the heights, Sophia burst out laughing. She could have destroyed her son's creation with the stroke of a finger. But first, she needed to recuperate something that Yaldabaoth had taken from her. Before she could re-join the Pleroma, she had to retrieve that part of her own life-force which had gone missing with her error. Yaldabaoth held that spark within himself. Her mission, now, was to get it back intact.[33]

## 18.

Sophia whispered into Yaldabaoth's ears: 'Your human is a little more than a doll. But if you breathe on his face, you will see him come alive and rise on his feet.' The young god fell for his mother's trick. He breathed on Adam's face, transmitting to him his otherworldly spark. Adam opened his eyes, looked at his creator and asked, 'Who are you?'. 'I am God, your father', replied Yaldabaoth, 'now rise and stand on your legs'. Adam tried his best to push himself up but could do no more than flounder about on the ground. Yaldabaoth suddenly realized he had been fooled. He had passed to Adam a force powerful enough to overthrow him from his throne over Heaven and Earth. Luckily, though, Adam was still inactive and unaware of his true power. Yaldabaoth immediately ordered his archangels to lock him up inside the garden of Paradise, where he was to be kept in the dark about the true nature of his soul.

Sophia summoned her assistant Zoe, 'life', and sent her to Paradise with the task of revealing to Adam his true origin, as a lost child of the Pleroma, and of helping him become a fully functioning human being, in view of liberation. To prepare for her mission, Zoe took a new name, Eve, and used some matter from Yaldabaoth's Earth to fashion for herself a female body. When she saw Adam lying on the ground of Paradise, she took pity on him. 'Rise up Adam, become alive!' she said. Her words coursed through Adam, igniting a mysterious energy within him. He finally stood on his legs and bowed to Eve. 'I don't know who you are, but I shall call you "Mother of the Living", because you truly gave me life.'

In Paradise, however, nothing could stay hidden from the eye of the authorities. 'Isn't that the enemy who threatened to destroy our world?' the archangels cried, rushing towards Eve. They had no idea how powerful she was. Eve blinded and scattered them, and while they lay unconscious on the ground, she moved her spirit, Zoe, out of her body and into a tree that grew nearby, the Tree of Knowledge. When the archangels awoke, they saw the body that Eve had left behind. They moved cautiously around it, then they seized it and raped it to produce from her a new progeny of slaves. Zoe looked at them from the Tree of Knowledge. Their violence did not affect her. The authorities could only abuse her body, made of the same lowly substance as their own.

Now the authorities turned to Adam. They sedated him, then erased his memory. When he woke up, seeing Eve's body next to him, he asked the archangels who that creature was. 'We made her out of your rib', they replied, 'to give you a companion who will submit to you.' Adam nodded, and Eve, still empty of the spirit of Zoe, did not object. The couple remained together in Paradise, mindless and subservient to their masters.

For Sophia, however, the battle to recuperate her spark had just begun. She asked her divine family for help, and out of the Pleroma emerged a spirit, called Christ, who descended at lightspeed towards Paradise. Disguised as a serpent, the wisest of beings, Christ coiled itself around the Tree of Knowledge, where Zoe still resided. When the serpent saw the couple walking about, he called Eve. 'Did your God forbid you from eating from the trees of this garden?' the serpent asked her. 'No, he told us only not to eat from the tree upon which you are. If we eat of it, we will die', replied Eve. 'Your God is lying to you;

you shall not die. Rather, if you eat of this tree, you will become superior even to your creator.' Eve looked at the tree, where the spirit of Zoe hid. She picked some fruit, tasted it and gave some to Adam. A sudden flash of understanding brightened their minds: they realized their condition as prisoners of an evil God, who feared and hated them. They saw themselves naked of knowledge and felt ashamed. But even though they felt disgusted by the lowliness of their bodily substance, they found each other's form enchanting. They fell in love with one another and resolved to start together a new life of knowledge and rebellion.[34]

## 19.

When the archangels found Adam and Eve hiding from them in the bushes, they immediately realized what had happened. Unable to retaliate against the serpent, whose power was far beyond theirs, they banished the couple, casting them out of Paradise to the lowest dimension of the universe, Yaldabaoth's footstool, the Earth. In that wild realm, plagued by pain, death and disease, they would surely succumb to the weakness of their bodily shells.

Adam and Eve were alone against the world. Eve was pregnant with the poisonous seed of the archangels. She gave birth to Cain, Abel and other children who carried within themselves the influence of the authorities. Then she made love to Adam. Their union produced another child, Seth, resplendent with the spark of Sophia and the wisdom of Zoe. Seth began a progeny of his own, an 'unmovable race' that kept alive the legacy of the Pleroma. From them, the Gnostics would eventually emerge.

Yaldabaoth sent a Flood upon the Earth, to destroy all of Seth's progeny. But Sophia intervened and ensured their survival. When the descendants of Seth established themselves in the cities of Sodom and Gomorrah, Yaldabaoth gathered a storm of fire and sent it against them. The Sethians escaped and scattered throughout the world, hiding among the ignorant masses.

Over the centuries, the bloodlines of Seth and the archangels intertwined. It was too late, Yaldabaoth had to admit, to annihilate humanity. Instead, he established the rule of new authorities over the people: the zodiac to control their destinies, and kings and priests to ensure their repression. The world became a Hell of suffering, where humans were enslaved to their ignorance and plagued by the weakness of their bodies.

But Sophia did not lose heart. She asked the Pleroma to send down again the spirit of Christ, who had already helped Adam and Eve in the guise of a serpent. This time, Christ took on the body of a boy called Jesus. He began roaming Palestine, teaching people about their divine nature and their true home beyond this world. God stirred up his fellow countrymen, the Jews, against him, and since that was not enough, he drove to madness one of Jesus's closest friends, Judas Iscariot, who betrayed him. Jesus was captured by the earthly authorities and was nailed to the cross, as per God's wishes. But the spirit of Christ had fled Jesus' body before he was killed. Hidden among the crowd at the foot of the cross, Christ looked impassively at Jesus breathing his last.

After the body of Jesus had been buried, Christ showed itself again to the apostles. They saw him in its true likeness, as a shapeshifting being, now young, now old, now female, now male. Christ consoled them, explaining that God could do him no harm.

God had no power over them either. They too belonged to the otherworldly Pleroma, far beyond the darkness of this world. He told them to spread this secret *gnosis* (knowledge) to all people, because anyone who acquired it was destined for salvation. Their mission was to organize a universal rebellion against the rule of God and his authorities.

Christ prophesied that in the end times, the prison of this world will be shattered, and God's authority will be overthrown. The human bodies will vanish, while our spirits, free at last, will be allowed to return to the otherworld to which they belong. Together with us, Sophia shall be rescued from her exile and forgiven for her past mistakes. Indeed, she is the soul and the innermost essence of every human. The voice inside ourselves that does not accept the suffering of this world, the longing that sometimes we feel for an elsewhere which we have never seen – those are the voice and the longing of Sophia. Our salvation will also be the redemption of our true mother.

Having said this, the spirit of Christ faded and disappeared. Its story had ended. That of the Gnostics had begun.[35]

## 20.

After this wild cosmic drama, it is not easy to return to a plain historical narrative. What vicissitudes could rival the adventures of Sophia, the malevolent schemes of Yaldabaoth or the heroism of the 'unmovable race'? The facts of history seem inordinately dry next to those of myth. Unless, of course, history is interpreted as the unfolding of a myth. And that was how the Gnostics experienced the events of their time in the Late Ancient Mediterranean.

The Gnostic communities gathered like a rebel network of cosmic migrants. They did not want to build a permanent home on Earth, but to sabotage the world before embarking on an exodus beyond the vault of the sky, beyond Heaven, beyond God, towards the ineffable elsewhere of the Abyss. Anyone who wished to join them, rich or poor, freeborn or slave, was welcomed into the secrets of their knowledge. Women were especially welcome. What was forbidden to them by other cults was allowed and encouraged among the Gnostics; many of their priests, teachers and prophets were women, and the form of the female body was considered an image of Eve, Zoe and Sophia.

The Gnostics gathered around charismatic figures, followed sets of rituals and distributed different offices among the faithful. But they did not take any of that too seriously. They had to use the imperfect language of the world, since 'truth did not come into the world naked, but in symbols and images. The world cannot receive truth in any other way'.[36] Yet, they knew that worldly identities, hierarchies and social conventions were just part of God's evil plan to keep people enslaved to their ignorance.

They developed different strategies to accomplish their mission. Some pursued the path of asceticism, renouncing all that Yaldabaoth's world had to offer. Their impeccable behaviour made them a hard target for their opponents. Others, on the contrary, gave ample opportunities to their critics. Those 'libertine' Gnostics trusted that liberation would come automatically after death, thanks to their knowledge of the truth, and thus dedicated their lifetime to the work of sabotage. Their reasoning was straightforward: since this wretched world is the product of an evil God, then the social and natural laws that keep it functioning must be equally evil. Thus, for example, instead of procreating children who would be submitted to God's rule, they preferred to collectively eat their semen and menstrual blood in ritual orgies.[37] Others, again, combined libertinism with a reinvention of social practices and beliefs. In his treatise *On Righteousness*, the Gnostic thinker Epiphanes, son of Carpocrates, advocated for a form of Gnostic communism that was radically opposed to the institutions of private property, the judiciary system, monogamy and marriage, as well as to the discriminatory belief that animals and plants are not worthy of human dignity.[38]

All of them, ascetics, libertines and communists, considered themselves 'the kingless generation', whose only allegiance was to the otherworldly spark burning inside them.[39] They were the children of the 'non-existent God', the Alien God, the silent Abyss, eternally alive and beyond comprehension. They were foreigners to the world and its language, citizens of an elsewhere shrouded in mystery.

## 21.

Despite their valiant efforts, the Gnostics ultimately failed in their war against the world. By the time they had been stamped out of history, the Hermeticists too had vanished, while the last Pagans had retreated to the deep *pagus* (countryside), where they clung to remnants of their faith under a cloak of folk traditions. Across this spiritual wasteland, the dominant religions solidified their hold. By the end of Late Antiquity, the symphony of Mediterranean imagination had been reduced to a trio of monotheisms: Judaism, Christianity and, soon to come, Islam.

Only one voice remained to break this eerie harmony: Manichaeism. To this date, its echo has not yet entirely faded. When we use the term 'Manichean' today, we are accusing someone of being so rigid as to be blind to the subtleties of the world, especially in terms of right and wrong. This enduring infamy reveals how Manichaeism was also destined for a complete historical defeat. But the sensitivity of its principles, and the range of its historical influence across vast stretches of time and cultures, testify to much more than is captured by today's slur. With Manichaeism, the imagination of the Late Ancient Mediterranean will reach its furthest geographical distance, and with it, too, our story of this period will find its conclusion.

The story of Manichaeism began in 216 AD, when a baby boy named Mani was born in the region of Babylon. His family belonged to the old Parthian aristocracy, but his father yearned for a more spiritual kind of distinction than nobility of blood. Thus, when Mani was four, his father took him to a mystical community near the river Tigris. Mani was raised there, according to an ascetic lifestyle and schooled across the Jewish, Christian and Zoroastrian traditions.

At the age of twelve, when boys are typically preoccupied with the discovery of puberty, Mani saw the sky open above him. An angel descended from the heights and landed at his side. The angel, who presented himself as 'the Comrade',[40] revealed to the boy the existence of a secret world of Light, hidden beyond the world and inside every living being. Then the angel disappeared, promising to return. After that experience, Mani delved even deeper into his study of all religious traditions. He also worked hard to learn the techniques of any expressive medium, from painting to music, calligraphy to grammar, that would help him communicate his vision. Twelve years passed before he could see the Comrade again. When he finally returned, Mani's life took an irreversible turn. The Comrade ordered him to leave his village and to create a new community, whose members would seek the Light that shines within and outside the world. Mani left the landscapes of his youth together with a small retinue, which included his father, and began travelling across the Persian lands, now under the rule of the Sassanid dynasty. The group continued moving East until they reached the delta of the Indus River, then veered North to the Central Asian realm of Turan, where Mani converted the local king. During their years on the move, they did not cease developing their religion. They translated its message into the languages they encountered along the way and adapted it to the sensitivities of the different cultures. After all, the same truth had always spoken with different voices to different people.

> Wisdom and deeds have from time to time been brought to mankind by the messengers of God. So, in one age they have been brought by the messenger, called Buddha, to India, in another by Zarathustra to Persia, in another by Jesus to the West. Thereupon this revelation has come down, this prophecy in this last age through me, Mani, the messenger of the God of truth to Babylonia.[41]

## 22.

Mani's cosmology was profound yet simple, like a fable. He unravelled complex metaphysical knots into a clear narrative, where evocative imagery trumped abstract explanations. In the best tradition of Mediterranean syncretism, he drew inspiration from multiple sources. He borrowed especially from the mythology of Zoroastrianism, the ancient religion of Persia, where two opposite forces, roughly equal in power, contended for dominion over the universe. Mani pushed Zoroastrianism in a novel direction, similar to how Christianity had transformed Judaism. He created a story at once grandiose and humble, a cosmic epic whose protagonists resided inside the body and soul of every living creature.

In the beginning, his story went, the universe was divided into two realms, ruled by two absolute principles: pure light and pure darkness. They were perfectly separate from each other, and the universe hung in balance between them. The darkness, however, was agitated by its turbulent nature, so one day it decided to attack the realm of light. The Lord of Light, Zurvan, prepared his defences against the Lord of Darkness, Ahriman, and his 'authorities', the Archons. He evoked a warrior of light, called Ohrmazd, and fashioned him as the archetype of the primeval man.

Unlike most creatures, Ohrmazd did not keep his soul inside his body, but he wore it outwardly like an armour. Dressed in his soul-armour, Ohrmazd travelled to meet the incoming forces of darkness on the border between the two realms. In a terrible battle, Ohrmazd was defeated, and the Lord of Darkness took him prisoner.

Zurvan thus evoked another being, Mithra, and sent him to rescue his champion. Through force and cunning, Mithra managed to retrieve Ohrmazd's body, but not his armour of light, his soul. The Lord of Darkness had hidden it on planet Earth, where his authorities guarded it like a treasure. Mithra did not give up. He built a system of planets and stars, an enormous mechanism to extract the light from Earth and return it to Zurvan. To set this machine in motion, Zurvan summoned an androgynous being, The Third Envoy, and dispatched them to the solar system. The Third Envoy took their abode in the sun, appointed their twelve daughters to preside over the houses of the zodiac and began drawing the light by using the moon like a bucket. Even today, we can see the moon filling up every month and then pouring its light towards the sun, until it is empty and ready for a new load.

Some of the light, however, had been hidden by the Lord of Darkness inside the bodies of his Archons. The Third Envoy showed themselves in their androgynous, naked splendour, and the Archons could not control their excitement: the male ones spilt their seed on the ground of the Earth, while the female ones produced spontaneous abortions. Their seed turned into plants, while their abortions became animals, both of whom are carriers of particles of light.

Overwhelmed by Zurvan's offensive, the Lord of Darkness created two humans, Adam and Eve, in the shape of the androgynous Third Envoy. He stored all the remaining light in them and sunk them into a condition of ignorance about their true nature. Zurvan responded by playing his last card. He sent another envoy, the Jesus of Splendour, to enlighten humans about their rightful place in the realm of light. Since that day, and until the inevitable victory of Zurvan at the end of time, each creature's soul is entangled in a cosmic fight to escape the grip of the authorities of darkness and to return to its home of light. Once the last soul has been saved, the material world will finally vanish, and the original state of perfect separation between pure light and pure darkness will be reconstituted.

## 23.

Every day, the followers of Mani were engaged in the war against darkness. Some of them, the Elect, dedicated their entire lives to the good fight. They renounced all worldly attachments, including property, a fixed address, labour and sexual intercourse. They pursued a life of purity and tried to cause no harm to any living being, whether animal or vegetable. Others, the Hearers, made up for their limited commitment by providing for the needs of the Elect. They prepared and served their daily vegetarian meal, where they witnessed the physical process through which the Elect incorporated in their stomach the particles of light carried by the plants. Having purified them with their metabolism, they would bring them with themselves after death in their final journey towards the realm of Light. In return for their service, the Elect absolved the Hearers for the sins they had incurred against the plants while preparing their meals.

Mani's religion stood out from the brutal context of Late Antiquity. Its mythology was dreamy and hopeful, and not overly complicated. Its ethics combined a unique sensitivity to any form of suffering with deep metaphysical insights. It is no wonder that many intellectuals were attracted to the Manichaean communities. Among them was a certain Augustine, a native of Thagaste in Algeria, whose nine years as a Manichean Hearer taught him much of what would eventually render him the greatest philosopher of his time, and a Father and Saint of the Catholic Church.

The religion of Mani found a receptive audience among the merchants as well, whose worldly affairs fitted comfortably within a doctrine that did not demonize the world. The possibility of a two-layer membership, too, allowed them to gain salvation by catering to the needs of the Elect, rather than by giving up their life. Carried by the merchants, as well as by professional missionaries, Manichaeism spread across borders. Mani instructed his missionaries to remain flexible, adapting his doctrine to the local cultures. As long as the fundamental message remained unchanged, he saw no problem in modifying the letter. He personally worked on a reform of the Aramaic alphabet to render his writings more easily translatable into the languages of the neighbouring countries. To those who had sworn allegiance to a realm beyond the world, the borders imposed by competing empires and ethnicities were just lines drawn in the sand.

This estrangement from the historical dynamics, however, would eventually exact its price. As Jesus Christ had warned his disciples, those who do not swear allegiance to the world would always attract the wrath of those who derive their power from the superstition that the world is everything. 'If you belonged to the world, the world would love you as its own. Because you do not belong to the world, but I have chosen you out of the world – therefore the world hates you.'[42]

## 24.

While Mani was preaching in Central Asia, a new sovereign ascended the throne of Persia. He had a reputation for being a wise monarch, interested in more than wealth and power. Thus, at the beginning of the reign of Shapur I, King of Kings, Mani and his growing entourage decided to return to the Persian heartland. The prophet of the Light asked to be admitted to Shapur I's presence to expound his doctrine. The king agreed, and in a single audience, he was enchanted by Mani's cosmology. Shapur I bestowed his royal blessing upon Mani, extending his protection to anyone who went in his name. Mani seemed destined for an unusually easy career as a prophet.

But in 272 AD, the benevolent Shapur I died. The following year, Wahram I ascended to the throne of Persia. Mani was not paying much attention to what was happening at court. Perhaps, he thought that the triumph of his religion could no longer be derailed by political events. He was about to leave for a new journey to the East when a messenger handed him a summons to the court of Wahram I. He left his instructions to his disciples and took the road to Ben Lapat, where the king resided. The atmosphere he found at court was less than friendly. He was immediately challenged by the Zoroastrian priests, who accused him of spreading an unpatriotic doctrine that endangered the spiritual foundations of Persia. Then, he was interrogated by the king himself. 'How come God gave his revelation to you, while he did not reveal the same to me, who am lord over the whole country?' Wahram I asked. 'It is God who is Lord', Mani replied.[43]

Publicly belittling the authority of the King of Kings amounted to an act of sedition. Wahram I gestured to the guards to seize Mani. They clamped irons on his hands and feet, then wrapped layer upon layer of chains around his body until the prophet was crushed beneath their weight. Mani was left on the floor to asphyxiate. Only a handful of disciples dared to stand beside him, while his breathing grew fainter. It took Mani twenty-six days to die, in what had been, in effect, his crucifixion.

## 25.

Like the Passion of Jesus Christ, Mani's death only emboldened the activities of his church. The 'messengers of the light' relocated their holy see to the Iraqi city of Ctesiphon, and from there they established new strongholds in Egypt, Algeria, the Iberian Peninsula, Gaul, Italy and Dalmatia. Wherever they went, they met with a warm welcome from the populace and the hostility of the political authorities.

In Roman lands, the Pagan emperors distrusted a religion that came from enemy Persia, while their Christian successors numbered Mani's doctrine among the heresies. The Manichean believers were arrested, deprived of their possessions and sentenced to forced labour. Their leaders were burnt alive, together with their sacred scriptures. By the end of the sixth century, the Manichean church was virtually extinguished everywhere in Europe and North Africa. When its message briefly resurfaced during the European Middle Ages, among the Bogomil sect in Bulgaria and the Balkans and with the Cathars in Southern France, the official Church lost no time in organizing their extermination.

Things were no better in Persia. The Sassanian kings banished the Manichaeans, forcing them to move their holy see to Samarkand, in modern-day Uzbekistan. The arrival of the Islamic rulers, a few centuries later, unleashed a new wave of persecutions that pushed them even further to the East.

Only among the Uyghur people of Chinese Turkestan, near modern-day Mongolia, would the seekers of the Light find, at last, a haven. In the Uyghur kingdom, Manichaeism returned to its old splendour. Not only was it tolerated, but it eventually rose to the status of an official state religion. Manichean missionaries restarted their activity, travelling northwards to Siberia and eastwards to the Chinese empire, where they were welcomed at the court of Empress Wu Zeitan and engaged in public discussions with peers from the local currents of Buddhism, Taoism and Confucianism.

It looked as if, after centuries of wandering, the Manichaeans had found a permanent home. At the beginning of the thirteenth century, however, the Mongol emperor Genghis Khan led his army across the border. He attacked the Uyghur kingdom, conquered it swiftly and moved on in all directions. In a few years, the Mongols took over China and Central Asia, reaching as far as the Middle East and Eastern Europe. Their new empire, built on a rough warrior's ethics, had no room for Mani's message of non-violent struggle against the darkness. Smothered by military repression, the flame of the Manichean church finally went out.

## 26.

In 1292, during the reign of Genghis Khan's grandson Kublai, the Venetian merchant Marco Polo and his uncle Maffeo were travelling along the south-eastern coast of China. The two Venetians stopped for a break in the city of Fuzhou, near the coast facing the island of Taiwan. Having heard of their curiosity about anything unusual, a local man, a learned Muslim, asked them if they would be interested in meeting a strange group who lived apart from the rest of the population. They didn't worship idols, nor fire, nor did they follow the precepts of Muhammad, Buddha, Lao Tzu, Confucius or Christ. Marco and Maffeo asked to be introduced to them, but those mysterious people were not keen on meeting strangers. They feared that the two travellers might be undercover police agents, sent by the emperor to investigate their secret. After days of negotiations, the Polos were finally allowed to visit their community. They learnt that the small group followed a religion which dated back over 700 years, but whose name had been forgotten even by its believers. Their faith had been banned for such a long time that they no longer had any teachers to guide their cult and help them interpret their scriptures. All they had was a handful of books, which they could not understand and thus used simply as talismans.

Marco and Maffeo asked to see the books, and to their great surprise discovered in them some passages from the Bible. Clearly, they thought, these must be long-lost Christians, scattered thus far by history's winds! Their idea was met with indifference until the Venetians pointed out that, as Christians, they would be under imperial protection and allowed to practice their cult without fear. At once, the community agreed to send two emissaries to the imperial court to proclaim themselves Christians.[44]

Marco and Maffeo Polo travelled on, satisfied with having returned a few lost sheep to the fold. Modern scholars, however, believe that those people knew perfectly well who they were and what the nature of their scriptures was. They were the very last Manicheans, who had miraculously escaped persecution by the Mongols. They had good reason for feigning ignorance in front of the Venetians, who did indeed work for the Mongol emperor.

And there was something perfectly fitting in their claim to have 'forgotten their own name'. By adhering opportunistically to another denomination, the last Manichaeans of Fuzhou preserved the essence of the Mediterranean imagination, with its disavowal of conventional names and its ironic distance from worldly institutions.

It is also fitting that our journey through the age of Late Antiquity should end with them. When they realized that they had been defeated by history, they did not squander their last energies in a frontal attack against the powers of the time. They abandoned the battlefield and moved on in silence, shrouded under ever-changing identities. Like the last Pagans, the Hermeticists and the Gnostics, they chose occultation over surrender. To the world where the Archons of history reigned supreme, they left nothing of themselves but a shell.

Like the worshippers of Osiris, whom Rutilius had met in the *pagus*, they passed as eccentric simpletons. In fact, they were putting into practice the lesson they had learnt from Ohrmazd, the hero of Mani's cosmogony, who had lost his soul after wearing it outwardly as an armour. Unlike him, they kept their otherworldly spark well-hidden inside themselves, like the voice of an inner guide. Their aloofness revealed their kinship to the other dreamers of Late Antiquity, who had not let history's darkness take over their inner realm.

After the twilight of Late Antiquity, the dawn of the early Middle Ages cast a dim and unsettling light over the Mediterranean. Centuries of religious repression had spared little of its old creative fervour, and most of its coasts languished in a state of material and intellectual impoverishment. But from the South-East, across the sands, a new wind was beginning to blow. A new age of violence and splendour was about to envelop the Mediterranean, forcing its people to mine again the depths of their imagination for ways out of an inhospitable world.

Of this challenge, and of the unlikely alliance that ensued between the imaginations of the Christian North and the Islamic South, we shall say more in the next chapter.

# Meanwhile in the Mediterranean...

## Sixth century to fifteenth century

*622 AD* – The Prophet Muhammad travels from Mecca to Medina, which becomes the traditional starting date of the Islamic era.

*661* – Mu ʿāwiyah I assassinates Muhammad's son-in-law, Ali, and founds the Umayyad caliphate.

*732* – At the Battle of Tours, Frankish and Umayyad troops fight for control of South-Western Europe.

*750* – The Abbasid dynasty defeats the Umayyads and takes over the caliphate.

*8th–11th centuries* – The Mediterranean is ravaged by frequent Viking raids.

*800 AD* – The Frankish king Charlemagne is crowned emperor in Rome.

*969* – The Fatimid dynasty conquers Egypt and founds the city of Cairo.

*11th century – The Seljuk Empire conquers most of the Middle East.*

*1025 – The Persian scholar Ibn Sina completes his encyclopaedia of medicine, The Canon of Medicine.*

*1130 – The Normans complete the conquest of Sicily, formerly ruled by the Arabs.*

*1138–1204 – Life of the Jewish philosopher Moses Ben Maimon (Maimonides).*

*1054 – The Western and Eastern Christian churches part ways over doctrinal and political matters, inaugurating the Great Schism.*

*1096 – Pope Urban II calls for all Christians to unite to reconquer the Holy Land, launching the First Crusade.*

*1181–1226 – Life of Saint Francis of Assisi, founder of the Franciscan monastic order.*

*1207–73 – Life of the Sufi poet Jalal al-Din Muhammad Rumi.*

*1225–74 – Life of Saint Thomas Aquinas.*

*1258 – The Mongol armies conquer Baghdad, ending the Abbasid caliphal dynasty.*

*1347–51 – The Black Death.*

*1453 – The Ottoman armies conquer Constantinople, ending the Eastern Roman 'Byzantine' Empire.*

# 4

# *Translators*

# *The Middle Ages*

### 1.

In the second century after the Hijrah of the Prophet Muhammad, may the peace and blessings of Allah be upon him, the ninth century after the birth of our Lord, Jesus Christ, a Muslim commander, an Emir, was roaming the borderlands between Syria and Cappadocia. It was a dangerous territory, where every turn of the road could hide the ambush of *apelati* bandits or *akriti* Roman Christian soldiers. Mounted on a fast Arab horse, the Emir was riding in search of adventure. One day, having come across an isolated country mansion, he saw the daughter of a Roman general looking out from a window and instantly fell in love with her. He climbed the external walls, kidnapped the woman and rushed back to his horse. But the woman's brothers, on their way back from a hunt, saw him and chased him. They caught up with the Emir, surrounded him and challenged him to a duel. Defeated in combat by her brothers and conquered by the woman's beauty, the Emir offered to convert to Christianity and to join the Romans in exchange for being allowed to remain with her.

From their union was born the most famous hero of the Roman frontier, Digenis Akritas, 'the two-blood border lord'. His mixed origin placed him alongside the heroes of antiquity, whose blood combined that of humans and gods.

> [But] record not Homer; nor Achilles' tales,
> Nor Hector's; they are false! . . .
> But this man's deeds are true and well attested.[1]

Digenis Akritas was as precocious as Achilles. At the age of twelve, during a hunting expedition, he killed two bears, a deer and a lion with his bare hands. Then he ran away from home to join the *apelati* of the frontier. When the bandits tested him in combat, he defeated them one by one. Why join those who had proved to be below him? He left behind the *apelati* to travel further into the wilderness. While wandering in search of adventure, he discovered the daughter of another Roman general, locked by her father in a fortified mansion. The two youths fell in love and decided to run away together, but their escape was cut short by the men of her family and their soldiers. Digenis Akritas reined in his horse to fight them. He slaughtered them all, sparing only his beloved's father and her brothers.

Such feats of valour did not pass unnoticed. The Roman emperor, always on the lookout for new recruits for his army, dispatched a messenger to invite him for an audience at the imperial court. The invitation was coldly received. The Two-Blood Border Lord had little desire to enter state institutions and even less respect for the established powers. If His Highness wished to see him, he bluntly replied, he could come to visit him in person. Indeed, the emperor left his palace in Constantinople and travelled to the borderlands to meet the now fourteen-year-old Digenis Akritas and bestow upon him an aristocratic title. Little did he knew that such conventions had no value for him.

Meanwhile, not far from there, another warrior was going from glory to glory. Not a Roman but an Arab, not a Christian but a Muslim – not a man, but a woman. Her name was Fatima, and she too had been an exceptional child. When she was only five, she looked like a ten-year-old, and since her childhood, she had educated herself in the art of combat. Kidnapped at a young age by a rival Arabic tribe, she had been raised as a slave, tasked with the care of the camels and horses. Although she lived at the bottom of society, she held a veil draped over her face like a noblewoman, and never lost a chance to show her valour by joining the men in the most dangerous missions. Such were her warrior skills that she became known as Amira Dhat al-Himma, 'the Commander of noble ambition'. When she heard that her tribe was about to attack the one from which she had been kidnapped, she rode at the head of the army, defeated her father's soldiers, then skilfully negotiated to reunite the two tribes.

The only family she recognized, however, were her horse and her armour. She had no desire to ever have a husband. But reasons of political expediency decreed otherwise, and she was forced to marry a man she despised. She kept him out of her tent, throwing him into the dust every time he tried to approach her, until one night he mixed a powerful sleeping drug into her drinking water. Once she had fallen asleep, her husband entered her tent and raped her. A baby boy was born following this violence, but unlike either of his parents, the boy was black. His father rejected him, and his mother, the Commander, raised him alone, making him her companion in arms.

While Fatima trained her child to become a warrior, Digenis Akritas had to fight to protect his little encampment, set in a splendid meadow among the mountains. He fought lions, bandits, roaming soldiers, once even a dragon. Every night, he returned to his wife, the only thing in the world he held sacred. No bonds tied him to anyone except the love he felt for her and the fear of God that shook his heart. Ruthless and lawless, he felt no remorse whenever he killed, and when he raped, his only concern was that he had sinned against monogamy.

Unlike him, Amira Dhat al-Himma respected the laws of her group. She accepted the decisions of the caliph and of his successors, even when they went against her own interests. She felt responsible towards her people. Yet, the Muslim Commander did not give in to the temptation of separating friends and foes along the lines of religious identity. For both border lords, Christians and Muslims could alternatively be enemies or allies, depending on the situation and their mutual respect. Their attitude was shared by many other borderland warriors of their time, who easily swapped sides and allegiances across the two faiths. So too did Fatima's husband: when the Commander attacked him after the nightly rape, he sought refuge with the Roman emperor, forcing the people of his clan to convert to Christianity. It was not long before Amira Dhat al-Himma, too, joined the Christian emperor in Constantinople, lending her hand to fight his enemies.

After countless adventures, death met the two heroes according to their character. Amira Dhat al-Himma lived into her maturity, surrounded by the admiration of her people. She died while on a pilgrimage to Mecca, a blessing for a devout Muslim. Digenis Akritas, on the contrary, continued to live apart from society, although he eventually renounced the nomadic lifestyle to settle in a palace of his own construction. Some say that he died suddenly, while taking a relaxing bath with his wife, the first time he had ever lowered his guard. Others claim instead that death went to meet him face to face. It took the form of Charon, the mythical ferryman to the afterlife. Digenis Akritas and Charon fought in full armour, on the 'marble threshing floors', until the hero born of two bloods exhaled his last breath, without a friend to comfort him or a priest to forgive him.[2]

## 2.

Digenis Akritas and Amira Dhat al-Himma never once touched the arid soil of the borderlands. Their lives unfolded entirely in the voice of the folk storytellers, before moving into a handful of manuscripts where their tales were preserved. But their adventures reflected the real existence of thousands of people, living between Cappadocia and Syria in the ninth century AD, at the intersection of faiths, nations and cultures.

The feeling of displacement that emerges from the stories of Digenis Akritas and Amira Dhat al-Himma was familiar to the Christian majority living in Syria, at an awkward distance from the new Muslim overlords. Up until the seventh century AD, the people of the eastern Mediterranean coast had known a period of relative stability, first under the unified rule of the early Roman Caesars, then as part of the surviving Roman 'Byzantine' Empire. Despite frequent infighting between different Christian sects, their world had been dominated by one religion and by one, albeit progressively weaker, political power. Then, in the year 622 AD, history jolted forward. The Prophet Muhammad and a small group of followers brought the message of Allah from the Arabic city of Mecca to the nearby town of Medina, thus beginning the Islamic era. Just fifteen years later, in 637 AD, the city of Antioch and the whole of Northern Syria fell to the army of the 'rightly guided' caliph Umar. Islamic conquests proceeded at lightning speed, transforming the politics and culture of an immense territory. The Arabic warriors placed themselves at the head of their new dominions, restructuring society along lines of ethnic, as well as religious, separation. Non-Muslim *dhimmi*, whether Christian, Jewish or Zoroastrian, were subjected to special taxes and restrictions and had to renegotiate their status as foreigners within their own homeland.

Unlike the lords of the borderlands, they did not resort to violence to assert their dignity. They imitated the storytellers instead, using language as a tool to create new worlds for themselves. Their language of choice was Syriac, an Aramaic dialect that acted as the *lingua franca* of the eastern Mediterranean. Back in the last period of Roman domination, Syriac had already served as the trait d'union between the Christian era and the heritage of the old Greek world. Translators like Sergius of Reshaina had produced Syriac versions of some of the treasures of classical Greece, such as the medical works of Galen, the philosophical treatises of Porphyry and the logical works of Aristotle, alongside texts by Christian authors such as Pseudo Dionysius the Areopagite. The Syriac translators were especially drawn to texts on logic, which defined the rules for correct thinking and the grammar of philosophical argumentation. It was as if, to the mysterious pull that drags the worlds into the chasms of history, they were trying to oppose something that could still define, at least in the mind, the limits of what was rational, orderly and true.

With the arrival of the Muslims, the work of the translators intensified. Their effort ceased to be the solitary quest of a handful of individuals and became part of a broader project, aimed at creating a bridge between the splendours of the past and the ambitions of the new era of the caliphs.

## 3.

The story of the Christian translators, and of the Greek heritage in their custody, continued far to the south of Syria. It descended the blue ribbon of the Euphrates River, unfurled over the bright expanse of the Iraqi deserts, until it reached a valley where verdant fields stretched all the way to the banks of the Tigris River. There it stopped, to start a second life in a city of legends: Baghdad.

It is recounted that, one day, the caliph Al-Mansur, the second in the Abbasid dynasty, was journeying along the banks of the Tigris River, looking for the right place to establish his new capital. Everything about the city had to be perfect from the start. He asked his advisors about suitable locations, based on nearby resources and on the accessibility for both merchants and the army. Then he looked for signs of a higher order. He heard that the books of the Christian monks prophesied that a great city would be built on a site next to a little church, situated near the Tigris River. The prophecy specified that the builder would be someone bearing the name of Miqlas. Al Mansur gasped: Miqlas was how his nurse called him when he was a child. He went to inspect the site, spent a peaceful night inside the little church and when he awoke, after praying, he decreed that his capital would be built in that place.[3] To find the most suitable date to start the works, he consulted three astrologers, an Arab, a Persian and a Jew, who agreed on 30 July 762 AD. To source the materials, he ordered his builders to demolish the ruins of the imperial palace of Ctesiphon, the seat of the old Sassanian empire that had ruled Iraq before Islam, as if to transfuse its imperial spirit into the new foundation. The only thing left to decide was the name. He took two ancient Persian words, *Bagh*, 'God', and *Dadh*, 'founded', and combined them. Thus, he created Baghdad, the city 'founded by God'.[4]

This carefully crafted city was designed to align Heaven and Earth. The first nucleus of Baghdad was a perfectly round citadel, in the shape of the heavenly vault, whose walls opened in four gates, like the four rivers that flowed out of the Garden of Eden. Inside the citadel, al Mansur established his first palace.

In the decades that followed, Baghdad grew at a tumultuous pace. Hundreds of thousands of immigrants built their homes around the citadel, rapidly establishing the new Abbasid capital as one of the largest cities in the world. Baghdad became the fabulous setting of the tales collected in the *Thousand and One Night*, where the caliph Harun al-Rashid and his vizier Ja'far disguised themselves to roam the streets at night, looking for stories and wonderful adventures.

It was in this centre of commerce and exchange that the *dhimmi* Christian translators found new supporters, who helped them salvage the legacy of classical Greece.

## 4.

The folktales portray the caliph Harun al-Rashid, grandchild of the founder of Baghdad, as a splendid yet humane ruler. He took the time to listen to his subjects and, whenever possible, intervened to restore justice. There is little doubt among historians, about the splendour of his reign. An anecdote can give a sense of his greatness compared to his contemporaries in Europe. In 797 AD, the king of the Franks, Charlemagne, sent two of his noblemen, guided by a Jewish interpreter, to bring his regards to the caliph. To express his pleasure for the new acquaintance, Harun al-Rashid sent back a white elephant named Abul Abbas. The Frankish king, feverishly excited at receiving this exotic gift, could afford nothing better to send back than two Alsatian hunting dogs, to which the caliph responded with a mechanical clock made with gilded bronze. While the annals of Charlemagne record in detail the European adventures of Abul Abbas – who died accompanying his new master on a war campaign against the Danes – the annals of Baghdad make no mention of this negligible exchange of gifts with a minor and distant monarch.[5]

If his grandeur is historically attested, the humanity and long-sightedness of Harun al-Rashid are more uncertain. He had two favourite sons: the eldest, al-Ma'mun, who had been born from a Persian slave concubine, and the other, al-Amin, from a legitimate Arab wife. Al-Ma'mun, aware of his fragile position as a child of mixed background, grew into a studious young man under the loving guidance of his father's vizier, Ja'far. His brother, favoured by the court, dedicated little attention to his own intellectual growth. When the time came for the caliph to choose an heir, he picked the less talented al-Amin, who was of pure aristocratic and Arab blood. To make sure that his eldest son would know his place, Harun al-Rashid had his mentor, his own friend and loyal vizier Ja'far, executed.

Soon after the death of the caliph, the two brothers entered a brutal war, which al-Ma'mun swiftly resolved by conquering Baghdad and killing al-Amin. Then, one night, a strange man came to visit the dreams of the new caliph.

> He saw a man of reddish-white complexion with a high forehead, bushy eyebrows, bald head, dark blue eyes and handsome features, sitting on his chair. Al-Ma'mun said: 'I saw in my dream that I was standing in front of him, filled with awe. I asked, "Who are you?" He replied: "I am Aristotle." I was delighted to be with him and asked, "O philosopher, may I ask you [some questions]?" He replied, "Ask." I said: "What is the good?" He replied: "Whatever is good according to intellect." I asked: "Then what?" He replied: "Whatever is good according to religious law." I asked: "Then what?" He replied: "Whatever is good in the opinion of the masses." I asked: "Then what?" And he replied: "Then there is no more 'then.'"[6]

Aristotle's apparition to al-Ma'mun was well timed. Already under Harun al-Rashid, the Greek classics had become must-have luxury items. Partly for reasons of prestige, partly to strengthen the dialectics of the Islamic intelligentsia against its religious adversaries, Greek and Syriac speakers were hired by the Abbasid elite to translate works by the ancient Greek pagans. With al-Ma'mun, this informal trend became part of a state-sponsored project of unprecedented proportions, which opened new avenues for the Mediterranean imagination about the fundamental makeup of the world.

## 5.

According to an Islamic tradition, the Prophet Muhammad encouraged his followers to seek knowledge everywhere, even as far as China. For al-Ma'mun, such a 'China' lay just beyond the northern borders of his empire. While the Byzantine Romans increasingly neglected their classical heritage, the court of Baghdad began drawing legions of translators from the Syrian borderlands, wishing to extract from the ancient books any knowledge that could feed the Islamic intellectual revolution. Emissaries were sent abroad to find books on any available subject and bring them to Baghdad. Meanwhile, the caliph ordered the construction of a new library in the capital, ambitiously named *Bayt al-Hikma*, 'The House of Wisdom'. Circles of translators, mostly Christian *dhimmi* of Syrian origin, clustered around its silent rooms. Thanks to the generous sponsorships of the caliph and of his entourage, half-forgotten thinkers like Aristotle and Plato, Porphyry, Plotinus, Euclid, Ptolemy and Galen infused the still-young Islamic culture with a powerful combination of metaphysics, logic, rhetoric, ethics, mathematics, engineering, natural sciences, medicine and astronomy.

The appropriation of Pagan knowledge via non-Muslim translators did not pose an insurmountable ideological problem. Whenever something useful and true is found, it should not be discarded simply because of its provenance. In this cultural atmosphere, the Arabic language was easily stretched to accommodate a Greek term for a new discipline: *falsafa*, philosophy.

The Christian translators played a crucial role in the blossoming of Islamic philosophy, starting with the first in its lineage, the 'philosopher of the Arabs', al-Kindi. While unable to read Greek himself, al-Kindi employed a large team of translators, mainly from the Syrian Christian circle of the Hunayn family, to mine the classical Greek legacy extensively. Having mastered the ancients, al-Kindi began producing original texts on an astonishing array of topics, including metaphysics, logic, mathematics, ethics, psychology, mirror-making, manufacture and cryptography. In his effort to bring philosophy to the attention of his contemporaries, he insisted on the compatibility between rational enquiry and faith based on revelation. He did so through a combination of elements derived from both sources, as when demonstrating the non-eternity of the universe or the immateriality of the soul. Above all, his concern was to prove that philosophy, however vociferous in its argumentation, could in no way scathe the supreme majesty of God. Using the arguments of the Greek Neoplatonists combined with the Islamic notion of *Tawhid*, 'the oneness of God', he insisted that the distinctions of language can apply only to what is created, and thus finite. But God, being uncreated and thus infinite, exceeds anything that can be asserted through our limited linguistic means. God is above all qualities and definitions, and we should only fall silent about his nature. Through philosophy, al-Kindi not only reinforced the Islamic principle of the absolute unity and transcendence of God, but also dealt a powerful blow against the Christian idea of God as a Trinity, made up of three distinct persons, the Father, the Son and the Holy Spirit.

Perhaps unknowingly, his Christian translators had been working for the greater glory of Islam, and to the detriment of their own religion. And yet, if al-Kindi was right, how could any religion claim to have the correct definition of God? In absolute silence, the God of the Muslims and that of the Christians returned to the same ineffable unity, of which the sacred texts could speak only figuratively.

## 6.

The translation movement followed the fortunes of the Abbasid dynasty. Under al-Mamun, Greek philosophy was integrated into state legislation. The religious movement of Mu'tazilism, which combined Greek-style rationalism with adherence to the Quranic revelation, set the intellectual agenda, and anyone who disagreed with its tenets was persecuted by order of the caliph. But immediately after the death of al-Ma'mun, this persecution, known as *Mihna*, the 'test', came to a close. His descendants saw little value in strict logical arguments, favouring instead a less 'philosophical' approach to theological matters.

Meanwhile, at the peripheries of the caliphate, new local powers had begun carving out larger areas of autonomy. From the Maghreb to Iran, new dynasties became the de facto rulers of what had once been an undivided dominion. By the end of the tenth century, the power of the Abbasid caliphs was mostly nominal, with an array of local governments paying lip service to their role as successors to the Prophet. As the power of the Abbasids waned, so did the investment in the translation of old Greek texts. Along with the fading prestige of the Christian translators and their sponsors, the Christian communities of *Dar al Islam* were left at the mercy of the local rulers. For some of them, like the Christians living under the Fatimid dynasty in Egypt, life became especially hard.

One can imagine the mix of apprehension and hope with which these communities received the news, at the end of the eleventh century, of a great movement of Western Christians heading towards the Muslim-governed Holy Land.

The idea of a mass, armed pilgrimage under the sign of the Cross was first formalized in 1095, when Pope Urban II called upon the faithful to reconquer the land that had witnessed the life and death of Jesus Christ. At first, this plan roused little concern among the Muslims of *Dar al Islam*. The balance of forces was not in favour of the Crusaders. While the Islamic world had enjoyed centuries of expansion, the European lands were still emerging from a period of political and economic, not to mention cultural, decline. But the European nations could count on a bellicose aristocracy, a strong military tradition and a temporary surplus of population. With all the due differences, they shared some of the same traits of the early Muslim warriors, whose religious ardour had overcome seemingly insurmountable obstacles.

The journey of the Crusades began ignominiously. While the lords were still organizing their troops, the popular masses inaugurated the pilgrimage by unleashing a wave of violence against the Jewish communities of Europe, with massacres of unprecedented brutality. Satisfied with their crimes against the local 'infidels', they headed South-East towards the Holy Land, marching on foot along the curves of the Danube River, through the forested mountains of the Balkans and Northern Greece, into the territory of the Byzantine Roman Empire.

There, the post-Barbaric people of Europe, many of whom lived under the so-called 'Holy Roman Empire', encountered the true heirs of the old Roman world. Rarely, two peoples who claimed common ancestry had been so different.

## 7.

The arrival of the Crusaders at the court of Constantinople was recorded by an exceptional chronicler, Anna Komnene, the daughter of the Roman 'Byzantine' emperor Alexius I Komnenos.[7] Although her family had ascended to royal dignity only recently and through dubious means, Anna had been educated to an incomparably higher level of culture than the 'Western barbarians', as she called them, who were 'migrating en mass' through the Roman territories.[8] 'The arrival of this mighty host was preceded by locusts', she noted, ominously.[9] While quoting liberally from Homer and Euripides, she depicted the Crusaders as a strangely attired, motley horde, where every petty chief thought himself a king and a peer to the emperor. They spoke incessantly, ignored the rules of etiquette, and were so keen on war that even their priests bore arms, so that they seemed 'more commanders than priests'. Indeed, she wrote, 'this barbarian race is no less devoted to religion than to war'.[10] After three centuries under constant Muslim pressure, the Romans welcomed the Crusaders as a useful reinforcement in a phase of military crisis. But could they trust that their bellicosity would be unleashed exclusively against the Muslims? As the Western barbarians passed through the empire, a strong detachment of imperial troops escorted them all the way to the border.

On the other side, the Crusaders appeared even more incongruous among the local people. The Syrian author Usama ibn Munqidh depicted them in vivid colours, in his account of his meetings with the 'Franks, may God confound them'.[11] In a passage, he recounted the story of a Christian Arab doctor named Thabit, who had been called in by the Crusaders while their own doctors were away. He had been shown two patients, a woman suffering from general malaise and a knight with an abscess in a leg. Thabit visited them, comparing their symptoms with the Arabic translation of the ancient Greek medical treatises, and prescribed a diet for the woman and herbal treatments for the knight. The patients' health gradually improved until the Western physicians returned to the encampment. When they heard that the Crusaders had requested the services of an Arab, although a Christian, they were horrified. They dismissed Thabit's prescriptions and immediately imposed their own cures.

> A Frankish physician came to them and said, 'This fellow doesn't know how to treat them.' He then said to the knight, 'Which would you like better: living with one leg or dying with both?' 'Living with one leg,' replied the knight. The physician then said, 'Bring me a strong knight and a sharp axe.' A knight appeared with an axe – indeed, I was just there

– and the physician laid the leg of the patient on a block of wood and said to the knight with the axe, 'Strike his leg with the axe and cut it off with one blow.' So he struck him – I'm telling you I watched him do it – with one blow, but it didn't chop the leg all the way off. So he struck him a second time, but the marrow flowed out of the leg and he died instantly. He then examined the woman and said, 'This woman, there is a demon inside her head that has possessed her. Shave off her hair.' So they shaved her head. The woman then returned to eating their usual diet – garlic and mustard. As a result, her dryness of humours increased. So the physician said, 'That demon has entered further into her head.' So he took a razor and made a cut in her head in the shape of a cross. He then peeled back the skin so that the skull was exposed and rubbed it with salt. The woman died instantaneously. So I asked them, 'Do you need anything else from me?' 'No,' they said. And so I left, having learned about their medicine things I had never known before.[12]

## 8.

Underestimated by the Muslims, the Western 'Franks' concluded the First Crusade with unexpected success. Much of Syria, Lebanon, Jordan, Israel and Palestine and later Cyprus fell into their hands. What had started as a religious pilgrimage, although armed and drenched in blood, became for many an opportunity to amass immense fortunes. But the Crusader hegemony in the Levant would be short-lived. Despite the stream of reinforcements from Europe and the new Crusades launched by later Popes, the

Christian states progressively shrank under the Muslim attacks, until they finally vanished at the end of the thirteenth century.

The close encounter between the European Christians and the Muslims, however, lasted far longer than the brief parable of the Crusader states. Once again, it would be the translators who would create a bridge across different interpretations of the world.

As in the story of the doctor Thabit, the European societies of the early Middle Ages had much to learn from the scientific and philosophical culture of the Muslims, itself rooted in the classics of ancient thought salvaged by the translators. Despite their theoretical and empirical shortcomings, doctrines such as Greek Galenic medicine offered a more solid and structured approach to scientific problems than the folk remedies used by European physicians. For those who lived on the border between these two worlds, the poverty of European sciences became an opportunity to reinvent themselves as ferrymen of knowledge between languages and cultures.

A pioneer among them was the eleventh-century doctor Constantinus, known as 'Africanus'. In his youth, he had left his native city of Carthage, in Tunisia, to travel to Egypt and Iraq – according to some, reaching as far as India and Ethiopia – in order to acquire a complete education in the latest scientific developments. He briefly returned home before embarking again on a ship headed to the Southern Italian coasts. Once in the city of Salerno, he travelled inland to the monastery of Monte Cassino, where he settled down and joined the order of Benedictines. He had brought from his travels a series of Arabic medical treatises, which in the quiet of the monastery he translated with the aid of two assistants who polished his Latin prose. They produced, among other texts, the first comprehensive medical text in Latin, the *Pantegni*, an abridged translation of the tenth-century Arabic treatise *Kitab Kamil as-sina'a at-tibbiya* ('the perfect book of the medical art') by 'Ali ibn al-'Abbas al-Magusi. With typical Medieval disregard for the notion of authorship – oddly anticipating late modern ideas of 'uncreativity' and the authorial role of translators – Constantinus signed the work as if it was his own. His translations had a formidable impact on the development of European medicine, placing the monastery of Monte Cassino and the city of Salerno on the map of Medieval European sciences. For centuries thereafter, in no small part, thanks to Constantinus, doctors operating in Italy were requested to acquire a degree from the Medical School of Salerno as proof of their proficiency.

The timing of Constantinus' death, during the First Crusade, could be read as the symbolic closure of a pacific alternative to the military clash between two worlds. But what had been started by the Tunisian monk, and by numerous other translators operating in Southern Italy, was in fact the beginning of a new translation movement, which was to channel the sea of scientific Greek-Arab knowledge towards Europe.

## 9.

Mentioning 'Europe' in the context of the Middle Ages might sound anachronistic, and it is certainly imprecise if referring to a fully Christian Europe as opposed to a fully Muslim Arab world. Just as the Arabic-speaking territories were also populated by Jews and Christians, Medieval Europe was not entirely under the blanket of one faith. Large Jewish communities lived alongside the Christians – and often suffered persecutions at their hands – while a few pre-Christian pagans still survived in the rural areas of the North. Within Christianity itself, a multitude of 'heretical' groups rendered the religious composition of the continent even less homogeneous. But it was at its westernmost edge, in the Iberian Peninsula, that Medieval Europe hosted the most spectacular and longest-lived society ruled by non-Christians: *Al Andalus*, Andalusia.

Since the fall of the Western Roman Empire in the fifth century, Spain had been ruled by the descendants of the 'barbarian' invaders, first the Vandals (from whom, perhaps, came the name *Vandalusia*), then the Visigoths. Under their system of tribal allegiances, in a landscape of crumbling infrastructure, silted ports and rotting fleets, the golden days of Rome, when Spain had been a cradle of philosophers and emperors, felt like something from a very distant past. For three centuries, the treasures of the Iberian Peninsula, rich in fertile lands and mineral resources, remained enshrined in a suspended time, protected by the geographical barriers of a territory at the far end of the Mediterranean basin.

According to legend, the survival of the Visigoth kingdom of Spain depended on a secret hidden within an ancient tower. Every new king added a padlock on the tower's door, until twenty-six padlocks were piled on top of each other. Until, one day, a young king ascended to the throne. Tormented by curiosity, he broke into the tower. The walls of the inner chamber were covered with paintings of Arab warriors on horseback, wielding scimitars and spears. A parchment, resting on a pedestal in the middle of the chamber, read the following prophecy: 'Whenever this chamber is violated, and the spell contained in this urn is broken, the people painted on these walls will invade Spain, overthrow its kings, and subdue the entire land'.[13]

The Visigoth king must have given in to curiosity just before the year 711 when the Muslim Berber commander Tariq ibn Ziyad disembarked with his army on the southern coast of Spain, near a mountain that would carry his name, Gibraltar (*Jabal Tariq*, 'Mount of Tariq'). He swiftly defeated the Visigoths, establishing the first Muslim dominion in Spain. A few decades later, the last survivor of the Umayyad caliphal dynasty, Abd al-Rahman *al-Dakhil*, 'the immigrant', escaped his rivals in the Levante and chose *Al Andalus* as the seat of his new kingdom. Under the Umayyads and their successors, the westernmost edge of Europe experienced a period of splendour unmatched anywhere on the continent. A wise policy of peaceful intermingling between different cultures, ethnicities and religions sparked an intellectual blossoming where Jews and Christians, while still subject to some forms of segregation, were able to join their Muslim colleagues in the creation of new forms of literature and science. The result was a kaleidoscopic explosion of lines of thought, at times diverging, at times intertwined with each other.

## 10.

For a few decades, the Andalusian crucible seemed the realized utopia of a pan-Mediterranean union of minds. Its prosperous cities hosted thinkers such as Ibn Gabirol and Maimonides, two of the greatest Jewish philosophers of the Middle Ages, alongside Sufi mystics like Ibn Arabi and polymaths like Ibn Tufayl, Ibn Bajja and Ibn Hazm. They influenced each other, sparred with each other and ventured together on untravelled paths of the imagination.

How could such different minds, often hailing from seemingly incompatible traditions, find a common ground for their intellectual pursuits?

An answer to this question was provided by the twelfth-century Andalusian jurist, mathematician, theologian, astronomer, physician and philosopher Ibn Rushd, also known by the Latin name Averroes.

While studying the Arabic translations of the classics of ancient Greek philosophy, Ibn Rushd had begun questioning what allowed all sentient beings to share the same ability to think while entertaining very different thoughts. His solution was daring and controversial. He held that every human – one might infer, every being endowed with understanding – not only had the same ability to think but shared the same, numerically identical mind. The minds of a Jew or a Christian, of a man or a woman, of a king or a slave, only appeared to differ, while being in fact the same, single universal mind, ultimately traceable to God, that looked at the world through different eyes. Since the ability to think constituted the highest essence of an individual, the fact that all people shared the same mind meant that there were no innate distinctions between them, except in terms of their accidental circumstances. Different bodies, upbringings and experiences presented the single mind that inhabited all thinking creatures with different opportunities to acquire knowledge and thus endowed it with different ideas and beliefs. As a reader can live countless lives by reading many works of literature, so this single mind experienced things in countless ways depending on its embodiments. After death, each of these windows would close, and the mind of each individual would return to its source – ready to see the world again through the windows opened by new births.

Ibn Rushd's ideas encountered fierce opposition in his own time, and even more so after his death. The critics were quick to point out his logical contradictions and a certain confusion in his use of definitions. Yet, if one had been meditating upon his theses while strolling through the streets of Cordoba or Seville, surrounded by men and women of different faiths, speaking multiple languages yet sharing in the same general conversation, their tenets would not have seemed extravagant. They posed a principle of unity within multiplicity and a conceptual ground for a policy of equitable coexistence of differences. Regardless of their philosophical shortcomings, they offered a vantage point for the imagination and opened vistas for a vision that went far beyond that of Ibn Rushd himself. They contained, in a nutshell, the essential lesson of the Mediterranean imagination: establishing the conceptual conditions for the flourishing of all, rather than chasing an impossible truth, should be the aim of our efforts to interpret the infinite mystery of reality.

## 11.

Ibn Rushd saw the last glimmers of Andalusia's golden age. Much had changed since the epic days when the Muslims had first set foot on Spanish land. The Umayyad dynasty had fallen in the eleventh century, replaced by a mosaic of small kingdoms (*reinos de taifa*). Soon afterwards, the fragmented landscape of Andalusia had been swallowed by invaders coming from Morocco, the Almoravids. Lastly, during Ibn Rushd's own lifetime, in the twelfth century, the Almoravids had also fallen, replaced by another invasion from Morocco: the Almohads. Of all the dynasties that had ruled Andalusia, the Almohads were by far the most intransigent. Their fundamentalism turned a land once open to multiculturalism, if not syncretism, into a hostile environment for anyone who did not subscribe to their religious tenets. A multitude of Jews, Christians, but also non-conforming Muslims chose to flee Andalusia: the Christians heading to the kingdoms of their co-religionaries in Northern Spain, the Muslims and Jews scattered all over the Mediterranean coasts. While Ibn Rushd had no qualms about entering the new political regime, securing an honourable position at court, other eminent thinkers decided to start a new life elsewhere.

Among these migrants was the great Jewish philosopher Maimonides, whose travels took him as far as Egypt. From his exile, Maimonides continued to intervene in the cultural debate of his lost homeland, taking a strong position in defence of those Jews (although the same applied also to the Christians and non-conforming Muslims) who had renounced their faith just to be allowed to remain in their homes. In a famous letter, he rebuked the all-too-easy condemnation of these people. What they did, they didn't do of their own volition, but were forced by the overwhelming violence of an oppressor.

> If [the coercion] is meant for [an oppressor's] own pleasure, [a Jew] may transgress and not be killed. [. . .] We do not find anywhere in the Torah God imposing as sentence a punishment on someone who is forced, whether for light things or grave

ones. Rather, [He punishes] someone who acts willingly ... but not someone who is forced.

It was right to celebrate as martyrs those who had resisted at the cost of their lives. But it would have been unfair to condemn the others. What counted was not the public display of one's own righteousness, but one's inner faithfulness. Thus, if a Jew was forced to go to the mosque or accept baptism lest they were persecuted and killed, they could do so without remorse. But deep in the secret of their heart, they must hold onto their faith even stronger than those who could publicly perform their piety.

Whoever comes to ask us whether he should be killed [rather than] acknowledge [the prophecy of Muhammad], we tell him to acknowledge it and not be killed ... and if he must do something with his hands, let him do it in secret.[14]

Maimonides' letter offered a theological justification for the practice of 'dissimulation', which had already accompanied (and would continue to accompany) Mediterranean people across the centuries. Whenever the powers that ruled history made their world uninhabitable, they knew how to withdraw to the innermost recesses of their hearts, nurturing there an altogether different vision of reality. Two very different lives, one public and one private, could run parallel to each other, with no necessity of conflating them under one sole judgement. For those who had been defeated at the great game of history, dissimulation was the mark of an invincible surrender.

## 12.

The fundamentalist regime of the Almohads, too, eventually passed. The Christian kingdoms of Northern Spain vanquished them in battle, and the Muslim domains of Andalusia shattered again into a mosaic of small kingdoms, progressively withdrawing within the borders of Granada, the last Muslim dominion until the end of the fifteenth century. The Christian conquest of Spain was a long and tortuous process, unlike how it is presented in the modern rhetoric of the so-called 'Reconquista'. Muslims and Christian rulers were often connected by bonds of alliance, and it was not unusual to see armies of the two faiths fighting together against common rivals.

While the situation among the rulers remained fluid, the demise of the Muslim states had drastic consequences for the common people. Suddenly, the Muslim population of a conquered city found itself foreign in its own homeland, subject to even worse restrictions than those imposed by the Almohads. Forced to choose between conversion, exile or execution, many followed Maimonides' advice and ostensibly gave up their faith. They became *Moriscos*, joining the *Marranos* (converted Jews) in the ranks of the *conversos* (new Christian converts). Like the Jews before them, they had to learn the art of dissimulation, establishing a stark distinction between their public persona as obedient Christian subjects and the secrets they harboured in their heart.

Cut off from their religious communities, both *Moriscos* and *Marranos* could hold onto their original faith only by memory, without the aid of now-forbidden texts. They dissolved their tradition into the crucible of their imagination and distilled it into something new. Out of this secret brewing, they created forms of worship that combined traditional rituals with elements taken from the rites of the Catholic oppressors. To compensate for the loss of some parts of the liturgy, they intensified the emphasis upon asceticism and renunciation. They assigned new power to the few prayers they could remember, as if the divine essence was hiding inside their very words. They also learnt the mystical value of silence, discovering the infinite wealth that harboured within their innermost depths. It is not surprising that the most celebrated Christian mystic of Spain, Saint Teresa of Avila, hailed from a family of *Marranos*.

But the pressure exerted on non-Christians also contributed to producing the opposite tendency. Instead of seeking refuge in the 'interior castle' of mysticism, some started questioning the very value of religion. Short of openly declaring themselves atheists (as it would have brought upon them even greater persecution), they recalibrated their own moral compass along thoroughly secular coordinates.

> Pining for salvation in the afterlife, sacrificing one's life, enduring torments, ending up on the stake – why bother? Who had decreed this? Authority was dismissed, while the internal self became an alternative tribunal in which – before there had been any trial – the *Marrano* could absolve herself, rejecting any faith and emancipating herself from any bondage. The extreme tension between Judaism and Christianity helped prompt a growing indifference towards religion in general. Neither Jews nor Christians, these *conversos* found an exit route precisely in this double negation, neither–nor.[15]

In this painful disenchantment, the first seeds of a modern consciousness were taking root.

## 13.

It was a tough life for the Spanish Jews and Muslims who held fast to their religion without the cover of dissimulation. Discriminated against and stripped of most public rights, they offered their services at the margins of Christian society. Some of them took advantage of the prohibition issued by the Catholic Church against lending money for interest, establishing themselves as bankers. Despite their assets, they were mostly defenceless against their Christian debtors, who could claim law and custom to avoid repayments. Others used their familiarity with ancient scientific texts to practise the medical profession. Their trade was at the mercy of the Christian authorities, who could strip them of their licences at any moment. Still others used their own precarious position, in between cultures and languages, to work as translators in the renewed effort to close the gap with the philosophical and scientific progress of the Arabic-speaking world. This new generation of translators converged in the city of Toledo, in central Spain. As they travelled from far and wide to reach it, they carried with them a centuries-old Mediterranean tradition.

We can almost see them, in their small carts pulled by mules, travelling across the changing landscape that had followed the expansion of the Christian kingdoms. Amidst the ruins of conquered castles, like props left on stage after a bloody play, a rewilding countryside encroached over the margins of the roads. Herds of sheep and cows had taken the place of ploughs and draft oxen, while the water reservoirs were slowly vanishing under a veil of dirt and fallen leaves. Fewer caravans of merchants stopped at the inns, where processions of pilgrims now rested along their way to the great sanctuaries of the North. The new society of the Christians was pastoralist, rather than agricultural, and much less connected with the networks of intercontinental commerce. The architecture, too, had changed. Stocky bell towers in the Romanesque style had replaced the vertiginous profiles of the minarets, whose few surviving examples had been converted for Christian use. The voice of the muezzins no longer announced the hours of prayer, while a new time was marked by the ringing of bells. In the deepest recesses of the countryside, in crumbling synagogues and mosques that could not legally be repaired, the survivors of the old regime cautiously murmured their invocations.

After such a journey, arriving in Toledo would have felt to our translators like a sudden dive into the past. Within the mighty walls rising along the curves of the Tagus River, the city still preserved a wealth of cultural and religious differences, with Jewish and Muslim communities living next to the growing Christian majority. Intellectuals from distant lands converged under the shade of the porticoes, where the Arabic and Hebrew letters were still respected. It was there, under the protection of enlightened patrons such as the archbishop Francis Raymond de Sauvetât, that Jewish, Muslim, *Marrano* and *Morisco* scholars joined their Christian counterparts in creating what would be known, across the centuries, as the Toledo School of Translators.

## 14.

Despite its name, the Toledo School of Translators was never quite a 'school': its members did not share a common institutional affiliation, and their projects did not fulfil a unified plan. The choice of books and authors that they helped to rediscover depended on the expertise of each of them and on the changing interests of their patrons. The wave of translations that emerged out of Toledo focused initially on scientific texts, including technical treatises on astrology and alchemy, and only later delved into the treasure of knowledge produced by Arabic-speaking philosophers.

This shift to philosophy was accelerated by the arrival in Toledo of a Jewish scholar well versed in both Arabic and logical speculations. Abraham ibn Daud, a native of Cordoba, was a polymath in the best Andalusian tradition, whose expertise extended to astronomy and history, as well as philosophy. Being a rationalist, he was an ardent admirer of Aristotle, the 'first master' of rational philosophy, and of his Muslim successor, the 'second master' Avicenna. Once in Toledo, he leveraged his scholarly reputation to introduce Avicenna's work into the debates of his time, championing the first-ever Latin translation of his books. By doing so, he was grafting the tree of 'European' philosophy with a rationalist branch, from which, in the following centuries, thinkers like Thomas Aquinas and Rene Descartes would flourish.

Ibn Daud possessed, in addition, a keen eye for the scholarly talent of others. He was instrumental in bringing to Toledo the philosopher Dominicus Gundissalinus, who would become one of the leading minds of the translation movement. Alongside Ibn Daud and Gundissalinus, the libraries of Toledo welcomed scholars from all corners of the Catholic world, such as the Italian Gerard of Cremona, the German Hermannus Alemannus, the Flemish Rudolf of Bruges, the English Alfred of Sareshel, and the Scottish Michael Scot, among many others.

The cosmopolitan atmosphere of the 'school', however, was not the sign of an authentic openness to different beliefs. Translations of sacred texts such as the Quran were undertaken with the explicit aim of confuting them, and the position of the Jewish, *Marrano* and *Morisco* translators remained socially precarious, despite occasional decrees offering them some protection. It is even believed that Ibn Daud himself may have met a martyr's end for his faith in Toledo.

Yet, there was a moment, in the middle of the thirteenth century, when it seemed like the utopia of an equitable *convivencia* (coexistence) had been revived, and a different world had found its pivotal centre in the work of intellectuals and translators of different faiths. This possibility, or perhaps this illusion, came to the fore during the kingdom of Alfonso X *el sabio* (the wise). It was under his influence that the Arabic and Hebrew heritage ceased to be treated as a repository of useful but dangerous knowledge. Alfonso X was a proficient poet, astronomer and astrologer, whose knowledge rivalled that of the translators he invited to his capital city of Toledo. During his reign, Jewish scholars in particular rose to unprecedented positions, some serving even as the king's personal physicians. Rising over the rigidity of much of his court, the king reformed crucial aspects of the culture of his time. As well as commissioning a new wave of translations of works by Jewish and Muslim authors, Alfonso X ordered these texts to be translated, no longer into Latin, but directly into the vernacular language spoken by the common subjects of his kingdom. With one stroke, Alfonso X showed the possibility of reviving a regime of peaceful coexistence between faiths, expanded the philosophical and scientific horizon of Christendom, and set the foundations for the establishment of local dialects, like Spanish, as national languages.

## 15.

Yet, even Alfonso X was not entirely immune from the prejudices of his time. When he commissioned the translation of the Talmud, for example, he tasked his scholars to commentate upon it in such a way as to harmonize it with Christian doctrine. The Jewish texts, he aimed to show, contained the same principles as Christianity, but the Jews had failed to deduce from them that Jesus was the rightful Messiah. Thus, while the sacred texts of Judaism were free from error, the Jews themselves were not absolved from the stubbornness with which they refused to embrace Christianity.

Even then, the atmosphere promoted by Alfonso X offered fertile ground for a new blossoming of the Mediterranean imagination. It was during the final years of his reign, partly thanks to his implicit patronage as an avid reader of Jewish mystical treatises, that some of the main texts of the Kabbalah first came to light. The most important among these was the Zohar, 'the book of splendour', which contained the essence of the Jewish mystical tradition. The book was presented by Alfonso X's subject, the rabbi Moses de León, as an ancient Aramaic text that he had rediscovered, but the medieval inflections in its language raise the suspicion that it was, in fact, his own original production. Regardless of its authentic authorship – a concept largely ignored both in Antiquity and in the Middle Ages – the Zohar immediately established itself as a foundational text for generations of mystics.

The perspective offered by the Zohar reveals reality as a field of dynamic energies in constant motion. Everything that we see around ourselves is not 'already there', as it appears to be, but is being created 'in real time' by a process that is constantly active within God's infinity, the *En Sof* ('that which is without end'). At every moment, God pours out of itself an immense creative energy, which irradiates, like light, throughout the universe. This creative light constitutes the substance and the true reality of all beings. Through its manifestation, God continuously creates the world. Yet, to do this, God also has to perform a second process: to leave enough room for the created beings to exist separately from their creator, God has to contract itself (*simsum*). To allow for the visible existence of the world, the invisible infinity of the *En Sof* has to withdraw. The existence of each single being in the universe is the result of this double movement of expansion and contraction, happening simultaneously inside the infinite essence of God.

The God of the Kabbalists contains within itself everything and its opposite: it is the light that shines forth and the darkness that hides itself; it is the being of all beings, the very stuff of anything visible, and a transcendent force that exceeds the very concept of 'existence'. It is at the same time inside and outside the world, public and secret, reachable and beyond grasp.

In a sense, it is the eternal archetype on which the Jewish *Marranos* fashioned their own life of secrecy and publicness, withdrawal and splendour.

## 16.

There appears to be a missing link in the Kabbalists' cosmological chain: how can the ineffable, invisible *En Sof* pour out of itself something so totally different as material reality?

For the Kabbalists, the passage between these two realms was not a sudden switch of registers. Between the ineffable Divinity and the sensible world lies an uninterrupted gradient of degrees of light and darkness, existence and mystery, combined in changing proportions. Each of these degrees corresponds to a *Sefirah* (plural: *Sefirot*, 'numeration'), defining one of the many dimensions that constitute reality.

The order of the *Sephirot* is usually depicted as a diagram or as a cosmic tree, yet the apparent fixity of the representation is deceiving. Just as God engages in a double process of emanation and contraction, so the process of manifestation, too, involves a double movement. The creative force descending from God to its creatures finds its balance, on the side of creation, in an ascending movement towards the divine mystery at the heart of all things. As they contemplate the mystery of the *En Sof*, moving their attention backward through the order of the *Sephirot*, the creatures of this world contribute to returning the creative energy of God back to its source. The Kabbalah itself, as an attempt to decode the structure of reality behind appearances, was part of this ascending movement towards God.

To proceed in this ascension, the Kabbalists looked for the clues disseminated in the created world, starting with the sacred texts describing the birth of the universe. Following an exegetic tradition that had started in Late Antiquity, many Kabbalists considered the first paragraphs of the Biblical Genesis as the exact sequence of orders through which God, the *En Sof*, simultaneously contracts itself and emanates the energy that constantly creates the universe. Thus, if one may dare a comparison to modern computer engineering, the opening of the Bible presents the programming sequence through which God writes the 'software' that runs our world. Like a computer program, this language should be read beyond its literal level: what seems like a succession of plain words is, in fact, a complex sequence of alphanumerical characters, where every letter corresponds to a creative act and can be interpreted both in its alphabetic value, in its numerical value, in reference to the shape of its written character, and in ways that connect it to other levels of signification. Every letter in the biblical text can be subjected to a process of substitution and permutation (*seraf*, the same Hebrew term that denotes the alchemical transformation of metals), which will unlock the secret meaning behind it.

The Kabbalists' intuition that language has such a creative effect on reality that God used it to create the universe – an intuition which approaches our own contemporary experience of immersive digital environments – reflects a frequent trope in the Mediterranean imagination, as well as in the imagination of nearby cultures such as Vedic India. Language is something far greater and more powerful than a medium of communication. Though always short of being able to convey the 'truth' about reality, language creates things, and it is through language the *chaos* of reality finds the form of an ordered *cosmos*.

This intuition echoed the daily grind of the Mediterranean translators of the Middle Ages. Through their work, they too were using language to give shape to new worlds. Whenever society declared them unwelcome, in the quiet tumult of their studios, they carved new spaces within their imagination of the universe. In the silence of their pages, they created the voice through which all worlds are made.

## 17.

How can there be expulsions, persecutions, discriminations in a universe that has been ordered by a benevolent God? How can the divine *En Sof* allow for the existence of evil?

For the Spanish Jews of the late fifteenth century, when almost the entire Iberian Peninsula had fallen to the Christians, such questions resonated with desperate urgency. Their generation would suffer the final, complete decree of expulsion from the Spanish lands. All remaining Muslims and Jews were given a few weeks to sell their possessions, pack their belongings and simply disappear. Anyone who failed to comply was subject to arrest, imprisonment, possibly execution.

A new wave of migrations departed from the westernmost edge of Europe, dispersing across the entire Mediterranean region. A favourite destination for the Jews was the Levant, where they became known as the Sephardi, the 'Jews of Spain'. A few of them managed to reach Jerusalem, then governed by Muslim rulers. It was in that holy city that a new Kabbalist master appeared, who tried to offer an answer to the question of the origin of evil. Isaac Luria, born in Jerusalem to a Sephardi woman and an Ashkenazi man of Mittel-European descent, infused a new breath into the Kabbalistic tradition.

Rather than a light that shines forth, Luria described God as an inexhaustible spring, projecting out of itself the shimmering, liquid energy of creation. The use of a different metaphor might seem like a small thing if it weren't for the fact that we humans think and construct our reality based on metaphors. When creation first happened, Luria continued, God established a number of 'vases' (the *Sephirot*) to retain the flow of its energy and transform it into the different dimensions of reality. Yet, these containers were not strong enough to hold the outburst, and the lowest *Sephirot*, connected to the more material realms, gave in and shattered, dispersing the energy throughout the universe. God immediately recuperated its lost flow, reconstituted the 'vases' and emanated a second, less vehement creative outpouring.

But the fragments of the first shattered vessels continued to float across the universe, holding within themselves the creative energy that they had soaked up. This trapped energy exercised a nefarious influence on all that existed, and, according to Luria, it accounted for the origin of evil. It was the duty of humans to recuperate these particles of the creative liquid and to return them to the divine flow that traversed and connected all things.

Luria's cosmic story carried an echo of the Late Ancient Gnostics and Manichaeans, who wished to redeem the divine particles that had been lost within the universe. But Luria was not a Gnostic, nor a Manichaean. For him, no other force but God inhabited reality, and no cosmic war could upset the balance of the universe. Humans had a responsibility to help God cleanse the world of what had been accidentally spilt, and they could do so through prayer, contemplation, ritual and the correct following of the divine rules of behaviour. He did not advocate an escape from the world but an active engagement with all that existed. The reason for this engagement, however, would be disclosed only to those who could look beyond the petty institutions of the world, towards the grand cosmic scheme where everything was one.

## 18.

The Jewish scholars were already accustomed to living anywhere as foreigners in a foreign land.[16] The dawn of the Renaissance age pushed their diaspora even further. Many converged in Italy, where the influence of the Pope, paradoxically, granted more safety than the fleeting moods of the secular monarchs. While Spain was falling into the grips of its own, fanatical brand of the Inquisition – whose main exponent, Tomas de Torquemada, descended from a family of Jewish *conversos* – the Vatican ensured a minimum level of tolerance throughout the Italian peninsula.

The atmosphere of the Italian Renaissance was favourable to their arrival. The intellectuals of the time were eager to explore the 'elsewhere', whether in space, time or culture. As well as launching a wave of translations from the Pagan classics, they took an axe to the restrictions that until then had limited the pursuit of knowledge. They no longer bowed to the established authorities, such as Aristotle's philosophy, as if to unquestionable truths. Every text had first to pass under the critical lens of the grammarians and the philologists, and then be tested for its actual contribution to the human quest for a dignified life. Not abstract principles, but the problem of how we might live amidst the stormy weather of the world became the guiding light of their intellectual work.

Renaissance humanism saw the human condition as an odyssey through an ever-expanding universe, where certainties were scarce and threats and horror all too real. Finding a way to infuse life with beauty, pleasure and virtue required the active engagement of all human capabilities, both physical and intellectual. In a world that no longer appeared as the immutable product of God's design, but as the outcome of human choices and mistakes, it was necessary to summon every possible resource to transform the harsh wilderness produced by human mistakes into a liveable and elegant garden. If these resources had to be sourced from elsewhere, among the Pagans, Muslims, Jews or even further afield, so be it.

The Renaissance did not reject the knowledge of the Middle Ages, but it reset its scope. It re-evaluated the human as a free agent in a manipulable world, and its freedom as both an empowering and a tragic existential condition. Bereft of the unshakable truths known only to the Divinity, humans were destined for the endless endeavour of trying to create for themselves a beautiful world out of an infinite reality.

In the task of understanding what the 'good' might be, and establishing the political conditions that might nurture its growth, the letters and sciences of every time and nation spoke a common language.

# 19.

Following the Jewish translators through Renaissance Italy will inevitably take us to the intellectual capital of the age: Florence. Before getting there, however, let us first take a little detour to the North, across the plains stretching between the Apennines and the Adriatic Sea. Surrounded by flat fields to the edge of the horizon, enveloped by a mist that linked the clouds to the agricultural canals, the town of Mirandola rose like a red circle of tiles and bricks over a green canvas. On its edge, in a low stronghold protected by a moat, lived the lords of the town, the Pico. As their dominion was small, so was also their claim to nobility. After generations of faithful service, the Pico family had finally obtained a fiefdom from the Holy Roman emperor, becoming Counts of Mirandola and of Concordia. Their land, however, stood in the middle of an area contested by much stronger rulers. They had to fortify their possessions and walk a dangerous path between diplomacy and war. Male members of the Pico family were expected to scheme and fight their whole lives, with the ever-present possibility of meeting a violent end.

In 1463, a boy was born to this family: Giovanni Pico, count of Mirandola and Concordia. 'A marvellous sight was there seen before his birth: there appeared a fiery garland standing over the chamber of his mother while she travailed and suddenly vanished away.'[17] From his earliest days, Giovanni distinguished himself by his prodigious intellectual talents. His mother, Giulia, the daughter of a famous poet, took care of sheltering him from the family atmosphere that had already led his brothers to the profession of arms. At fourteen, Giovanni was enrolled in the law faculty at the University of Bologna. The following year, after the death of his mother, he moved to Ferrara, where he entered the faculty of 'Arts', which meant, at that time, philosophy. He refined his Latin, learnt Greek, studied the classics, but excelled above all in the art of public disputation: in his way, he shared his brother's taste for duels and jousting. He moved again, to Padova, the seat of Italy's most famous university of philosophy, continuing his studies with renewed energy.

In Padova, Giovanni crossed paths with a young scholar who would weave into his life the centuries-old thread of the Mediterranean translators. Elia del Medigo had been born a few years before Giovanni into a Jewish family residing in Crete, then under Venetian rule. He had moved to Italy, travelling between different cities before settling in Padova, where he taught classes on Aristotle and Ibn Rushd, the Andalusian philosopher whose theories about the unity of all human minds we have already encountered. Giovanni was immediately fascinated with Elia's erudition and asked for his help to access, via his translations, the lesser-known works of the Jewish thinkers.

When Giovanni moved again, attracted by the magnetic pull of Florence, he asked Elia to come with him. He knew that the horizons disclosed by his translations would be fundamental to his future.

## 20.

Giovanni reached Florence in November 1484, when he was twenty-one years old. Brilliant, rich, elegant, he was also uncommonly beautiful. 'He was of feature and shape seemly and beauteous, of stature goodly and high, of flesh tender and soft: his visage lovely and fair, his colour white intermingled with comely ruddies, his eyes grey and quick of look, his teeth white and even, his hair yellow and not to piked.'[18] He wrote poems for his lovers and had no difficulty entering the most exclusive literary circles in the city.

In another historical age, perhaps, his education and his charm would have sufficed to grant him an eminent position among his contemporaries. But not so in the Florence ruled by the Medici family, in the midst of an unprecedented cultural blossoming. To stand out, Giovanni needed something special, something that nobody among his Florentine peers had yet acquired. He turned again to his friend Elia del Medigo. He wanted to know more about the secrets of the Kabbalah and that mysterious *Zohar* which had not yet been translated into any language. But Elia, a good Aristotelian and Averroist rationalist, warned the young Giovanni about the obscure metaphors used by the Kabbalists, which could easily lead even a cultured reader astray. He taught him a little about the Kabbalah but declined to take him into the depths of its mystery.

Thus, Giovanni started to study Hebrew and Aramaic on his own, and after a few months of intense dedication, he learnt them well enough to write a simple composition. He realized, however, that it would take him years before he could read the Kabbalistic texts in the original. He went looking for other Jewish scholars who could translate the ancient texts and disclose the wisdom he craved. He hired a travelling erudite of dubious reputation, going by the name of Flavius Mithridates, previously known as Guglielmo Raimondo Moncada, but born as Shemuel ben Nissim Abul-Farag. A native of Sicily, originally from a Jewish family, Flavius had converted to Christianity at a young age. He had enjoyed a meteoric career, which had taken him from ordination as a simple priest to occupying teaching positions in the most prestigious universities in Rome. He had gone as far as joining the personal entourage of Pope Sixtus IV before a sudden scandal had decreed his fall. Suspected of having taken part in a murder, he had fled Rome and, after a period of wandering, had reached Florence.

Giovanni was not bothered by Flavius' shady past. His tempestuous moods, his possessiveness and even his arrogance seemed a small price to pay to learn what Elia had refused to teach him. Flavius did not fail to repay his patron's trust. He produced a prodigious quantity of translations and commentaries on the texts of mystical Judaism, which, however, he often tweaked to match his own theory about the harmony between Kabbalism and Christianity. From him, Giovanni acquired some of the ideas that would form the cornerstone of his unique philosophical identity and of Renaissance philosophy in general.

## 21.

It all happened in one year, the annus mirabilis 1486. Giovanni was twenty-three years old. He had fallen in love with Margherita, and she loved him back. But romantic love, praised as it was by the poets, was not the criterion according to which marriages were arranged. Margherita was married off to a member of the Medici family and followed her husband to a town outside Florence. The two lovers, however, did not give up. Giovanni hired a gang of mercenary thugs and took position outside the town. Margherita made sure of going for a walk at a time and place previously agreed with Giovanni. The armed party rushed in, made a big display of a fake kidnapping and ran away. They had barely left the town when a cloud of dust appeared on the road behind them. Margherita's husband had hastily summoned

200 armed men and was running in their pursuit. The two parties met under the walls of a tower, where, after a skirmish, all of Giovanni's mercenaries were killed. The two lovers fled inside the tower, where they were held 'prisoners' by the landlord, who saw the advantage of saving them in view of a future repayment. After a long negotiation, Margherita was 'freed' and sent back to town. She was welcomed back by her husband, who chose to save his honour by believing in the ruse of the kidnapping. Giovanni did not leave the tower until Lorenzo the Magnificent, head of the Medici family, instructed the landlord to release him and offered him his protection. True to his character, Lorenzo had no doubts when choosing between the medieval rules of family honour and the bond he shared with the Humanist intellectuals.

Back in Florence, Giovanni bore the brunt of his tarnished reputation. He found solace in his friendship with Girolamo Benivieni, who became his life companion and perhaps even his lover. In that same year, he published his first book, *The 900 Thesis*, accompanied by the text for a public speech which was to become the manifesto of the Renaissance: *The Oration on the Dignity of the Human*. Giovanni was making use of all that he had learnt from the Greek classics, Muslim and Zoroastrian philosophy, and especially the Jewish mystical tradition. He took this combined heritage of the whole Mediterranean and developed it further in a daring direction. Moving systematically, he sketched the blueprint for a universal philosophy, where the different dimensions of reality appeared simultaneously through the angles developed by thinkers of any era and provenance. Since reality is infinitely varied, and deeply penetrated by the ineffable spirit of the Divinity, then only the concerted effort of all human minds can hope to obtain even a minimal image of its true structure. Rationalism and mysticism must proceed hand in hand, since for every aspect that can be observed and analysed, infinitely more remains beyond the grasp of mind and language.

The prime example of such complexity is right before our eyes: the human, in all its limits, is a perfect case of how much more there is to reality than what meets the eye.

## 22.

The *Oration on the Dignity of the Human* was a small gem of philosophical thinking, literary style and youthful bravado. Giovanni addressed it to the highest prelates in the Vatican, with whom he hoped to hold a public disputation about his book *The 900 Theses*. Laying out his case for the exceptionality of the human being, he began by quoting first a Muslim, and then a Pagan.

> Most esteemed fathers, I have read in the ancient texts of the Arabians that when Abdallah the Saracen was questioned as to what on this world's stage, so to speak, seemed to him most worthy of wonder, he replied that there is nothing to be seen more wonderful than man. This opinion is seconded by Mercury's saying: 'A great miracle, Asclepius, is man.'[19]

'Mercury' was none other than Hermes Trismegistus, while 'Abdallah the Saracen' was, most probably . . . Giovanni's own invention! No such quote can be attributed to an Arabic writer of this name, while something similar can be found in the Greek playwright Sophocles, when the chorus of his *Antigone* sings: 'Wonders are many, yet of all Things is Man the most wonderful'.[20] It is possible that Giovanni, finding a reference to Sophocles too banal, wished to impress the 'most esteemed fathers' by immediately bringing in a sense of the breadth of his intellectual horizons.

His most daring feat, however, came when he put his own ideas directly into God's mouth. He imagined what the Divinity might have said to Adam, setting the dialogue at the very beginning of the universe, after the first few days of the Creation. God had already created the stars, the sky, the animals and the plants – the only remaining task was to give shape to the human, a creature with broad enough understanding to appreciate the magnificence of God's work. But there was a problem: God had exhausted all his gifts on his other creatures, having assigned to each of them a specific nature and a set of unique abilities. With all the archetypical forms already taken, what else could he have given to his latest creature, the human?

> The Master Creator decreed that the creature to whom He had been unable to give anything wholly his own should share in common whatever belonged to every other being. He therefore took man, this creature of indeterminate image, set him in the middle of the world, and said to him: 'We have given you, Adam, no fixed seat or form of your own, no talent peculiar to you alone. This we have done so that whatever seat, whatever form, whatever talent you may judge desirable, these same may you have and possess according to your desire and judgment. Once defined, the nature of all other beings is constrained within the laws We have prescribed for them. But you, constrained by no limits, may determine your nature for yourself, according to your own free will. [. . .] We have made you neither of

heaven nor of earth, neither mortal nor immortal, so that you may, as the free and extraordinary shaper of yourself, fashion yourself in whatever form you prefer. It will be in your power to degenerate into the lower forms of life, which are brutish. Alternatively, you shall have the power, in accordance with the judgment of your soul, to be reborn into the higher orders, those that are divine.'[21]

Thus spoke Giovanni, through God's mouth. The human was not any specific thing, but it was a creature that could decree its own form. Around the eternal kernel of its soul, which it shared with all living beings and with God itself, the unique form of each person was the product of their free volition. The place of the human in the universe, the scope of its ambition, even its own identity: everything was performatively created and defined by the human, while nothing was decreed by its nature.

If one wished to find the origin of late modern 'queer theory', with its stress on the performativity of identity and its rejection of any claim to their 'natural' essence, they would need to look no further than the opening pages of Giovanni's *Oration on the Dignity of the Human*.

## 23.

Giovanni printed *The 900 Theses* at his own expense, distributed it among the universities of Europe, submitted it to the Vatican Curia and waited to be summoned for a public disputation. He was still refining the last details of his *Oration*, when he received a response from the Papal intellectuals in Rome. Instead of a courteous invitation to a debate, he was given a stern injunction to correct his work, which contained 'mistaken' and possibly heretical theses. In hindsight, the only surprising thing was Giovanni's own surprise. He could not believe that the 'most esteemed fathers' had failed to grasp the depth of his philosophy, preferring instead to remain entrenched within the precinct of orthodoxy. He replied with a half-hearted letter in which he apologized for having caused trouble while not taking back anything of substance in what he had written. A second message came from Rome. No longer an injunction, but an arrest warrant. Giovanni left Florence and fled to France. His book was the first printed volume to be universally banned by the Catholic Church. The Papal warrant reached him in his exile: he was arrested in France, promptly extradited to Rome . . . and then he was saved, at the last minute, once again, by Lorenzo the Magnificent. The head of the Medici family sent an armed escort to take him back to Florence, where he would reside under protection in a villa outside of town.

This misadventure forced Giovanni to recalibrate his worldly ambitions, but not the breadth of his intellectual pursuits. He hired another Jewish translator, the philosopher and rabbi Yohanan Alemanno, an esteemed Kabbalist and translator from both Hebrew and Arabic. Thanks to his help and under his guidance, he delved even deeper into the meaning of the esoteric texts, acquiring a clearer understanding of the mystical interpretation of the Jewish scriptures. He wrote new books, where he gave an astonishing display of acumen and intellectual virtuosity. In his *Heptaplus*, in just a few pages, he managed to provide seven parallel readings of the first few paragraphs of the book of Genesis, showing how every word in the Biblical account of the creation could be interpreted from different angles, and then recomposed to create a grandiose vision of reality as a gallery of mirrors, where every speck of dust reflected the totality of the universe, and a divine harmony reigned supreme.

The tone of his writing, however, was changing. He was no longer the wide-eyed youth who trusted in the infinite possibilities of the human. The real task of every person, he now believed, was to return to God. The human was indeed endowed with the ability to fashion itself in whichever way it saw fit, but experience had shown him that worldly institutions had smothered this potential. And since the world had failed its task, only by overcoming the world, he realized, could one find true freedom.

Giovanni ceased writing love poems, shut off his amorous relationships, except for his faithful Girolamo Benivieni and moved towards an increasingly ascetic lifestyle. He met a Dominican friar, Girolamo Savonarola, a fiery preacher of worldly renunciation, and started to follow him. He hadn't yet reached the age of thirty, yet he had only a few years left to live.

## 24.

A bank of clouds can hang for a long time before breaking and unleashing a storm. The clouds, it seemed, had been gathering for a while when the storm finally hit the Mediterranean in the fateful year 1492. The wind started blowing from the West, where, in January, the Catholic monarchs conquered Granada, the last Muslim stronghold in Andalusia, and ordered the conversion or expulsion of all non-Christian subjects. If ever the dream of a peaceful coexistence between faiths had seemed possible, now it felt truly over. Then, in April, Lorenzo the Magnificent died. The great patron of the Renaissance, a true friend of Giovanni and his lifetime protector, was no more. The cultural scene was deprived of its light, and Florence fell into dangerous political instability. Finally, in October, unbeknownst to all but his crew and the native people on the island of Hispaniola, Christopher Columbus reached the shores of America. He sent inland a Jewish translator, the Spanish *converso* Luis de Torres, to try his Hebrew and Arabic on the natives. A few months later, Luis de Torres also died, probably killed by his own comrades. It was the beginning of a massive wave of genocide and colonization, which would devastate the Americas and push the Mediterranean to the margins of history.

By the time he was thirty, Giovanni felt like a relic of the past. He spent most of his time at home, or listening to Savonarola's sermons about the coming deluge, the end of the world and the need for repentance.

In November 1494, Giovanni was overwhelmed by a violent fever. A few days later, he was dead. 'He had lived 31 years, 8 months and 24 days', his beloved Girolamo Benivieni noted in the horoscope he wrote for Giovanni. Many years later, Girolamo Benivieni would request to be buried next to Giovanni, in the church of San Marco in Firenze. Above them, the tombstone still reads: 'To ensure that after death, the bones of two people whose souls were conjoined by love in life would not be separated'.

The death of Giovanni Pico della Mirandola, count of Concordia, was truly the end of an era. The Renaissance continued as a cultural and artistic movement, but the optimism and the sense of vast horizons, of which the young philosopher had been the standard-bearer, receded into the twilight.

The very map of the world was being redrawn. In the West, a new world had appeared – a world whose inhabitants the Europeans hardly recognized as humans – while in the East, the rise of the Ottoman Empire had closed the routes between Europe and Asia. In the North, the explosion of the Protestant Reform had ignited a Europe-wide war between Protestants and Catholics, which would bloody the continent for over a century. The last vestiges of the past, such as the Jews still residing in Christian lands, were either expelled or confined to the ghettos, the first of which was instituted in Venice in 1516.

The thread with which the Mediterranean translators had been weaving since the end of antiquity seemed to have finally exhausted itself. No more mixing of the cultures and faiths that history had set apart. No more combining different voices in the pursuit of a universal aim. From then on, what did not fit in a pre-established category was to be banned to the realm of the monsters.

Once again, history seemed intent on crushing any possibility of a world where multiple lives might flourish together. The beginning of Modernity could not have looked gloomier. But the people of the Mediterranean knew that it is always possible to escape what appears inevitable. Only this time, they had to adopt a different strategy. They left aside the scholarly work of the translators to take on the rough and noble art of treason.

To the practice of this art, and to a close encounter with its Mediterranean masters, we will dedicate the next stop in our journey.

# *Meanwhile in the Mediterranean...*

## *Fifteenth century to seventeenth century*

1492 – *Lorenzo 'the Magnificent' de Medici dies in Florence. Cristoforo Colombo reaches the shores of America. The Christian monarchs Isabella and Ferdinand complete the conquest of Spain. The persecution against Jews and Muslims in Christian lands intensifies.*

1502 – *Juan de Cordoba of Seville is granted by the Spanish monarchs the right to send African slaves to the Caribbean, thus inaugurating the transatlantic slave trade.*

1514–34 – *The Ottoman Empire gains control over the whole Mashriq.*

1517 – *Martin Luther launches the Protestant Reformation, rapidly followed by other reformers across Europe.*

1520–66 – *Suleiman I 'the Magnificent' rules over the Ottoman Empire.*

1527 – *A largely Protestant army, led by Charles V, the Holy Roman Emperor, mutinies, attacks Rome and sacks it.*

*1529* – *The Ottomans lay siege to Vienna.*

*1536–1798* – *The kingdom of France and the Ottoman Empire stipulate a formal alliance.*

*1540* – *Ignatius of Loyola founds the Society of Jesus.*

*1542–59* – *The Italian peninsula is devastated by the war between Francis I of France, allied with the Ottoman Sultan Suleiman I, and the Holy Roman Emperor Charles V.*

*1545* – *The Catholic church reacts to the Protestant Reformation by launching its own 'counter-reformation'.*

*1550–51* – *Scholars gather at Valladolid to debate the human rights of the Native people of America.*

*1571* – *The Ottoman Empire conquers Cyprus.*

*1578* – *The Portuguese king Sebastian I is killed at the Battle of Ksar el Kebir, where his army is annihilated by the troops of the Sultanate of Morocco.*

*1568–71* – *The 'Morisco' population in Spain revolts against Christian rule, but their insurrection is violently repressed.*

*1593–1606* – *The Habsburg and Ottoman Empires fight each other to exhaustion in the inconclusive Long War.*

*1617* – *The construction of the Sultan Ahmed 'Blue' Mosque in Istanbul reaches completion.*

*1623* – *The construction of Saint Peter's Basilica in Rome reaches completion.*

*1667–1699: The war between the Ottoman Empire and the 'Holy League' – formed by the Holy Roman Empire, Poland-Lithuania, Republic of Venice and Russia – ends the Ottoman expansion in Europe.*

# 5

# *Traitors*

# *Modernity*

### 1.

A northern wind swept the beach, swirling clouds of sand among the myrtle bushes and the bluestem grass. A few stone throws from the shore, where the water turned dark, the profile of a raft appeared and disappeared between the waves. The tree trunks that made up the hull creaked and shifted, letting the water in. The sail, a patchwork of rags and clothes, flapped like a tattered flag. Only the riggings, a tangle of horsehair ropes, still held the vessel together. Fifty men were crammed onboard. Naked and skeletal, they were what remained of an expedition force of 400 soldiers and eighty horses, dispatched from Spain a few months earlier to conquer the mysterious land of Florida. Misfortune had haunted them since their departure. Storms, desertions, diseases had thinned their ranks, yet they had trudged on, through the marshes and the forests of the new continent. The leader of the expedition, Panfilo de Narvaez, boasted an impeccable record as a *conquistador*, proven by the massacre of thousands of natives on the island of Cuba. He had invested his personal wealth in the mission and had no intention of stopping until they had plundered the treasures of some hidden city.

By the time the raft was battling the ocean waves, however, Panfilo de Narvaez was no more. He had led his men into the forest without any logistical preparation and had brought them to the brink of despair, without food, without water, at the mercy of the arrows of the natives. When he had been forced to acknowledge that they could proceed no further, he had ordered the building of a makeshift fleet to try to return to the territory controlled by the Spaniards. He had taken for himself the sturdiest-looking raft and the few soldiers still capable of rowing and had set off immediately. It was time, he had declared, for each person to fend for themselves. Then, a powerful storm, like the hand of God, had descended upon them all. Panfilo's vessel had been swallowed by the waves and sunk in the water. The other rafts had been scattered by the winds. Those who were aboard the one just off the coast, now struggling to stay afloat, had good reason to think of their impending death as the final annihilation of the expedition.

But they did not die. Not all of them. Shipwrecked on the beach, the survivors huddled together, soaked and shivering.

> [We] were naked as the day we were born and had lost all that we had with us, which though it was not worth much, was everything to us at that time. And since by then it was November and the cold was very great and we were in such a plight that one could have counted our bones without difficulty, we looked like the very image of death.[1]

The natives hesitated a while before coming closer to this ghostly bunch. One of the Spaniards crawled towards them, begging for help. His name was Alvar Nunez Cabeza de Vaca, the expedition's treasurer. Many years later, having returned to Spain as the sole survivor from that group on the beach, his testimony would tell the tale of their adventure.

The natives took Alvar and his men to their village, where they were fed and clothed. A few days later, they were joined by the survivors from another raft. Questioned about their vicissitudes, they confessed that hunger and desperation had driven them to cannibalism. Four Spaniards had been eaten by their own comrades, and the natives who had discovered them 'were so indignant about this . . . that undoubtedly if they had seen this when it began to happen, they would have killed the men, and all of us would have been in dire peril'.[2]

A harsh winter came, depleting the food reserves of the village. Weak and hungry, prey to diseases, the Spaniards died one after another until only fifteen remained alive. The villagers, who could no longer afford to keep them as guests, enslaved them and put them to work on the heaviest chores. Fatigue did the rest, and Alvar soon found himself alone. He was worked to the bone until his fingers were so sore that he could not pick his own food without crying. Instead of letting him die, his masters converted him to another function. Such a strange-looking creature certainly harboured some special power, and it was time for him to put it at the service of the village. They taught him how to blow on the ill parts of a body, and during the medical procedure, they told him to chant his own Latin prayers to Christ, the Virgins and the Saints. Somehow, his attempts at healing worked, and he was spared his life.

As soon as he had sufficiently recovered, Alvar ran away from his masters. He moved from tribe to tribe, in search of better conditions, until he realized that his exceptional status as a foreigner allowed him to act as an intermediary between groups often at war with each other. Six years passed, during which he travelled the territories of the Southwest of today's United States trading shells, hides, ochre and arrowheads, and learning the different languages. During one of these trips, he came across three Spaniards, slaves to a local tribe. 'We gave many thanks to God because we were together, and that day was one of the happiest we had had in our lives'.[3] They were Andrés Dorantes, Alonso del Castillo and Estevanico, a Black 'Moor' from Morocco, who had been brought into Narvaez's expedition as a slave. Together, the quartet decided to try to find a way back to the Spanish-owned lands.

Thus, the adventure of Alvar Nunez Cabeza de Vaca and his comrades began. From the East of modern-day Texas, they marched West, towards Mexico. Along the way, they sustained themselves by performing feats of faith healing. In every village they entered, they visited the sick, blowing on their bodies and chanting their Latin prayers, at first with some scepticism, then increasingly sure of their actual ability to heal. Their fame spread throughout the region. Now, even before approaching a village, people brought them the sick and implored them for a cure. In his retelling of their adventure, Alvar sounds sure of having acquired the power to channel the grace of God towards his patients. He does not distance himself from the natives' belief that he and his companions were 'children of the sun', who had descended from the sky. Once, he claims, he even managed to resurrect a dead person.

The four healers marched forward, half-naked and dishevelled like so many Johns the Baptist. Whenever they left a village, some of the inhabitants would accompany them to their next stop. Progressively, they amassed a following of hundreds. They learnt to speak six of the local languages, and anytime they received a gift of goods or food, they distributed it among their people. They had recreated across the ocean one of those mystical folk movements that were also traversing Europe during those same years.

They performed surgeries using sharp stones, healed the wounds with blowing and prayers, and taught their followers that the true, secret names of their ancestral divinities were in fact those of God, Christ, Mary and the Saints. They kept walking West, across the Rio Grande, through mountains and plains. They saw herds of bison grazing in the valleys and species of animals and plants that did not exist in the old world. They mingled with people whose customs surprised them, such as those who lived without leaders, those who held transexual women as the strongest warriors, and those who kept everything in common. At times, they felt like they had entered a different reality governed by other rules than those of the rest of the Earth. But they also suffered hunger and thirst and endured the dangers of travelling unarmed in a land torn apart by tribal warfare. Over the years, they walked nearly 4,000 kilometres through modern-day Texas, New Mexico and Arizona until they reached the western coast of Mexico.

There, at last, they found the first sign of what they had been chasing all along. In a new village, they noticed a person wearing an ornament made from a belt buckle of European origin. Clearly, the Spaniards had to be somewhere in the vicinity. As they journeyed Southward along the Pacific coast, the signs of the Spanish presence became unmistakable. Once populous villages lay in ruins, their inhabitants hiding in the forests and in the mountains. Everything was burnt and shattered. Could such devastation have been caused by the 'civilisation' to which they had longed to return?

Their first meeting with a group of Spanish soldiers dispelled their doubts. Frustrated after weeks of meagre pillaging in the now-deserted region, the soldiers tried to enslave the natives who accompanied the four healers. Alvar protested with their commander, while at the same time urging his followers to run away.

> The Christians were angry at this, and had their interpreter tell [the natives] that we were men of their race and that we had been lost for a long time, that we were unlucky and cowardly people, and that they were the masters of that land, whom the Indians must obey and serve. But the Indians paid no heed to what they were told; rather, they talked with one another saying that the Christians were lying, for we came from where the sun rises and they from where it sets; and that we cured the sick and they killed the healthy; and that we had come naked and barefoot and they well dressed and on horses and with lances; and that we did not covet anything, rather we returned everything that they gave us and were left with nothing, and the only aim of the others was to steal everything they found. . . . From this fact appears how often men's thoughts are frustrated, for we wanted only to seek freedom for the Indians, and when we thought we had done so the exact opposite occurred.[4]

Most of the natives eventually managed to escape, while Alvar and his comrades were taken by the Spanish to Mexico City. Alvar departed towards Europe, while his three comrades remained in 'New Spain': Andrés Dorantes and Alonso del Castillo as free men, and the Black Estevanico, who had shared their same hardship, as a slave once more.

Estevanico's adventures, however, were not yet over. At the service of a new master, he was ordered to guide a new expedition heading North of Mexico to the fabled 'seven cities of gold'. He never returned from that journey. He disappeared among the natives, probably having simulated his own death: like an initiate in a mystery cult, the only path that could lead him to a new life had to pass through a symbolic death.

Once in Spain, Alvar published the memoir of his travels and gained a reputation as an expert on the New World. He was asked by the king to cross the ocean once again, to take the position of governor in the region of Rio de la Plata, in today's Argentina and Uruguay. His past adversities felt like nothing in comparison to the bitterness that he was to experience there. Soon after his arrival, the local landowners accused him of favouring the natives at the cost of Spanish interests. They arrested him on charges of treason, and when they went to confiscate his goods, they found a sealed box containing the full ceremonial dress of a shaman. No further proof was needed. He was sent back to Spain in chains. He would never return to the lands that had seen his metamorphoses: free man to slave, pious Christian to syncretic faith healer, Spanish subject to something novel, queer, irreducible to any of the denominations in whose name, then as now, social groups justify their crimes.

## 2.

In 1542, when Alvar published his memoir, the Spanish Dominican friar Bartolome de las Casas was also penning the conclusion of his famous book *A Short Account of the Destruction of the Indies*. The explorer and the friar had brought back a similar impression of the New World and shared the same indignation at the atrocities they had witnessed. Both had the misfortune of accompanying the conquistador Panfilo de Narvaez – Alvar on his last expedition, Bartolome on that where he had made his name by massacring the native people. Both rejected the official rhetoric around the Spanish conquest, which they recognized as a catastrophe of apocalyptic proportions, rather than as a process of 'civilization'. But a fundamental difference set their two accounts apart. Even though the Dominican warned those responsible that they would not escape the fire of eternal damnation, he did not disown his fellow countrymen: he was a Spaniard talking to other Spaniards.[5]

Not so with Alvar. Over the course of his narration, the subject of his story progressively shifts. At the beginning of his book, the narrative 'us' denotes the members of the Spanish expedition, while the native people are referred to as 'them'; by the final chapters, however, the roles are inverted. When Alvar describes his long-awaited meeting with the Spanish soldiers, he casts his former countrymen as 'them' and the group of his native followers as the 'us' with whom the reader is invited to identify.

If Alvar is part of the colonial history of America, his existential transformations also give him a place in the history of the Mediterranean. His story of shipwreck, capture and slavery reflected the lives of many of his contemporaries, caught amidst the constant warfare stirring the Mediterranean waters during the sixteenth century. The Sea had become the main stage of the conflict between the Christian nations, grouped in variable alliances, and the Muslims, gathered under the banners of the Ottoman Empire. No stretch of coast was safe. After each clash, the victors would carry away with them hordes of men, women and children, to be sold as slaves in their home ports. It is estimated that between the sixteenth and the eighteenth centuries almost nine million people experienced life as a slave in the Mediterranean region. While some of them were of Sub-Saharan origin, most of these slaves came, in fact, from the coasts of the Middle Sea.[6]

The experience of slavery was to leave an indelible mark on the Mediterranean imagination of early Modernity. In the bustling streets of the North African and Ottoman cities, legions of Christian slaves could be seen labouring on public works, embarking as rowers on the fleets, accompanying their masters on their daily business, or trading goods on commission. Equally, for a traveller walking through a European port or visiting a well-to-do European family, encountering Muslim slaves was not uncommon. They could be seen heading inside the hulls of the warships, working on construction sites, labouring in artisanal workshops or hurrying between domestic chores in the houses.

But falling into slavery was not the end of one's life, and the rest of Alvar's adventure resonated equally deeply with his Mediterranean readers. In his incredible journey of personal transformation and integration into a new society, thousands of

Christian and Muslim ex-slaves found an echo of how they too had managed to invent a new life in a foreign land.

## 3.

The institution of slavery marks the nadir of human imagination. The possibility of looking at another person while denying that one is faced by another self testifies to the dangers that come with our imagination's ability to select and recompose its perceptions of the external world. Even more brutally than war, which it often follows, slavery disables the very possibility of founding the social contract on relationships of solidarity, implying that fear and constriction should be counted instead as the most effective bonds among people.

No form of slavery can ever be mild. But even the institution of slavery has a history of its own, with significant variations in the role it has taken within society. During the classical age of the Roman Empire, for example, the productive system was so reliant on slave labour that it would have been impossible to abolish it without having to rethink the entire social structure. Likewise, in the southern parts of the United States until the mid-nineteenth century, slavery played such a fundamental role for both the economy and the citizens' sense of identity, that its preservation was deemed a sufficient reason to create a Confederacy and to ignite the Civil War. In cases of this kind, it is possible to talk about 'slave societies'.

Things were different in the early Modern Mediterranean. Despite the large number of slaves and their impact on the economy, no Mediterranean society of that period founded its survival or its self-identity on the institution of slavery. For both the Christian and the Muslim states, it would be more correct to speak instead of 'societies with slaves' – even though this distinction does not imply any lessening of the suffering.[7]

The specificity of slavery in the early Modern Mediterranean becomes clearer once it is compared to the simultaneous 'transatlantic trade' of enslaved African people towards America. For those who suffered enslavement in Africa and were shipped across the ocean, the arrival in America meant a complete and irretrievable separation from everything familiar. They entered an economic and political system that was founded, not only on their exploitation, but on their intentional dehumanization. The African Americans of the early centuries had no hope of ever returning home, nor of ever integrating into their new society, and had to expect that their condition would be inherited, as if naturally, by their descendants. Their status as 'ontologically slaves', even more than their labour, stood as the foundation of the Western project in America.

In the early Modern Mediterranean, on the contrary, the condition of slavery was generally temporary, and it was regulated by a complex series of international negotiations. The European and Muslim powers were evenly matched, with a predominance of the Muslims up to the seventeenth century, and a progressive strengthening of the Europeans after that date. The northern and southern shores of the Mediterranean looked at each other with apprehension and mutual respect. It was in everyone's interest to treat prisoners not too harshly, to avoid retaliation on their own subjects imprisoned on the other side.[8]

The wider economy of slavery also played a role. Much of a slave's value consisted in the possibility of exacting a ransom – and a 'damaged' prisoner, or even worse, one who had died, could become worthless. Mediterranean slaves were able to hasten their release with the help of their families and charitable organizations from their countries of origin or by ransoming themselves through their labour. Once the period of slavery was over, the ex-slaves were often encouraged to integrate themselves into the society of their captors. Many decided to stay, beginning a new life with a different name, different customs, a different language and, importantly, a different religion. For those who took this path, integrating meant becoming 'renegades': they died to their old identity and were reborn to an utterly new condition.

## 4.

'Around five in the morning, we saw two large ships sailing towards us.'[9] Thus, drily, the seventeenth-century Dutch gentleman Emanuel de Aranda begins the story of his capture by Barbary corsairs and of his years as a slave in Algiers. It was often as simple as that: a journey by sea, the silhouette of a sail emerging from the horizon and the realization that one's life was about to take a sudden turn. When it was clear that the enemy could not be escaped, everyone on board readied themselves for the incoming metamorphosis. The rich would throw their treasures overboard and change into modest clothes, trying to pass for meagre prey whose ransoming terms would be reasonably low. Under the deck, the slaves on the rowing benches would hold their breath and slow the oars, hoping for liberation. Instead of beating them as usual, the guards would address them almost gently, wary that their positions might soon be reversed.

Like the invisible force that spun the Medieval 'wheel of fortune', a gust of sea wind was enough to turn a nobleman into a slave, or a slave into the master of their former masters. For the Muslims, this was *qadar*, the mysterious, yet merciful, will of God. The destiny of every person had been written into God's plan for the universe since the beginning of time and thus had to be accepted unquestioningly. For the Christians, as for the Pagans before them, the unpredictability of events was instead the effect of *Fortuna*, a semi-divine force that could disarray the order of the world like a whimsical breeze – as it was often symbolically depicted.

Fortuna, or destiny, taught Mediterranean people that the world was like a theatre play, where a person's role could change at any moment.

From the marbles that crowded the walls of the churches, effigies of skulls beckoned to the faithful, whispering their constant *memento*: 'What you are now, I was once, and what I am, you shall soon become'. Among the Muslims, the storytellers reminded their listeners that a miserly animal encountered on the road could once have been a person who had been dragged out of their humanity by the force of destiny and cast into a new form. All things in this world were in constant flux, especially identities and social positions. Nobles and plebeians, women and men, Christians and Muslims, shared the same existential precarity, at the mercy of more-than-human forces. Regardless of their differences, their vulnerability rendered them one sole community under an omnipotent sky.

The eternal law of transformations overwhelms those who dare oppose it. Destiny, or fortune, leads the willing and drags the unwilling. Who could blame the 'renegades' for having embraced it, by betraying their country, their culture, their religion, to the point of becoming the 'enemy'?

## 5.

Once in the hands of foreign captors, every new slave began to think how they could escape, or at least alleviate, their state of complete subjection. Learning the local language and customs was essential to survive the ordeals of everyday life. Converting to the local religion, while not automatically leading to liberation, was certainly an advantage.

Transferring one's faith between Islam and Christianity was not necessarily a major change. The difference between the two religions could be seen as just a matter of details: 'an insignificant detail . . . easily found anywhere: a little bit of water, that of baptism' – as Pope Pius II wrote to the Ottoman Sultan Mehmed II, inviting him to embrace Christianity[10] – or a little bit of skin, that of circumcision. Both religions descended from the same original revelation, preached the same fear of God, and encouraged the same compassion towards one's fellow beings. And for a Christian, in particular, becoming 'Turk' – as the early Modern Europeans generally called the Muslims – opened up possibilities that would have been unthinkable in Europe. The early Modern Muslim world offered a welcoming atmosphere of tolerance and unparalleled levels of social mobility. While Europe was still stuck inside the trappings of feudalism, the Ottoman Empire enjoyed a society where the aristocracy did not exist, peasant servitude had been abolished, and religious minorities were respected. To be sure, the Ottoman Empire was not a paradise, and in many respects it was just as brutal as the Christian states. Yet, it had learnt to balance the heaviness of its system of absolute monarchy with the provision of unique opportunities for social advancement of the common folk.

A case in point was the Ottoman practice of the *devshirme*, 'the collection'. Every year, state emissaries visited the Christian provinces in the Balkans to select a cohort of children who would be trained to become the special 'slaves' of the sultan. Traumatically separated from their families, they were deported to the agricultural regions of Anatolia, where they spent a few years working the land, learning Turkish and converting to Islam. When they had reached a suitable age, the 'collected' children entered the elite force of the Janissaries, which constituted the backbone of the Ottoman army and enjoyed a wide range of privileges. The most promising among them progressed even further, joining the administrative organs of the state up to the most prominent political positions. For centuries, the uppermost echelons of the Ottoman Empire were occupied by former Christians, slaves of humble origin – much to the dismay of the European diplomats, who had to negotiate with these commoners raised to positions of power. Most of them accumulated immense fortunes; but when they died, all their possessions would return to the sultan, of whom they remained technically the slaves. Thus, the creation of aristocratic dynasties was avoided.

On occasion, Christian slaves in the Ottoman Empire could rise even higher. A prime example is the story of Roxelana, a

Ukrainian woman who was captured by the Tatars and sold on the slave market in Istanbul. After converting to Islam, Roxelana entered the imperial harem, where she became the sultan's favourite. The sultan Süleyman eventually married her and recognized their son, Selim II, as his legitimate heir. Such was Roxelana's influence over the imperial court that her detractors suspected her of witchcraft.

## 6.

Far from the palaces of Istanbul, between the rocky shores of South-Western Europe and the sands of the Maghreb, slavery was inextricably linked with one of the oldest Mediterranean traditions: piracy. Pirates had been traversing the Middle Sea since the Bronze Age, when the difference between a merchant and a raider was down to the opportunity of the moment. Briefly, during the heyday of the Roman Empire, piracy was virtually erased from the region, but it quickly returned as soon as the Sea was no longer under the dominion of a single political power. Yet, in no other historical period did Mediterranean piracy reach such power as during the Early Modern era, with unprecedented levels of organization and integration into society. Hundreds of ships and thousands of Christians and Muslims alike dedicated their lives to raiding the coasts and capturing the passing ships. Although their victims continued to see them as just pirates, the Early Modern sea-raiders would be better qualified as 'corsairs': irregular troops in the ongoing war between the Christian and the Muslim states. They planned their attacks in accordance with the changing alliances of the state to which they belonged, targeting exclusively the fleets and coastal towns of the enemy.

A sudden ringing of bells, followed by a precipitous escape to the inland at the cry '*Mamma, li Turchi!*' (oh, dear mother, the Turks!), were common features in the life of Christian communities, especially on the coasts of Italy. The ships of the Muslim corsairs of the Maghreb arrived at astonishing speed, often under the cover of darkness, and rarely returned to their port without a supply of slaves for the markets of Algiers, Tunis or Tripoli. Women and children fetched a higher price, not least because of their possible sexual exploitation, while most of the men were destined for work in the fields, in the quarries and, in great numbers, on the rowing benches of the warships.

Thus began, for example, the second life of Giovan Dionigi Galeni, the son of a family of fishers in a Calabrian village on the Southern coast of Italy. The Algerian corsairs kidnapped him when he was still a teenager, enslaved him and chained him among the rowers on one of their ships. The young man did not lose heart: he converted to Islam, changed his name to Uluç Alì, worked his way to regaining his freedom through his service and eventually began his own business as an independent corsair. From that point onwards, his story mixes with legend. With his own fleet, Uluç Alì wreaked havoc all over the coasts of the Christian nations, particularly his native Italy. So spectacular were his successes that the Ottoman sultan promoted him first to naval commander, then to *pasha* of Tripoli, and again to *bey* (governor) of Algiers. In 1571, the war between the European Christians and the Muslims reached its climax: at the naval battle of Lepanto, off the coast of Greece, the Ottoman forces experienced a catastrophic defeat, losing almost 200 vessels and over 20,000 men. Uluç Alì was the only Ottoman captain to return from the battle with his fleet intact, having defeated his immediate adversaries in the field. The sultan promoted him to *kapudan pasha*, commander of the entire Ottoman navy. An old man, approaching death in his sumptuous palace in Istanbul, Uluç Alì bequeathed to his slaves a Turkish village of his own foundation, which he had named, with a hint of nostalgia, 'New Calabria'.[11]

## 7.

The golden age of Mediterranean piracy ran parallel to that of piracy in the Atlantic Ocean. But while, in the Americas, the corsairs were simply a tool for the European powers to unsettle each other's routes towards the colonies, the Mediterranean corsairs strove to stabilize their own position as an autonomous geopolitical entity. In America, the pirates controlled only small enclaves along the coast; in the Mediterranean, their territorial domains were the size of states. On the Christian side, the island of Malta functioned as an advanced base, from which hundreds of raids were launched every year against the coasts of the Maghreb. In Italy, the city of Livorno acted as the main marketplace where Christian pirates, slave traders and ransom negotiators ensured that the pirate economy would be replenished by a steady financial flow.

But it was on the Barbary coast of North Africa, between the sixteenth and eighteenth centuries, that the corsairs achieved true splendour. The coastal areas of today's Algeria, Tunisia and Libya were formally submitted to the authority of the Ottoman sultan, though in practice they were largely autonomous. Their government consisted of a mixed body composed of the representatives of the Ottoman Janissaries, the local Arab notables and the *taifa* (guild) of the corsairs. Since the local economy received great benefit from its activities, the *taifa* often took a predominant role, and the governor of each state, the *Bey*, was often chosen from among its associates.

Interestingly, most of the people who sat in the government were ethnically 'foreign' to the local Berber society: the Janissaries typically came from the Christian regions of the Balkans; the Arabs were the descendants of the invaders who had taken over the region in the seventh/eighth century; and the *taifa* was composed, for the most part, of Eastern Mediterranean sailors and European renegades. Arabic, the official language, was often accompanied by a *lingua franca* that combined all the Mediterranean languages. But the ethnic provenance of the North African corsairs was not limited to the regions surrounding the Middle Sea: the renegades from Italy, Spain, France and Portugal were joined by the English, Flemish, German and Polish, in a cosmopolitan community that defied any possible idea of 'purity'.

Women, too, were active as corsairs. Most notable among them was Sayyida al Hurra, 'the sovereign lady', a formidable corsair and queen of Morocco in the early sixteenth century. Born in Andalusia, she had been raised in Morocco after her family had to flee persecution from the Christians. As an adult, Sayyida al Hurra took her revenge by relentlessly attacking the Spanish fleets and coastal cities. By coordinating her efforts with Hayreddin Barbarossa (the leader of the Algerian corsairs, born in Greece to a Christian Orthodox woman), she increased her military might to the point that the Christian states had to beg for a truce. Imagine the dismay of the European diplomats! Not only did they have to deal with the 'ignoble commoners' who occupied the top positions in the Ottoman government, now they were also forced to negotiate with the former slaves, renegades and women of the corsair *taifas*, whose fleets had paralysed their sea commerce, humiliated their armies and terrorized their people. Truly, to their eyes, the southern and eastern coasts of the Mediterranean were an otherworld, where the conventions of European society were upended.

What looked like a nightmare to the European aristocracy, however, felt like a dream to some of their subjects. While still fearing the 'Turks', the dispossessed and discontented of Europe looked at this otherworld with fascination, sometimes with hope. 'I'd rather be governed by the Turks than by the priests!' were the last words on the scaffold of a sixteenth-century rebel from Bologna, then under the Papal state.[12] 'Might the Sultan soon arrive!' echoed a contemporary anonymous pamphlet from Venice, depicting the 'Turks' as the force that might cleanse Europe from its injustices.[13]

## 8.

The renegade corsairs rarely had special regard for the prisoners who came from their own country of origin. The distance between a free person and a slave, and perhaps an unconscious repulsion for what reminded them of their past life, prevailed over a sense of kinship based on provenance. Some, like the Venetian renegade Ali Piccinino, leader of the *taifa* of Algiers, were infamous for their cruelty towards their European slaves.

But solidarity existed between the slaves themselves, even when they belonged to opposite factions. Thus, in 1642, the Dutch slave Emanuel de Aranda and his companions welcomed, like long-lost brothers, the Turkish slaves who had been sent from Europe in exchange for their freedom. They were in Ceuta, Morocco, when they met 'the five Turks, who welcomed us and wished us good luck. They came with us for a drink at a tavern and they asked us about their friends in Algiers, then we told each other about our adventures and our misfortunes. Those were the happiest moments of our lives, in the past and in the future.'[14] A few decades later, while walking through the port of Marseille, Count Marsigli of Bologna spotted among a group of galley slaves a Turkish man who had been his master during his time as a slave in Algiers: 'we recognised each other and we hugged', and the count rushed to the ship's commander to buy the Turk's freedom.[15]

Not all slaves, however, enjoyed an equal standing. The racist prejudices of their masters created an informal hierarchy even among those at the bottom of society. European traders preferred Turkish slaves over Arabs and Arabs over Black Africans. Slave traders in the Ottoman Empire would pay a higher price for a European than for a Black African. Besides racism, these rankings were due to considerations of return on investment. While purchasing a European slave could yield a large ransom, paid by their families or by charitable institutions, there were no equivalent channels of exchange with Sub-Saharan Africa. Furthermore, the Black African slaves, knowing that no external help would come to rescue them, often sank into a state of severe depression, defined by the European traders as 'suffering of fantasy'.[16] Prostrated yet indomitable, many of them let themselves die or resorted to suicide rather than live the rest of their days as slaves.

It was hard for the Black African slaves to integrate into their host societies even after liberation. The colour of their skin marked them out, especially in Europe, and the absence of a substantial local Black African community left them isolated. Yet, at times, their exceptionality was also the source of an extraordinary destiny. Such was the case, for example, of Benedetto Manasseri, born in Sicily in 1524 to two Black African slaves. He was liberated at birth by his family's master, who had promised his mother that her firstborn would be free, while his parents and siblings continued to live as slaves. A sensitive and lonely young man, he could not bear the racism of his fellow citizens and decided to withdraw to the mountains, where he lived long years as a hermit. He later joined a Franciscan monastery and, according to tradition, performed miracles to heal the poor who flocked to visit him. His reputation as a man of wisdom grew to such an extent that even the Spanish viceroy of Sicily frequently asked for his advice. He became the object of popular devotion already during his lifetime, and after his death, he was declared a saint by the Catholic Church. To this day, Saint Benedetto il Moro ('the black') is venerated as one of the patron saints of the city of Palermo.[17]

## 9.

As they moved across the Mediterranean, the slaves brought with them not only their personal stories but also new bodies of knowledge. They pioneered new art forms, like the Black African slaves in the Iberian Peninsula who celebrated their conversion to Christianity with music and dances that caused consternation among the local ecclesiastics. They popularized novel flavours, like the Turkish ex-slaves who opened some of the earliest coffee houses in Tuscany, Austria and Germany, between the seventeenth and eighteenth centuries. They also brought new technologies, such as the techniques of shipbuilding introduced by the Northern European slaves in the Maghreb. Once ransomed and back at home, they also created a new literary genre, the 'memoir of slavery', which included some of the finest pages by Miguel de Cervantes, for five years a slave in Algiers.[18]

Sometimes, they ended up shaping entire intellectual fields, as happened in the sixteenth century with the slave-turned-convert, Leo Joannes Africanus de Medicis, also known by his Arabic birth name al-Hasan ibn Muhammad al Wazzan. His story epitomizes the twists and turns of life in the early Modern Mediterranean and the unique contribution to the advancement of knowledge provided by slaves and renegades. Al-Hasan was born in Granada around 1488, while the Catholic kings were completing their conquest of Spain and expelling all Jews and Muslims from their domains. His family had to flee to Morocco, then under the rule of Sultan Muhammad al-Burtuqali ('the Portuguese'), so-called because of the years of captivity he had spent in Portugal during his childhood. When al-Hasan finished school, he accompanied his uncle on a diplomatic mission on behalf of the sultan. He traversed the Sahara Desert to the golden city of Timbuktu, then ventured across the Maghreb to the banks of the Nile. Over the years, he visited the Arabian Peninsula, Iraq, Persia, Constantinople, Armenia, reaching as far as southern Russia. In 1518, while journeying homeward, his ship was attacked by Spanish corsairs. Captured, he became a slave – but his exceptional knowledge spared him from ending up in the common slave market. Instead, he was offered as a gift to Pope Leo X. He remained in captivity until he agreed to convert to Christianity, and at his baptism, in the church of Saint Peter, the Pope himself acted as his godfather. Thus, al-Hasan assumed the name of the Pope, Leo, his surname Medici, and the nickname *Africanus*, 'the African'.

Leo Africanus lived freely in Rome, where he worked with Jewish scholars to compile the first-ever trilingual dictionary: Latin-Arabic-Hebrew. But his name was to be made immortal by another work, which he wrote in Italian: *The Cosmography and Geography of Africa*. Through its pages, Europe gained the first glimpse of parts of Africa which no Christian traveller had yet seen. Leo described the places, the people, the nature and the customs, with a flair for storytelling and a taste for classifications. Amazingly, he wrote it entirely from memory, since the European libraries of his time had very little, if anything, to offer in this area. Despite its inaccuracies, his work remained for centuries a benchmark of African geography, influencing generations of explorers, scientists and writers. In 1532, already a celebrated authority, Leo left Italy to return to the Maghreb. He settled in Tunis, where he changed his name again and converted back to Islam. It was as if he had journeyed full circle. Had his years in Italy and his conversion to Christianity been only a dream? Perhaps, as in the play of the Spanish author Calderon de la Barca, *La vida es sueño*, all Mediterranean lives of that period had something of the quality of a dream. Fleeting, unpredictable, at the mercy of all imaginable events – before the awakening that would finally dissolve them.[19]

## 10.

Learning more about Africa and the Mashriq was a priority for the European powers. The Ottoman Empire controlled the Maghreb, except the kingdom of Morocco, and Asia Minor all the way to Mecca. Its power elicited the respect and fear of its adversaries. In the aftermath of its only major defeat during the sixteenth century, the naval battle of Lepanto, it took only a few months to reconstitute the strongest fleet in the Mediterranean. By 1683, the Ottoman Empire was besieging Vienna for the second time. Even during the hostilities, the European states, starting with Venice, could not afford to break off diplomatic and commercial relations with such a formidable partner. The Ottoman Empire was not only the otherworld dreamed by the discontented of Europe, or the nemesis that terrified its aristocracy, but an empire that had the serious potential of becoming universal, extending its power all over the world.

However, with time, the Ottoman Empire began to show signs of fatigue. It refused to embrace the latest technological developments, from printing to clock-making. Its banking system did not evolve, its military still rested on the laurels of earlier ages, its bureaucracy was burdened by increasing corruption. Meanwhile, the old virtuous traditions, like the absence of a hereditary aristocracy, were beginning to wane.

The decline of the Ottoman Empire reflected the twilight of a wider region. The Mediterranean had ceased to be a key node of global commerce, supplanted by the new routes connecting Europe to the American continent. New explorations had opened the way to East Asia, and what once used to pass exclusively through the Middle Sea now travelled along other paths. During the eighteenth century, the Christian territories of the Mediterranean did not fare much better than the Ottoman Empire. Spain and Portugal were chasing the last rays of their golden age, most of Italy had been colonized by foreign powers, and France, with its continental and transoceanic ambitions, had steered its attention away from the old Sea.

The eighteenth century also saw the decline of piracy. The states of the Maghreb, like the corsair state of Malta, could no longer afford to maintain massive fleets. Arming a ship with cannons, as the new age demanded, was beyond the economic possibilities of most corsair captains. The Mediterranean slave trade, too, thankfully, substantially decreased. The latest models of ships no longer required hundreds of arms to power their oars, while, on land, new technologies had reduced the demand for workers. Moreover, the new doctrines of the Enlightenment rendered the possession of slaves increasingly unacceptable among the European elites. The local dispossessed, although free in theory, were now to bear the full brunt of then nascent capitalist exploitation, while the disappearance of the corsairs sheltered the powerful from those sudden gusts of wind, which in the earlier centuries had placed them at the mercy of Fortuna.

By the mid-nineteenth century, the soaring trajectories of Northern Europe and, to a lesser extent, North America were already beyond anyone's reach. The Mediterranean had become a land of exotic oddness, good for the fantasies of the first tourists and orientalists and for the colonial ambitions of the dominant nations. The Ottoman Empire, with its antiquated modes and its decrepit infrastructures, was now 'the sick man of Europe'.

Yet, for all its frailty, this dying world still had an important role to play in the history of the imagination. While disappointing 'the magnificent progressive destinies' of full modernity, it remained the only ground where the improbable, sometimes the impossible, could grow.

## 11.

When one feels the ground sinking beneath one's feet, it is natural to jump upwards, as if to reach in mid-air for an invisible support. Likewise, in a catastrophe, a sense of foolish light-heartedness can sometimes emerge. Even though it might not reverse the generalized collapse, the 'inner emigration' of unjustified joy remains a force capable of redeeming what can no longer be fixed.

In the Mediterranean of the eighteenth century, this feeling of lightness took the form of new art and music, following the impulse of those who, from the height of their social position, had been the first to notice the incoming storm. An inexhaustible stream of joy flowed through the theatres, chambers and oratories of the Italian elites. Composers such as Antonio Vivaldi, Pietro Locatelli, Francesco Geminiani, Francesco Veracini, Leonardo Leo, Nicola Porpora, Giovanni Pergolesi and many others, seemed to magically dispel the clouds of the age. Sadness was not entirely banished, but in their compositions, even the most terrifying themes, like a massacre, a sea tempest or a crucifixion, wore such light garments that even a human heart could bear them. The Italian baroque and *galante* music of the period, like the rose-and-azure paintings of Giovanni Battista Tiepolo and Sebastiano Ricci, or the white that brightens Giovan Battista Piazzetta's works, were a breeze wafting through a room that was closing in.

Likewise, in the Ottoman Empire, the chain of military defeats and territorial losses found its counterbalance in the elites' exercises of lightness. In the Ottoman cities, elaborate fireworks punctuated the course of the seasons, while new architectural styles combined a stately majesty with a delicate sense of the small pleasures of life. Dancing women made their first appearance in the Ottoman miniatures of the period, amidst gilded interiors and paradisiacal landscapes. In the gardens of the affluent, a new craze for the rarest varieties of tulips condensed into a colourful mist, their intricate patterns reflecting on the turbans and clothes of the garden strollers.

Such a splurge of money on art and music, at a time when many suffered economic hardship, could seem outrageous – but it can also be read, in hindsight, as an attempt to salvage something from the catastrophe. As in the belief, common to Judaism and Islam, that even at the worst of times there is always one saintly person, living in hiding, whose heart contains the balance and salvation of the world, so the foolish lightness of the eighteenth-century Mediterranean acted as a shelter for the very possibility of holding onto joy in the face of disaster.

Like two sailors staring into each other's eyes as their ship goes under, the Southern European and Ottoman shores of the Mediterranean did not cease to look at each other for inspiration. Motifs *a' la turca* (Turkish style) entered the standard repertoires of *galante* music, while baroque and rococo ornaments made their way into the palette of Ottoman art and fashion. Far from the condescending orientalism of the Northern European powers, the fascination for the 'other' endured in the Mediterranean countries as a form of mutual reassurance that the same destiny, even though it was one of defeat, enveloped them all.

## 12.

While the affluent elites embarked on vessels of art and music, a different tension animated the Mediterranean intellectuals. Echoes of the Enlightenment filled their discussions and their writings, propelling them in the pursuit of a new idea of freedom. Society needed to be reformed, they claimed, its culture purged of superstitions, its structures freed from the fetters of privileges and corruption. The achievement of freedom had to pass through the creation of a new way of life, in accordance with the eternal values of reason.

At first, the Mediterranean revolutionaries trusted in the strength of their philosophical arguments to stir the people in the direction of reform. But as history progressed into the nineteenth century, it became apparent to them as well that the material situation of the Mediterranean required a different approach. With dismay, the heirs to the French Revolution discovered that the populace preferred the established injustices of old over a blind plunge into a future built on abstract concepts. To conquer the hearts of the people, they needed to create a story that was as simple as the old narratives, yet capable of mobilizing even stronger emotions. Thus, filled with good intentions, they combined their rational arguments for freedom with the emotions stirred by a new idea: the nation.

Until then, the feeling of belonging to a 'nation' had been mostly a means for the scattered minorities, like the Jews, to maintain a semblance of autonomy in times of persecution. In the hands of nineteenth-century intellectuals, however, the 'nation' became something else entirely: no longer the invisible home of the homeless but a powerful divinity that could break the surface of the Earth into discrete parts and split humanity into groups unbound by anything common. Combined with an increasingly 'scientific' racism, the nation became the form in which different ethnic groups entered a zero-sum game to determine which one had been chosen by nature to rule over all.

Having ignited this explosive idea, the revolutionaries witnessed their call for reform gaining acceptance among the populace. New clandestine groups sprouted all over the Mediterranean, coalescing around notions of cultural and ethnic purity and calling for the complete political autonomy of each people. Terms that until then had been used merely to describe a geographical region or a linguistic group, like 'Italy' or 'Greece', turned into political battle cries. To help the common folks come to terms with the idea of belonging to these new imagined communities, the intellectuals delved into historical research to prove – on a 'factual' basis, as was the ambition of the time – the ancient, if not 'natural', origin of the various national denominations.

It was not long before 'nation' replaced 'freedom' as the propulsive force of the era. If the relics of the old regime needed to be overthrown, it was no longer because of the suffering they had inflicted on actual living individuals: the sin of the old monarchies, especially of the multicultural empires, was to have failed to fulfil the unique destinies of the different nations that composed them. Thus, for the Mediterranean revolutionaries, the British Empire became a model of reference: its combination of liberalism, monarchy and aristocracy had ensured the global hegemony of a single nation, England, while also preserving its national character from being contaminated with the spirit of its 'lesser' subjects (be they the Irish or the Indians). The Mediterranean intellectuals were not oblivious to the plight of the British working masses, nor to the oppression endured by the colonies – but in their eyes, the real subject of history was the nation, not the person.

## 13.

It might raise a wry smile to observe how the European revolutionaries sought refuge from their political misfortunes in that very Ottoman Empire that embodied everything they despised. The Ottoman Empire was backwards, corrupt, poor, mired in religion and deaf to the autonomist aspirations of its ethnic components. Yet, whenever a liberal or a national revolution failed in a European country, the conspirators flocked to its cities. Istanbul teemed with foreign revolutionaries, whose presence was tolerated as long as it did not pose an immediate threat to the local authority.

In the mid-nineteenth century, just as the last Mediterranean pirates vanished, a new generation of renegades set out on their journey. Turkish reformers migrated to France and Britain to learn the ways of modernity, while exiled Europeans gathered in Ottoman cafes to discuss plans for future revolutions in their countries of origin.

Not all Mediterranean intellectuals subscribed to the cult of the nation, though. For the utopian socialists, the communists and the anarchists, national divisions were just a means for the ruling elites to better control their subjects. In their eyes, a revolution that did not upturn the structures of society in view of universal liberation could not really call itself a revolution. Like the Gnostic 'saboteurs' of Late Antiquity, they wanted to subvert all established powers, through violence if necessary, until every person could reclaim their right to live in a world that resembled a paradise.

> Expelled from every nation,
> we will move from land to land,
> preaching peace,
> rejecting war.
> Peace be among the oppressed,
> and war to the oppressors.[20]

The Italian anarchists, in particular, moved to the Ottoman Empire in such great numbers that they formed its third largest anarchist community by provenance, after the Turks and the Armenians.[21] Among them hid an accomplice in the assassination of Italy's king Umberto I: Cesare Camilieri, known as Asan bin Abdullah after his conversion to Islam.[22]

Another strand of European intellectuals also looked favourably to the Ottoman world. Those who still held onto the ideas of the French Revolution praised it for its tolerance and freedom, unmatched anywhere in Europe. In his polemical writings, the Italian revolutionary Alfio Grassi contrasted the tyrannical rule imposed by the British on their colonies with the autonomy enjoyed by Ottoman subjects of any ethnicity. While the European nations were still struggling to obtain their constitutions, he remarked, the Quran acted as a charter of fundamental rights for the Ottomans, and the *muftis* and *ulamas* functioned as an effective counterforce to the power of the sultan.

> Well before 'civilized' nations had constitutions, chambers and an opposition party, the Ottomans had already established one and the other, and relied on these three foundations as the pillars which were intended to sustain the Empire.[23]

He was echoed by the Italian writer Giorgio Libri-Bagnano, who denounced the hypocrisy of those Europeans – particularly the French – who supported the anti-Ottoman revolt of the Greeks based on arguments of ethnic and religious identity.

> [You should] fight for the Greeks, not because they are Christians, but because they are oppressed! Attack the Turks not because they are Turks, but because they are oppressors![24]

For the peoples who could not claim a special status as Christians or Europeans, the alternative to the Ottoman rule was, most frequently, colonization by the French or the British. Thus, after years in the liberal circles of London and Paris, the Libyan intellectual Hassuna D'Ghies returned to his native Tripoli with a changed heart. His country's only hope for freedom, he realized, was within the tattered but protective fold of the Ottoman Empire. The Italian colonial conquest of Libya in 1911 would eventually prove him right.

For Algeria, too, falling out of the Ottoman shadow coincided with colonial occupation. What the Ottomans used to request, the French took by force. As witnessed by an exceptional chronicler, the Swiss-born anarchist writer Isabelle Eberhardt, life under colonial conditions had nothing to offer except disillusionment and humiliation. Rather than accepting that the price of survival was the status of lesser subjects, she saw the Algerian people withdrawing to the remotest margins of the desert, under 'the warm shadow of Islam', or within the stupefying clouds of *kif*.

> Even in the darkest purlieu of [the] underworld, such men can reach the magic horizon where they are free to build their dream-palaces of delight.[25]

During her brief life, mostly spent between the docks of Marseille and the hypnotic desolation of southern Algeria, Isabelle too followed this path. Although European by birth, she was persecuted by the colonial authorities; though educated to secular values, she became a Muslim and a Sufi initiate; born a woman, she lived most of her life dressed as a man. When she died in 1904, at twenty-seven, drowned by a flash flood in the desert, her writings remained, testifying to a practice of radical withdrawal, where the spirit of the Mediterranean imagination survived almost intact.

# 14.

On the Balkan border between the Ottoman and the Habsburg Empires, the rise of nationalism paved the way for a new age of war. Since the mid-nineteenth century, the Ottomans had been retreating from their Balkan territories, leaving behind a region rife with tension. After centuries of peaceful coexistence, Muslims, Christians, Jews, Slavs and Turks were discovering a new distaste for their reciprocal differences. Especially among Serbian intellectuals, fantasies of Slavic purity and Christian supremacy combined with the invention of a new mythology around the supposed destiny of their own nation. Differences that until then had little relevance to everyday life, suddenly turned neighbour against neighbour. Revolts, wars and waves of repressions ensued. In the same years when the anarchists and the communists were rallying the proletarians of every land to recognize their common cause, the people of the Balkans were set on a different trajectory.

Not all of them, though. Among the Albanian communities dotting the Adriatic coasts, a minority of voices spoke in counterpoint to the spirit of the age.

Girolamo de Rada belonged to one of the earliest Albanian diasporas, in the Southern Italian region of Calabria. He never left Italy and never visited Albania, but he dedicated his writing to championing Albanian culture and praising the beauty of the Albanian language. In his view, the rise of nations posed a fatal risk to those small communities that had no means with which to assert their rights through military might. He envisaged the creation of a federal Europe, composed of self-governing peoples, where peace might be achieved thanks to the absence of a dominant culture, rather than by imposing pockets of cultural homogeneity. Disappointed with the course of historical events, he eventually looked to the Ottoman Empire as the only political formation that could ensure the survival of those minorities, like the Albanians, who were 'scattered and exhausted on different shores'.[26]

From Istanbul, the Albanian Muslim Shemseddin Sami Frasheri seconded his idea. For Frasheri, the spirit of the Albanian people had its closest expression in the mystical ways of the Bektashi Sufi, the religious sect of the Ottoman Janissaries.[27] The Bektashi blurred the boundaries between Sunni and Shia Islam, adopted ritual elements from both Christianity and Turkish shamanism, had a laxer attitude towards religious prohibitions, welcomed women, and insisted on the mysterious, ineffable nature of the divine revelation. They were an initiatic cult, where the adept learnt to overcome the hard distinctions imposed by society, in view of a mystical understanding of the world as thoroughly inhabited by God. For a stateless people like the Albanians, as for the deported young men who formed the Janissaries, the overcoming of societal divisions was not a far-fetched fantasy, but a necessity for everyday survival.

## 15.

The summer of 1914 will remain in the memory of those who lived through it as the most beautiful summer they ever remembered. For in their consciousness, it shone and flamed over a gigantic and dark horizon of suffering and misfortune which stretched into infinity.[28]

28 June 1914: a Bosnian Serb nationalist assassinates Archduke Franz Ferdinand, heir to the Habsburg throne of Austria-Hungary. A few months later, war ravages Europe and its

neighbouring countries, including the Ottoman Empire. Nobody had ever seen a war like it. The arsenals of weapons accumulated during the years of peace poured onto the battlefields like a storm of steel. The same technologies that had brought 'progress' into the lives of millions of people were exacting their blood tribute. Chemical weapons made their debut, alongside explosives of a magnitude as yet unseen. A battle no longer lasted until sunset, but raged on for months, furiously grinding together the trees, the soil, the buildings and hundreds of thousands of lives inside the bomb craters. As if the romantic age of single acts of heroism had been gone for millennia, multitudes of soldiers fought and died together in the same instant, like a single body of sewn-up flesh and metal.

> I live like an animal, an animal that is hungry, tired. I have never felt so stupefied, so devoid of thoughts. . . . [I have become] a true infantry soldier, a simple executor of chores, a particle of a multitude. Everyone commands me, from the corporal to the general; they all have this right, which is absolute and unappealable, and if they wish they can erase me from the list of the living. [. . .] Habit is so strong, enslavement so effective, that we advance in good order, docile and swift like automatons, towards the only place in the world where we would not want to go. [. . .] The artillery roars, crushes, disembowels, terrifies. Everything roars, spurts, and wavers. We find ourselves in the centre of a monstrous vortex, fragments of sky collapse and cover us with debris, long luminous trails collide and crumble with short-circuit flashes. We are prisoners of an apocalypse. The Earth is a building on fire with sealed doors.[29]

Among the warring countries, none paid a higher toll than Serbia, whose nationalist wing had sparked the events leading to the Great War. In less than five years, Serbia lost a quarter of its population. Massacres of unprecedented brutality also occurred at the opposite edge of the Ottoman Empire, where the Christian Armenian minority was exterminated by the Muslim majority, for fear that they might be an enemy 'fifth column'. Meanwhile, to the South, the war had brought about the disintegration of the common area across the Maghreb and the Mashriq. From the chaos that ensued, France and Britain carved out a new region, branded as the 'Middle East', which would prove an inexhaustible source of ethnic conflicts, nationalist rivalries and religious wars down to our present day.

By 1918, nothing remained of the old political structures of the syncretic Mediterranean. Brightly coloured and freshly starched, new flags soared over the ashes of the multi-ethnic empires of Ottoman and Habsburg. Loud like a trumpet, the spirit of the age called for anyone lingering in an opaque area of mixing to declare themselves in unequivocal terms. Everyone had to align with the character and destiny of their assigned category: the Greeks with the Greeks, the Turks with the Turks, the Jews with the Jews and so on. Just as the globe had been sliced by the grids of modern cartography, so the living, too, had to conform themselves to the logic of a world that was being reorganized like a natural history museum or a commercial warehouse.

## 16.

The twentieth century wanted to channel the youthful energies of 'progress' into a plan for the total development of human potential. But such ambitions came at a cost. In return for the advancements brought by the scientific reorganization of society, institutions had to become inflexible: their function was not supporting life but correcting it. Inside the factories, the thrilling speed of the new means of production and transportation was accompanied by an unbearable acceleration of work rhythms. On the streets, the spotlights illuminating the new goods and services cast the shadow of an unprecedented impoverishment of the masses. Meanwhile, in the realm of the imagination, the narrative of humanity's march towards perfection started singing with a second voice: without undue sentimentalisms, it was now imperative to sacrifice those whose contribution to 'total' progress had proved suboptimal. Whether individuals or entire peoples, the weak and 'degenerates' had to succumb for the greater good of all. In short, humanity had entered the age when it would test its ability to annihilate itself.

Halting the unfolding of events no longer seemed possible. Thus, searching for a way out of the inevitable, the Mediterranean imagination resorted to a solution that appeared absurd, if not impossible. It responded to the merciless precision of the age by mixing all political positions and identities. It defied the new military and industrial complex by reviving the spirit of past pirate adventures. It presented poetry and art as a community's strongest weapons, and the pursuit of beauty and pleasure as the true aim of social life. And it chose the most ravaged land, the coast of the Balkans, as the stage where an entire world would enact its own funeral in the guise of a wild party.

The year was 1919. Peace had returned almost everywhere, except for the war still raging between the Greeks and the Turks.

The victorious powers of Western Europe rested contented with their gains. Among the victors, only the Italians, whose ranking among the world's powers was entirely self-assigned, felt that their war efforts had not been adequately repaid by the terms of the armistice. Confronted with the tragedy of half a million dead soldiers, and as many permanently disabled, the Italian populace turned its discontent into a nationalistic lament: until all the 'Italian' territories had been liberated and reunited with the motherland, every drop of blood would have been spilt in vain. The most blatant example of this 'injustice' was right on Italy's doorstep: the majority-Italian port town of Fiume, previously part of the Habsburg Empire, was about to be assigned to the newly founded kingdom of Yugoslavia.

Thus, it started in the Balkans, on the long wave of Italian nationalism. Yet, in just a few weeks, it became something else entirely: a pan-Mediterranean project aimed at establishing life on new foundations – poetic, revolutionary, contradictory, and, ultimately, impossible.

It was the beginning of the strange and short adventure of the Free State of Fiume.

## 17.

'Fiume is the fifth season of the world.'[30] Rarely has a rogue state been described in such poetic terms. But at Fiume, poetry was the general common denominator. At the head of the expedition that had taken over the town in September 1919, there was none other than the Italian poet Gabriele D'Annunzio.

In fact, D'Annunzio was more than a poet: an acclaimed novelist and playwright, he was also a decorated war hero many times over, an aviator, a transgressive performer, a fashion innovator, a pioneering advertiser, an egomaniac and an avid consumer of cocaine. His seemingly inexhaustible creativity had made him an international celebrity, and his inventions had taken hold of the Italian imagination. In later years, when the Fascist Party seized power in Italy, the regime would appropriate elements of his aesthetics, casting an enduring shadow on his legacy. However, as we shall see, D'Annunzio himself was not reducible to fascism.

When he led the first detachment of deserters from the Italian army into the town of Fiume, D'Annunzio was aware of entering a dangerous game. Although he declared himself to be interpreting the patriotic wish of Fiume's Italian population, he knew very well that he was weakening Italy's position at the post-war negotiating table. The Italian government, furious at D'Annunzio's stunt, ordered the army to surround the town. Fiume was isolated, cut off from the railway system and from access to food and supplies. By itself, the town had only days before it would have to surrender. Its survival depended entirely on D'Annunzio's ability to fire up the popular imagination. With a stream of communiques, he made clear that what was at stake was much more than a small territorial annexation. He and his deserters were part of a global movement fighting the abuses of the powerful nations over the weaker ones.

> From the indomitable Irish Sinn Fein to the red flag that in Egypt unites the Crescent and the Cross, all uprisings of the spirit against the devourers of raw flesh and against the

exploiters of defenceless peoples will reignite with our spark that flies far away. All the insurgents of all races will gather under our banner. And the unarmed will be armed. And force will be opposed by force. . . . Our revolt welcomes white and coloured races alike; it reconciles the Gospel and the Quran, Christianity and Islam. . . . Every insurrection is an effort of expression, an effort of creation.[31]

Rejected by the Italian government, Fiume called to itself all the rebels against capitalism and Anglo-American imperialism: the then nascent fascists, but also the syndicalists, the anarchists and the communists. 'I stand for communism without dictatorship. No wonder, considering that my entire culture is anarchic. It is my intention to make this city a spiritual island from which an eminently communist action can radiate towards all oppressed nations.'[32] The anarcho-communism of Fiume, however, had little in common with the harshness of 'Lenin's doctrine, which has lost its way in blood. Here the Bolshevik thistle turns into a rose of love.'[33] It was a form of 'Latinised Bolshevism'[34] that combined the cult of action, a genuine attention to the plight of the oppressed and to the demands of the workers, with a decadent aesthetic and the ambition of bringing about a spiritual revolution through art. All this, within a hopelessly besieged town and through the efforts of the international brigade of deserters, rebels, criminals and artists who had responded to a poet's call.

## 18.

Speaking from the balcony of the palace of government to a frenzied crowd shouting his war cry 'Eia eia alala!' – a spectacle and a motto that would later be appropriated by the fascists – D'Annunzio announced the launch of a new constitution, *La Carta del Carnaro*. It was the most visionary constitutional text of its time. It established a republic based on socialist principles, ruled through a democratic system, and geared towards a spiritual revolution fuelled by art and poetry. The literary style of the charter was D'Annunzio's, but its contents were mainly the work of the revolutionary syndicalist Alceste de Ambris. It is worth pausing for a moment to browse through its articles, starting with those guaranteeing equality for all citizens:

> Article 4 – [The State] recognizes and confirms the sovereignty of all citizens without distinction of sex, lineage, language, class, or religion.
>
> 12 – All citizens of both sexes have full authority to choose and engage in all industries, professions, arts, and crafts.

16 – Citizens are endowed with all civil and political rights upon reaching the age of twenty. Without distinction of sex, they become legitimate voters and eligible for all offices.

The constitution protected minorities, whether religious or ethnic:

> 7 – The fundamental freedoms of thought, press, assembly, and association are guaranteed to all citizens. Every religious worship is admitted, respected, and can build its own temple.
>
> 52 – In middle schools, the teaching of the various languages spoken throughout the State is mandatory.

Equality was guaranteed by institutions that were set to safeguard and nurture the individual:

8 – The statutes guarantee to all citizens of both sexes: education in clear and healthy schools; remunerated work with a minimum wage sufficient for a decent living; assistance in sickness, disability, and involuntary unemployment; retirement pension for old age; inviolability of the home; *habeas corpus*; compensation for damages in case of judicial error or abused power.

To avoid exploitation, the institution of private property was limited to its honest acquisition through labour:

3 – [Fiume] is a straightforward government of the people which has as its foundation the power of productive labour and as its order the broadest and most varied forms of autonomy.

9 – The State does not recognize ownership as the absolute dominion of the person over the thing but considers it as the most useful social function. The only legitimate title of ownership over any means of production and exchange is labour.

Although workers were at the centre of the constitution, work itself was not idolized. As in Marx, the ultimate aim of the economic system was the abolition of work:

19 – [Out of the ten guilds that reunite the workers of Fiume,] the tenth guild has neither profession nor count nor name.... It is consecrated to the complete liberation of the spirit above the painful breath and the sweat of blood. It is represented, in the civic sanctuary, by a burning lamp inscribed with an ... allusion to a spiritualized form of human labour: 'Labour without labour'.

These political and economic provisions, however, were only means to a higher end. Fiume's revolution had to bring about a transformation of the spirit. Just as Oscar Wilde supported revolutionary socialism because, by liberating people from need, it elevated them to the appreciation of beauty, so D'Annunzio saw the transformation of life into art as the ultimate revolutionary objective. Beauty and culture were to be pursued in every field:

50 – For every people, culture is the brightest of long weapons. ... For the people of Fiume, it becomes the most effective tool of health and fortune against external threats. ... Therefore, [Fiume] places at the top of its laws the culture of its people.

63 – A college of *Edili* is established. ... It convinces workers that adorning even the humblest dwelling with some sign of folk art is a pious act; ... it aims to restore to the people the love of beautiful lines and beautiful colours in the things that serve everyday life; it encourages entrepreneurs and builders to understand how new materials – iron, glass, concrete – demand only to be raised to a harmonious life towards the invention of a new architecture.

64 – In [Fiume], Music is a religious and social institution. ... A great people are not only those who create their god in their own likeness, but also those who create their hymn for their god. If every rebirth of a noble people is a lyrical effort, if every creative feeling is a lyrical power, if every new order is a lyrical order, then Music, considered as a ritual language, is the exalter of the act of life, of the work of life.

Fiume's revolution was ultimately summarized by D'Annunzio as a religious effort towards a kind of 'progress', which was altogether different from the zero-sum 'progress' championed by the capitalists, the racists and the social Darwinists:

> 14 – [The State] holds three religious beliefs above all others: Life is beautiful, and man, remade whole by freedom, has the right to live it magnificently; The whole man is the one who knows how to invent his own virtue every day in order to offer his brothers a new gift every day; Work, even the humblest, even the darkest, if well executed, tends towards beauty and adorns the world.

## 19.

The religious tone of Fiume's constitution might lead to an easy misunderstanding. The spirituality of D'Annunzio and his followers was diametrically opposed to the bigoted conservatism of the official Church of the time. Fiume was a 'city of life', pervaded by an atmosphere of intense eroticism. Nudism was widely practised, even by the most prominent figures of government, in the name of a more authentic connection with nature. Women and men engaged in a polyamorous season that brought the local hospital's ward for sexually transmitted diseases to its knees. Homosexuality was not merely tolerated, but it became a constitutive part of the ethos and aesthetics of the revolution. Looking from his balcony at some of his men going hand in hand towards a known cruising spot, D'Annunzio favourably remarked: 'Look at my soldiers, they walk together in couples like the warriors of the ancient Theban legion'.[35] The beauty of naked bodies and the fire of youthful passions were living symbols of what the revolution wished to achieve.

'An endless party' is a recurrent description of D'Annunzio's Fiume by those who took part in it. Street parties animated the days and nights of the town, amidst dancing, improvised parades, concerts and wild performances. Daring and dangerous practical jokes were celebrated as a novel form of art. Rivers of cocaine sustained the general excitement, in a joyous inversion of what would later become the regular use of amphetamines among the troops of the Second World War. The collective effort, it seemed, was aimed at suspending the flow of time. Indeed, Fiume could look no further than the instant of its present: clipped at the back by the recent past of the World War, its future rested inside the enemy cannons encircling the town. The revolution could live only for as long as the imagination allowed to extend the present.

But how could they survive when access to food and supplies had been cut off? In this regard, too, the Mediterranean imagination aided the revolution. Looking into the past history of the region, D'Annunzio found the story of the Uscocchi pirates, who during the sixteenth century had fought against both the Venetians and the Ottomans, attacking their ships and selling the crews as slaves. The new Uscocchi of Fiume were tasked with a similar mission: capturing the passing ships, or hijacking those still in the ports, to take them to Fiume. The best targets were the cargo ships carrying food, clothes and weapons, but any kind of load could be resold, and the ships themselves could be held for ransom. A governmental department was dedicated to these kinds of activities: the Office for Sleights of Hand (*ufficio colpi di mano*). Their exploits became legendary, as when they slowly substituted each member in the crew of a cargo ship with their own men, or when a commando hid inside the coal deposit for days before suddenly emerging to take over the helm. They also targeted the besieging army, as when they kidnapped an Italian general who had derided the 'immoral ways' of the people of Fiume. The activities of the Uscocchi were crucial to feeding the starved town, but they were also an element of the 'endless party' of D'Annunzio and his followers. More than military actions, they were gestures of concrete poetry, trying to suspend the inevitable.

## 20.

After sixteen months of siege and five days of bloody fighting, on 29 December 1920, Fiume capitulated under the bombardment of the Italian navy. Far from bringing peace, the 'Blood Christmas' of Fiume started the countdown for another, much darker revolution. Less than two years later, Mussolini's black shirts marched on Rome, inaugurating the 'Fascist era'.

The 1920s shook the Mediterranean with the convulsive rhythm of a fever. Waves of reactionary, nationalist revolutions surged in quick succession, installing dictatorial regimes in Turkey in 1920, in Italy in 1922, in Spain in 1923, in Albania in 1925, in Greece and in Portugal in 1926 and in Yugoslavia in 1929. Despite their efforts, the anarchists, socialists, and radical democrats had failed to stem the totalitarian flood that would soon lead to the Second World War. In this scenario, the experience of Fiume stood as a unique attempt to defuse the violence of the age through aesthetic sublimation, and to compose the contrasts between political extremes within a higher spiritual perspective. D'Annunzio's charisma, at the time far more recognized than Mussolini's, was supposed to guarantee the good success of this march against the course of history. But the impossible remained unachieved. And the catastrophes that followed engraved within the collective memory of the Mediterranean the lesson that achieving the impossible is, at times, the only possibility for a dignified life.

After the fall of Fiume, D'Annunzio's followers scattered to the winds. Some moved to the extreme right, converging within the Fascist Party. Others joined the antifascists, holding onto an untimely dream of collective freedom and individual dignity. Others again, like D'Annunzio himself and the Futurists who had animated the cultural atmosphere of Fiume, took an ambivalent position towards the new totalitarian regimes.

The following decades would swallow them all.

It would take millions of deaths, dozens of razed cities, the Holocaust and the invention of atomic weaponry for something like Fiume to happen again. It would return in the 1960s, when the political pendulum swung to the opposite side of the totalitarianism of the early twentieth century: the torch of Fiume came alight again in the hands of the counterculture. The red thread between these two moments was clear to the anarchist thinker Hakim Bey, among the ideologues of rave culture:

> If we compare Fiume with the Paris uprising of 1968 (also the Italian urban insurrections of the early seventies), as well as with the American countercultural communes and their anarcho-New Left influences, we should notice certain similarities, such as: – the importance of aesthetic theory (cf. the Situationists) – also, what might be called 'pirate economics,' living high off the surplus of social overproduction – even the popularity of colorful military uniforms – and the concept of music as revolutionary social change – and finally their shared air of

impermanence, of being ready to move on, shape-shift, relocate to other universities, mountaintops, ghettos, factories, safe houses, abandoned farms – or even other planes of reality. No one was trying to impose yet another Revolutionary Dictatorship, either at Fiume, Paris, or Millbrook. Either the world would change, or it wouldn't. Meanwhile keep on the move and live intensely.[36]

Like the ghostly reincarnations of Alexander the Great, the cosmic flight plans of the Gnostics, and the border-crossings of the medieval translators, the imaginary flame of Fume was never fully smothered.

Yet, the vitalism of the counterculture did not exhaust the adventures of the Mediterranean imagination in the twentieth and twenty-first centuries. Besides those who wished to extend the present or to jump towards the future, there were also those who looked longingly towards the past, and those who placed their hopes far beyond the realm of time. From such infinite distances, they drew the inspiration to find a way out from an increasingly shrinking world. These new agents of the imagination will be our guides through the next chapter, where our journey will proceed along the path traced by writers of lost pasts, esotericists, philosophers and migrants of all provenances. Their dreams and their creations will take us to the threshold of the contemporary Mediterranean imagination – where the rest of our story is still being written.

# *Meanwhile in the Mediterranean . . .*

## *Seventeenth century to twentieth century*

*1643* – *The Peace of Westphalia ends the Thirty Years' War, inaugurating the Modern order of International Relations.*

*1716–18* – *The Austro-Ottoman War ends with a clear Ottoman defeat.*

*1718–30* – *The 'Tulip Period' flourishes in the Ottoman Empire.*

*1740–8* – *The War of the Austrian Succession rages from the Mediterranean to the Atlantic.*

*1768–74* – *The Russo-Ottoman War ends with a clear Ottoman defeat.*

*1789–99* – *The French Revolution.*

*1803–15* – *The Napoleonic Wars involve most of Europe and parts of the Southern Mediterranean.*

*1811–28* – *Anticolonial wars in South America establish the independence of most of the Spanish and Portuguese colonies.*

*1884–5 – The European colonial powers gather at the Berlin Conference to decide the partition of Africa.*

*1895 – The Italian inventor Guglielmo Marconi creates the first radio transmitter.*

*1914–18 – The First World War rages across the planet, but especially in Central Europe, Turkey and the Mashriq.*

*1917 – The Russian Empire dissolves, replaced by the Soviet regime.*

*1919 – The Austro-Hungarian Empire dissolves.*

*1922 – The Ottoman Empire dissolves.*

*1922 – Mussolini marches on Rome, starting the 'Fascist era' in Italy.*

*1930s – Right-wing dictatorships are established in Austria, Portugal, Greece, Spain and Germany.*

*1939–45 – The Second World War rages across the planet, killing tens of millions – in addition to the millions killed in the same years by the Holocaust.*

*1949 – The United States and its allies create the North Atlantic Treaty Organization (NATO).*

*1954–64 – Algeria, Morocco and Tunisia become independent from France.*

*1955 – The Soviet Union and its allies create the Warsaw Pact of mutual defence.*

*1991–2001 – Ethnic wars ravage the lands and peoples of former Yugoslavia.*

# 6

# *Migrants*

## *The contemporary age*

### 1.

Enveloped by chitchat and the clinking of silverware, brushed by the waiters swirling through the smoke-filled room, Joseph Roth was writing at his usual table. A small group of people, as elegantly dressed as those hard times allowed, sat around him. For some of them, the clothes they were wearing were the only things they had salvaged from home.

Busy cafés had always been Joseph's favourite place for writing. The noise did not bother him; sometimes he even liked to take part in the ongoing conversations. Whenever he spoke, the others listened. Exiled Germans, Austrians, Poles and Ukrainians huddled around him as if seeking warmth from the last glowing ember of their lost homeland. He addressed each of them courteously, the embodiment of an old gentleman.

Joseph passed his delicate hands through his thinning blond hair. He took a sip of Hennessy. He was barely in his forties. A youthful spark still brightened the azure of his eyes. But at first sight, he gave the unmistakable impression of an old man. Old, slow, increasingly lost in thought as the glasses of liquor marked the passing hours. Under the table, he kept his shoelaces undone to give some relief to his swollen feet.

His friends were discussing the state of things back home, in what had been the Austro-Hungarian empire. The German nationalists were again pushing for *Anschluss*, the reunification of all ethnic Germans. Rumours had it that nationalist agents were flocking to Austria disguised as tourists, to incite ethnic pride among the locals. 'The situation in Austria is hopeless, but not serious',[1] quipped a man sitting at the next table. Joseph looked up from his notebook. His voice croaked as he repeated what had lately become his refrain, 'It's disgusting! Disgusting!'

Ah, if only things had gone differently! If only the handsome Austro-Hungarian cavalrymen, attired as if heading to a ball rather than to slaughter, had prevailed over the modern artilleries in the Great War! If only the old, ancient, venerable emperor Franz Joseph had lived into the hundreds! But no, all was lost. Their world had passed into the endless night of history, buried among the dead civilizations.

Even those who had mocked it for its slowness and stuffiness, as writer Robert Musil had done by calling it 'Kakania', had to admit that the empire had been the last oasis of peace in that new, murderous Twentieth Century. In the *halakhah*, the religious law of the Torah, twenty is the earliest age when a prisoner can be given a death sentence: but wasn't it death which awaited them and the whole of Europe? Gathered in that café, on the ground floor of a small hotel in the heart of Paris, the group of refugees felt as if they had been the first witnesses of the impending catastrophe.

Joseph looked like an old alcoholic, determined to kill himself one glass of Hennessy at a time. He mumbled and ranted against the new world order, against nationalism, against the desire of his age to bring everything to the efficiency of a well-oiled killing machine. In between drinks, however, it was clear to him that his self-destruction was not madness. It was only right that the orphans of the old world should follow it into oblivion. He was not going to leave much, apart from his writings. Money, he never had. No children. His wife, Friedl, languished in a mental asylum in Austria. He would not live long enough to see her meet her end. She would die alone, and so would he.

But his writing would live. He took another sip. Drinking gave him focus. The noise, the waiters, the chitchat about the *Anschluss* finally vanished. Time stops on the page. On the tip of his pen, it is still the golden age when Franz Joseph sits on the imperial throne, and all is well. The magical silence of the night sky still spreads over the Galician villages, near the Russian border, where the forest murmurs, the swamps resound with the croaking of frogs and the Jews follow without fear the rhythm of prayer and of the Sabbath. In the town barracks, the imperial officers are still leading the regular existence of a battery of clocks, albeit ones that have been synchronized on the wrong historical time. There is no incentive to seek innovation because everything is precisely as it should be: straight, round and edgeless, like a butter knife. The empire might have become geopolitically irrelevant, with 'ruinous sums of money spent on the army, but only just enough to secure its position as the second-weakest among the great powers'.[2] But its real strength has never been in the military: the essence of the empire is an atmosphere, where life feels possible even for those who are homeless in every land. Under Franz Joseph, even the Jews are protected from the violence that is unleashed against them in nearby countries.

To be sure, the old empire was not heaven – but what followed its fall was certainly hell.

A loud clamour suddenly erupted in the café. The waiters darted towards the door. Joseph leaned over his table, peeking at a throng of sharp suits flooding the entrance. Judging by how quickly they had monopolized the attention of the staff, they must be the entourage of someone important, that is, in that day and age, someone despicable. A whisper ran through the smoky air. Yes, it was a famous politician, one of those pushing for an alliance between the French and the German nationalists. 'It's disgusting!' Joseph cried, painfully raising himself on his feet. He stretched up his arm, waving, 'Waiter! Waiter! Why did you leave our table? To look after that bad politician? He's just a bad minister. Me, I am a good writer!'[3] Those around him roared with laughter, cheered on by the customers at the other tables.

Joseph won this one. A final, futile victory before the drunken intemperance of a Jew would be no longer possible, not even in Paris.

## 2.

Joseph Roth came from the edge of Europe, where the Ukrainian steppes begin their immense flow towards Russia and Asia. He was born in a small town, to a Jewish family of modest means.

When he was an infant, his father suffered severe mental illness and left home to join the cult of a thaumaturge Rabbi. Joseph grew up under the wing of an overbearing mother, having never met his father. For the rest of his life, he would not tire of inventing fictional versions of his family history, often introducing himself to new acquaintances as the illegitimate descendant of an Austrian aristocrat. He left home as soon as he could and spent the following years inching Westward, towards the capital of the Austro-Hungarian empire, Vienna. Despite being poor, he styled himself as a dandy. He attended classes dressed in the finest clothes, sported a monocle and carefully distanced himself from his peers. Yet, people were his true passion. He loved walking the busy streets, brushing against the variety of human types that animated the convulsive atmosphere of the city. He would walk for miles, before sitting at a café to write down his impressions. Those were the years of the *feuilletons*, when newspapers dedicated entire supplements to brilliant and often acerbic analyses of social life. Thus, Joseph became a journalist. His job took him to Berlin, where he witnessed the rise of National Socialism, and, from there, to Paris.

He could not see himself ever returning to his native town, with its inhabitants whose 'voice smells of onions'[4]. He had no intention of settling in the German-speaking lands, where life for an intellectual, let alone a Jew, had become impossible. He dreaded even the idea of owning a flat, preferring the freedom allowed by hotel rooms. But if there was one place in the world that felt like home, it was Paris. The French capital offered him the perfect combination of cosmopolitanism, anonymity and a hint of the Mediterranean spirit.

When travelling through the 'white cities' of Southern France, he remained enchanted by an atmosphere that reminded him of the dream of his lost homeland. The medieval towers of Avignon, the fishermen huts on the coast, the verdant marshes, the sun-bleached towns spoke of a long history in which Muslims, Jews, Christians, heretics, Europeans, North Africans and Roma people, despite centuries of conflict, had renounced drawing firm divisions between each other. The French Mediterranean offered the fugitive Joseph a glimpse of an existing alternative to the Northern obsession with purity. It was a land of beauty that had peacefully slipped out of the historical race for power – a world on its own, floating between the waves of the sea and the survival of an enchanted past, sheltered from the raging present. In France, far from his roots, Joseph felt as if he had entered a dimension aligned with his own radical foreignness. Without irony, he could say of himself: 'I am a European, a man of the Mediterranean if you will, a Roman and a Catholic, a Humanist and a Renaissance man.'[5]

## 3.

Like the 'Mediterranean', as we have explored it in this book, far exceeds its supposed geographic boundaries and transcends any stringent definition, so also Joseph Roth was irreducible to the limits of any exclusive identity. He was one of the greatest novelists of his century, the author of stylistic wonders like *The Radetzky March*, but earned his living working as a journalist. He was a Ukrainian who felt Parisian but identified as Austro-Hungarian. He was a lifelong socialist who yearned for the monarchy. He was a Jew who styled himself a Catholic. However, to say that he 'was' any of these things would be misleading. Before wearing an identity, he subjected it to the typical Mediterranean cure: cutting and stretching it beyond recognition until it fit his own existential narration.

His being Austro-Hungarian, for example, was more of a mythological trope than a definition: the lost empire, of which he wrote so lyrically, was a fairyland with only faint resemblances to actual history. It represented for him the idea of a realm sheltered by the sacral figure of the emperor from the nationalist violence of his present, a land where 'a lot of peoples might exist, but no nations'[6]. Speaking through one of the characters of *The Radetzky March*, he cried: 'How much longer, how much longer? This era no longer wants us! This era wants to create independent nation-states! People no longer believe in God. The new religion is nationalism.'[7] Yet, while the empire still stood, Joseph had not looked to the throne with unquestioning adoration. In his youth, he had been a fierce critic of the Austro-Hungarian government, of its classism and of its stiff, snobbish ruling class.

His Jewishness, too, oscillated with the rhythm of his moods. While depicting the Jewish characters of his fiction with profound empathy and continuing to oppose the antisemites in public, he saw no problem adopting antisemitic language in his own private correspondence. But it was his passion for Catholicism, above all, that betrayed his taste for mythological reinventions. For Joseph Roth, Catholicism was the accomplished form of Judaism, where the Jews' millenary statelessness took on the form of a magnificent cosmopolitanism.

His conversion to Catholicism – never quite completed, as he was not baptized – had little to do with spirituality. Like many professed Catholics, his inner disposition was rather towards atheism. In his novels, God was either indifferent to the plight of his creatures, or seemingly invested in procuring their suffering. Yet, Joseph also believed in miracles, and saw the ever-present chance of the miraculous breaking through the everyday as a force capable of rescuing even the most wretched lives.

In his being everything and nothing, a perennial foreigner to any fixed idea or identity, he kept himself at a hygienic distance from the abstract notions worshipped by his contemporaries, such as the ideas of race and nation. To the lust for political control, he opposed the ironic lightness of creative reinvention. He treated his own life, and the world around him, like he did his literature: with a quasi-magical ability to bring to life what was dead, and a desperate faith in the possibility of redeeming through narrative what could no longer be salvaged through action.

## 4.

'Alcohol created around him a partition behind which he could isolate himself and find the courage to resist. And resisting for him meant continuing to write. . . . He lived as long as he was able to write.'[8] Towards the end of his life, Joseph Roth was losing the ability to write. His last novella, the story of a drunken vagrant who found and squandered a large sum of money, he dictated to a friend sitting at a typewriter, while another friend at his side related it to him as a second-hand anecdote. A few weeks later, in May 1939, while the last spring of peace was blooming in the parks and squares of Europe, he died in a Parisian hospital.

The death of Joseph Roth, closely followed by the suicide of the writer Stefan Zweig, marked the final moment as the curtain fell on the late age of Austro-Hungarian literature. Despite the encroaching darkness, it had been a marvellous and scintillating season of culture. Its protagonists, like Roth and Zweig, had been mostly Jewish. The last generations of Austro-Hungarian Jews before the Holocaust counted writers like Elias Canetti, Franz Kafka, Karl Kraus, Leo Perutz and Arthur Schnitzler; musicians like Gustav Mahler and Arnold Schoenberg; philosophers like Martin Buber and Karl Popper; the psychoanalyst Sigmund Freud; and figures such as Hugo von Hofmannsthal and Ludwig Wittgenstein from the recently 'assimilated' Jewish families.

Across the vast territories of the Austro-Hungarian Empire, from the Adriatic Sea to the Russian border, the Jewish community consisted of small artisans and wealthy bankers, illiterate people and intellectuals, orthodox religious teachers and secular dandies. They spoke the language of the province where they lived, be it Polish or Bulgarian, they conversed with each other in Yiddish, and when they wished to use a literary tone, they wrote in the Austrian variant of German, with its taste for quirky wordplay. At home in many languages, they wrote and spoke as if always in translation.

Living in a multilingual empire profoundly affected their way of thinking. It led some, like Wittgenstein, to investigate the fundamental structures of language, and others, like Kraus, to lay bare the absurdity of media-speak and political communications. Among the writers, it gave rise to a literary style of unique grace and lightness. Hofmannsthal's dreamy verses, Roth's evocative descriptions, the dizzying spirals that drive the plots of the novels by Perutz and Lernet-Holenia showed a way of using language that did not aim to capture and exhaust its object. Mistaking the world for an orderly catalogue, where each thing was contained by a well-defined essence, was unworthy of a cultivated mind. To a historical age obsessed with 'actual facts' – behind which often hid the inventions of advertising and propaganda – the Austro-Hungarian writers responded by claiming that the value of an object did not consist in its 'actuality', but in its infinite 'possibilities'. Like those medieval theologians for whom every possibility eternally existed inside God's Mind, even though humans could only experience the few that were actualized, they challenged the idea of a fundamental difference between what was visible and what remained invisible.

In fact, 'three are one: the man, the thing, the dream'.[9] As in a dream, the characters of everyday life could seamlessly mutate into one another, or into multiple versions of themselves. None of these incarnations was absolutely true, nor false: since humans can approach the unfathomable mystery of reality only through the fictions produced by their imagination, then 'fiction' is the authentic metaphysical status of all worldly beings.

This metaphysical perspective went hand in hand with an ethical stance. While their contemporaries relished classifying things and people on the basis of their 'nature' – only to exploit or exterminate them accordingly – the Austro-Hungarian writers showed that everything that existed deserved the awe-filled respect that is owed to the whole of reality. Nothing and no one should be glorified or vilified based on a single aspect of its existence because every being contains within itself the infinite sum of all possibilities.

> If there is a sense of reality, and no one will doubt that it has its justification for existing, then there must also be something we can call a sense of possibility. Whoever has it does not say, for instance: Here this or that has happened, will happen, must happen; but he invents: Here this or that might, could, or ought to happen. If he is told that something is the way it is, he will think: Well, it could probably just as well be otherwise. So the sense of possibility could be defined outright as the ability to conceive of everything there might be just as well, and to attach no more importance to what is than to what is not. The consequences of so creative a disposition can be remarkable, and may, regrettably, often make what people admire seem wrong, and what is taboo permissible, or, also, make both a matter of indifference.[10]

The late Austro-Hungarian writers and intellectuals adopted the same cross-eyed gaze towards the world, which for millennia had characterized the Mediterranean imagination: a gaze that was able to grasp at the same time the uniqueness of each being, the limitless range of its possible metamorphoses, and the invisible thread that connects all existents, like pearls in an infinite necklace.

## 5.

When the Austro-Hungarian Empire was finally shipwrecked, its enormous body did not sink all at once. Tongues of St. Elmo's fire shot from its half-submerged extremities, taking form in the stories, the images and the atmospheres produced by its orphaned writers. It was the afterglow of nostalgia, which often recreates the contours of a vanished world.

The term 'nostalgia', however, does not do justice to the depth of this phenomenon. No two forms of nostalgia are ever the same, just as no two pains can ever be identical. At the very least, it is possible to distinguish between two different kinds of nostalgia – and in one of them, we can locate the Mediterranean spirit animating the late Austro-Hungarian writers.

Nostalgia can be a project or a projection.

In its mode as a project, the longing for a lost world turns into a plan of action for its re-establishment in the present. The past must be brought back in a material form, even at the cost of amputating the present (and its inhabitants) of any parts that do not fit on its Procrustean bed. This kind of nostalgia is ashamed of its own imaginary aspects and thus endeavours to turn them as soon as possible into actual reality. This is the form of nostalgia shared by political conservatives of every time and every nation.

On the other hand, when nostalgia is nurtured as a projection, the idea of materializing the past into the present appears not only superfluous but a step backward. With the disappearance of its material body, a lost world sheds the iniquities and the strictures that plagued it while it was still historically present. Once it turns into a dream, unshackled from its former connections with actual reality, it is no longer able to control its inhabitants with the rules and the beliefs that used to govern its society. It becomes a blank screen, ready to support the projection of fantasies that are more in tune with one's own ethical sensibility. Thus, in Joseph Roth's reinvention, the old empire lost its ingrained discriminations and its antisemitism to become a place of cosmic harmony. For Leo Perutz, it turned into a place where the magic forces of reality made themselves palpable. For Lernet-Holenia, it was a looping machine where space curved steeply, and time was suspended. For Werfel and Zweig, it represented a realm of pacified life and glamorous cosmopolitanism. None of them ever seriously thought of acting upon their fantasies to make the empire 'great again', as is typically the case with political conservatives.

When nostalgia takes the form of a projection, the disappearance of the past is not experienced as a moment of annihilation: although the old world has gone out of the realm of the visible, it has not fallen out of existence. The grief that one feels is authentic, but there is no reason to deduce from it that what once existed is now irretrievably lost. What we call 'death' is only a matter of perspective. Imagination is truly able to grant a new, immaterial life to the past, and art and literature suffice as its material reincarnations in the present.

This kind of nostalgia is a lens that reveals the analogic links weaving the fabric of reality. The ability of a melody, or a scent, or a weather pattern to superimpose the immateriality of the past onto the material substance of the present is not the trick of a hallucination, but a revelation of the equal metaphysical status of different dimensions of existence.

Nostalgia validated the intuition of the late Austro-Hungarian writers, exiles of a lost world and migrants across time, that many worlds exist simultaneously – and that the one socially dominant during a historical era is in no way more real than the others, rooted in the immateriality of dreams.

## 6.

But what if things had really gone differently? What if the old empire had not fallen? A swerve in the flow of the events of the Great War could have easily steered history in an altogether different direction. Let us imagine, for example, that an Austro-Hungarian engineer, while surveying the mountain tunnels on the border with the kingdom of Italy, had discovered a passage that, if sufficiently extended, allowed the Habsburg army to launch a surprise attack behind the Italian lines. By 1916, shortly after Italy entered the war, the Austro-Hungarian troops could have enacted this plan, obtaining a decisive victory. At the same time, it is reasonable to imagine that the German army, by far the most advanced at that time, could have found a way to penetrate the French lines, bringing the war on the Western front to a swift resolution.

With most of Europe under the control of the German and Austro-Hungarian empires, the impetus to continue the war would have faded quickly. The conquered areas, treated with leniency and preserved from unnecessary violence, would have fraternized with the occupiers, and these, in turn, satisfied with their accomplishments, would have clamoured for demobilization. The British Empire, struggling to keep its hold on its colonies, would have had no other choice but to accept an armistice.

In this scenario, by 1917, Europe was again at peace. Rather than issuing requests for reparations, the German Chancellor Walther Rathenau, heir to a Jewish family of industrialists, offered the defeated nations the possibility of joining together with the victors in the creation of a new, Europe-wide political entity: the Union of the Western Socialist Nations. France, Germany,

Austria and Italy would unite as a confederation run on socialist principles and aligned with the parallel efforts of 'our friend' Lenin in Russia. The success of this experiment, as compared with the Russian revolution, would be measured by the level of the workers' participation in the political and economic decisions that affected their lives. Internationalist socialism stemmed the perilous growth of nationalist movements and brought about the peaceful dismantling of the colonial possessions of the European nations across the planet.

Such radical transformations were inevitably going to arouse the opposition of the political conservatives. But the attempts of the German right to overthrow the socialist government could not prevail against the resistance of the organized workers, aided by the regular troops.

In the autumn of 1918 – while, in a parallel world, Europe was emerging from the Great War only to sink into a period of turmoil and totalitarianism – we can imagine the protagonist of this story, the engineer who first devised the idea of digging a tunnel between Austro-Hungary and Italy, sitting on a train on his way back from a visit to a nearby town. During the journey, he made the acquaintance of a man in his twenties, a certain Adolf Hitler. The young man declared himself satisfied at how the German people had fulfilled their 'destiny' by taking over Europe. Unencumbered by the urge to defend German supremacy, he felt free to pursue his true passion: painting.

Cured from its nationalisms, safe from the interference of the United States, and in good relations with revolutionary Russia, this version of Europe continued its *belle epoque* with a spirit of lightness and optimism unmatched in any century.

## 7.

The gates leading to this alternative Europe open in the pages of a unique novel, 'Contro-Passato Prossimo' (Near Counter-Past), found in the 1970s among the papers of the Italian author Guido Morselli. Drily written, like a bureaucratic record of recent events, the novel is not just a divertissement in uchronic literature. It is a polemic against the predominant idea of history as a linear succession of unavoidable facts, and of unactualized possibilities as non-existent fantasies. Keen to reveal the aim of his work, Morselli interrupts the flow of the narrative midway through the book, adding a fictitious conversation between himself and an editor, who is unconvinced by his project.

> *Editor*: It is well known that one should never put history on trial, rewriting it. You are venturing into a forbidden enterprise. How do you defend yourself?
> *Author*: My defense stems from a premise that . . . in philosophical jargon is called nominalism, and for which, in this case, one does not believe in History, as one does not believe in Society. There are only individual events (and) unique individuals, who put their (own) history on trial every morning, in front of the mirror. Otherwise, living would be for them nothing more than a stupid repetition of mistakes. In our daily experience, the alternative to the past . . . takes a quasi-necessity of its own. . . . I would like to make a contribution to the neglected, and indeed proscribed, critique *to* history.[11]

For Morselli, as for the late Austro-Hungarian writers, inventing a better past was not only possible but necessary. If the future can be shaped only by the powerful – so that, in the future, 'the strong do what they can and the weak suffer what they must'[12] – the past instead offers areas of intervention also to the meek and the dispossessed. As with nostalgia, the experience of powerlessness and defeat – the roots of the Mediterranean imagination – discloses a fundamental revelation about the sprawling nature of reality and about the coexistence of the visible world with worlds that never 'actually' were.

As rewritten by the imagination, the past is freed from its confinement within history. It is no longer a dead weight, conditioning the life of its inheritors, but it becomes an opportunity to reinvent one's own origin, identity and destiny, just like Joseph Roth had done with his own biography. The ability to act, too, is no longer limited to one's immediate proximities in the material realm, but it extends to all imaginable dimensions beyond the actual present.

This 'forbidden enterprise', as Morselli's interlocutor puts it, appears unreasonable only to those who happened to be born on the winning side of history. But for the foreigners, the exiles and the misplaced in every land, like the protagonists of our Mediterranean journey so far, reinventing one's own past can be essential for one's survival within a hostile environment.

The same cannot be said, unfortunately, in the case of Morselli's own life. Even the forces of imagination could not stem his sense of despair at feeling utterly inadequate to the present. Having received the umpteenth rejection from the publishing houses to which he had submitted his works, Morselli committed suicide in 1973.

What had remained beyond his grasp during his lifetime, however, came easily to him after the end of his material existence. Just one year after his death, his books were sent to press by the Italian publishing house *Adelphi*, gaining instant success, establishing Morselli as a key contemporary author, and fuelling a debate over the potential of 'fantastic' literature to open new perspectives on the 'real' world.

As he had predicted in the fictitious dialogue with the editor, his works also attracted the criticism of those who distrusted any attempt at rewriting history or transcending actuality. But such criticism was directed, more broadly, to the entire editorial project of the publishing house that had championed his work, *Adelphi*. *Adelphi*'s catalogue privileged the realm of possibility over that of facts, and it took pride in distancing itself from the din of the present to be better attuned to the silence that lies beneath the foundations of language. Accused of irrationalism and escapism, *Adelphi* became a symbol of the desire to resist the spirit of the age, and a sanctuary for the survival of the Mediterranean imagination during the harsh winter of the Twentieth Century.

## 8.

After twenty years of fascist dictatorship, involvement in the Holocaust and a catastrophic defeat in the Second World War, Italy entered the second half of the Twentieth Century teetering over a fault line in the new global order. The country stood at the meeting point between the Communist East, the post-colonial

Arab world and the bloc of Western states under American control. The Italian Christian Democratic Party, backed by the United States and the Vatican, kept in check the Italian Communist Party, the largest in Europe and a solid interlocutor of the Soviet Union. Between the 1950s and the 1980s, Italian politics were shaken by attempts at military coups d'etat, explosions of fascist terrorism and a creeping war between the state and the revolutionary movements of the extreme left. Politics took over the life and imagination of the Italian people to a degree unseen since the time of the Medieval communal republics. Before engaging in any aspect of daily life, whether work, community, religion or culture, individuals were expected, if not demanded, to declare their political position – where being 'political' meant subscribing to a precise ideology and belonging to a well-defined social collective.

The publishing industry was no exception. The promotion of an author or the decision to explore a topic from a particular angle were interpreted as political statements, and even the largest presses felt compelled to ponder the political implications of their every choice. A case in point was the prestigious Turin-based publisher *Einaudi*, whose editorial team included intellectuals of the calibre of Italo Calvino and Cesare Pavese. *Einaudi*'s list was carefully selected, not only to include the best of literature and philosophy but primarily to educate the readers in the 'orthodox' ideological positions of the left-wing of the day. At *Einaudi* worked the visionary Jewish editor Luciano Foà, whose main task was the acquisition of new authors and titles. At the beginning of the 1960s, Foà proposed commissioning the first complete critical edition of the works of Friedrich Nietzsche. For too long, he argued, the German philosopher had been appropriated by the far right, based on the edition of his works produced by his Nazi-sympathizing sister, Elizabeth. It was time to rescue Nietzsche's thought and to return it to its authenticity. His proposal was coldly rejected by *Einaudi*'s board. Nietzsche was certainly an important thinker, the board replied, but publishing such a politically compromised author would send the wrong signal to *Einaudi*'s readership. Frustrated by these ideological strictures, Foà resigned from his position and decided to invest his energies in opening a new window in the stuffy environment of Italian publishing. He called upon the help of his friend Roberto Bazlen, an extravagant character from the old Austro-Hungarian city of Trieste, a voracious reader and writer without oeuvre, the discoverer of such authors as Italo Svevo. Together, they would create a new publishing house dedicated exclusively to those 'unique' books where an author's direct experience of the primordial forces of reality emerges in its 'first-timeness' (*primavoltità*). Their catalogue would not be an educational syllabus, but a polyphony of kindred voices from any place and any century, finally reunited under one paper roof.

They gathered a cohort of professional readers versed in the most disparate languages, who could advise them on forgotten gems, and they sought the financial support of the socialist-leaning industrialist Olivetti family. To help with the selection of texts, they also hired the 21-year-old Roberto Calasso, the son of a famous anti-fascist jurist, who in due course would become the public face of the publishing house.

Thus, in 1962, the Italian book market saw the arrival of *Adelphi*, one of the most legendary publishers of the century, the inheritor of the borderless tradition of the Mediterranean imagination, 'which arises and develops in contrast to the demands of the surrounding environment, asserts itself only in a deserted world, in the dark night of the soul: the stronger the pressure, the more solid becomes the matter that opposes it'.[13]

## 9.

A publishing house can be many things: economic enterprise, political project, educational mission, vanity outlet. But it is rarely the case that it can only be described as a family of books. In the case of *Adelphi* (a variation on the Greek term for 'siblings', *adelphoi/ai*), only a sense of familiarity held together a catalogue spanning from scientific literature to ancient poetry, from obscure mystical texts to the latest literary experimentations. *Adelphi* was conceived as a library in the style of Aby Warburg, where the reader would inevitably end up picking, not the book they had originally looked for, but the title next to it, following an invisible link between them.

The titles selected by Foà, Bazlen and Calasso traced an unpredictable path between genres, authors, historical eras and geographical areas, proposing the practice of reading as a daring adventure into the uncharted territories of the mind. This ambition was already expressed by the logo chosen for the publishing house: the early Chinese character for 'new moon', with two stylized figures standing on a graphic sign resembling a boat or a smile.

To such an editorial venture, the legacy of the late Austro-Hungarian writers could not remain indifferent. From the beginning, authors like Roth, Zweig, Holenia and Perutz, not to mention von Hofmannsthal, Krauss and Kafka, constituted the backbone of the publishing project. Through their pages, creative nostalgia projected the gleams of an imaginary world that, like that of myth, 'never actually existed, yet is always'[14]. Alongside these exiles from history, the *Adelphi* catalogue hosted some of the most radical champions of the imagination, from Nietzsche, through Jorge Luis Borges, to the Italian scholar and poet Cristina Campo.

In her minuscule literary production, Campo – who said of herself, 'I have written little, and I wish I had written less' – encapsulated the very spirit of *Adelphi*. With her delicately hypnotic tone, where precision took on a lyrical quality, Campo unravelled the imaginary fabric with which human cultures, since time immemorial, have clothed the *chaos* of reality, forming it into a liveable *cosmos*. In her hands, the patterns on an Iranian carpet, the musical scales of a flute, the symbolism of a fairy tale, or the movements of a religious liturgy, revealed themselves as links connecting the ineffable realm to the familiar intricacies of the visible world. Each visual pattern opened the way to the invisible, each sound to silence, each letter to the ineffable – and vice versa. The highest products of human culture were not the most monumental, but those that, like tightrope-walkers, proceeded through the centuries with one eye intent on inventing the path ahead and the other fixed on the abyss below.

Guided by Campo, the reader could venture through the history of human culture as if through a marsh, where islets of language emerged from the dark waters of reality and the imagination blossomed in all its dazzling colours. A realm without borders, where identities cyclically sunk and resurfaced, and every lifeform unfolded a time and a history of its own: an ethereal Mediterranean, whose contours were constantly reshaped by the flow of invisible existential currents.

## 10.

Why are we venturing through this bookish dust when we set out to describe the latest adventures of the Mediterranean imagination? Are editors, writers and scholars really the best that we can find to carry on the torch that not long ago we saw brandished by pirates and revolutionaries? This retreat into the written page, reminiscent of the silent labour of the Medieval translators, is a reflection of the atmosphere of the age of Late Modernity.

So far, most of the protagonists of our Mediterranean journey have tried to escape their historical defeat either by physically fleeing their society – as did the renegades who deserted to the pirate states of the Barbary Coast – or by disconnecting their imagination from the idea of 'reality' held by their contemporaries – as did the Gnostics, Pagans and Manichaeans of Late Antiquity. Despite the risks and personal sacrifices that such radical migrations always involve, they could count on the fact that the societies of the time still lacked the technological means to exert total control over the lives and thoughts of individuals. With the advent of Late Modernity, the development of technology brought about a dramatic expansion in the possibilities of subjugation.

A first taste of this new scenario was offered by the totalitarian regimes of the early Twentieth Century, with their systems of total policing. Yet, as noted by the intellectual Pier Paolo Pasolini, despite their murderous brutality, totalitarian regimes had to settle merely for public displays of obedience to their commands. Their formidable claws were still unable to penetrate the hard kernel of the imagination of their subjects. Things changed, Pasolini continued, with the explosion of new forms of communication, from the first televisions to the omnipresence of the 'society of the spectacle'. By the last quarter of the century, the dominant powers in society were able not only to control external behaviours but also to instil effective forms of self-policing within their subjects. What used to be simple propaganda developed instead into the silent transformation of individual souls, while the laughable spectacle of totalitarian parades turned into the spontaneous processions of self-exploiting workers and consumers.

Thus, in the contemporary age, the pale sun of Late Modernity shines over a twofold struggle for autonomy: the fight to preserve the possibility of socially deviant behaviours (including one's active rebellion against perceived injustices), and the challenge to decolonize one's interiority from the socially dominant ideas, assumptions and diktats that pervade every person's sense of self and reality.

Hence, the renewed importance of writers, scholars and editors for the survival of the anarchic tradition of the Mediterranean imagination. Protected by harmless labels such as 'literature' or 'philosophy', the space of the page offers room for those alchemical operations through which an individual can still transform their historical powerlessness into fertile soil for the sprouting of new worlds.

This liberation struggle proceeds often invisibly, like a battle fought in a network of tunnels. It is an endless work of sabotage, carried out under the auspices of Harpocrates, the child-god of secrets who once protected the Mediterranean people of the Hellenistic era. Now as then, the inhabitants of Late Modernity are rediscovering the ancient art of concealment and dissimulation. Beneath a world saturated by the howling of police sirens, emails and advertising, the Mediterranean tradition continues to excavate its subterranean refuges, where nothing has yet been decided about what is permissible or inadmissible to be, think and do. There, in the suspended atmosphere of this network of tunnels, the waters of the Mediterranean are resurfacing, forming new swamps of language and ineffability, creating the only possible habitat for the wild flowering of the imagination.

## 11.

But it can hardly be satisfying to look at these writers' work from afar, nor can a purely academic gaze give us a sense of the spirit and atmosphere that animated the *milieu* of *Adelphi* and of Cristina Campo. Would it not be better to meet them and speak with them directly, even if doing so required us to shed some of our disbelief and plunge within a fiction of our own, as if into a dream? Thus, let us place our own hands, now, in those of Cristina Campo, and ask her to lead us into these secret corridors of the imagination. She does not immediately respond to our plea but takes one of her books, opens it on a random page and points to a line. She runs her fingertip along the letters, until resting it on the black circumference of a letter 'o', apparently identical to any other. As we fix our gaze into its gaping roundness, a breeze laden with the scent of water and earth envelops us. In the span of an instant, we are plunged into the cool air of a subterranean space. We stagger forward, running our hands along the damp earthen walls, looking for the reassuring presence of our guide. Small clusters of people emerge from the twilight, engrossed in a ceaseless murmur that fades into the low tunnel ceiling. Cristina takes us towards them. The distance between the groups is but a few steps, yet they look at each other with suspicion. This underground gathering does not give the sense of an organized movement, but rather a crowd of survivors after a shipwreck, feverishly intent on discussing their next move. We approach four men steeped in conversation, whom Cristina seems to know well. One of them, dressed in a white suit like an old English traveller, is in fact her life partner, Elemire Zolla. The others exude a slightly contrived aura of mystery, reminiscent of itinerant gurus. There is Ananda Coomaraswamy, the Hindu art historian, whose dark, slanted eyes impart an impression of melancholia, and René Guénon, the French/Egyptian Muslim mystic, nervously stroking his thin moustache. Standing by their side is the Swiss Sufi Frithjof Schuon, with his hands clasped and his white beard resting softly on an amber-coloured scarf.

'These are the Perennialists – Campo informs us – the explorers of the tradition common to all cultures.'

'Which tradition?' we dare to ask.

Schuon steps forward, and in a slow, measured voice, begins to explain how a single core lies at the heart of all great religions. 'It is a silent core, beyond any possible definition. Whoever calls it "God" is still far from grasping its essence, and only the mystic, who no longer uses their tongue to speak, can taste its flavour. All religious traditions hint at this ineffable One, which is the source of everything existing and the cradle of every possibility. But when the One reveals itself – Schuon adds arching his eyebrows and raising a finger – it manifests in different ways, to suit the sensibility of each culture. That is how religions are born, as the different glimmers of one invisible light. That is also how every creature acquires their individual soul, as the refraction of a single, indivisible soul. These outer differences must be respected, as divine manifestations, but without ever forgetting, mind you!, that only the One is the true substance of reality. This is the meaning of "esotericism".'

'And the origin of syncretism', interjects Elemire Zolla.

'That's precisely what Modernity has forgotten', interrupts Ananda Coomarswamy, adjusting the folds of his dress over his shoulders. 'Nowadays the world is in the hands of the secularists, who believe that reality is as small as the range of their measuring machines, or of the bigots, who stick to a literal understanding of the religious revelations. Both are blind to the ineffable dimension. Hence, they have no qualms about destroying sacred symbols which they do not understand, taking them for superstitions or for the products of a "foreign" tradition.'

'There is only one tradition!' René Guénon bursts out, his eyes darting like a bird of prey. 'But this age, this "reign of quantity" – he hisses – cannot understand how something can be at the same time one and many, unitary in its essence yet multiple in its manifestations. This confusion, which contemporary societies use to denigrate any form of mysticism, they call it "order". Yet it is a higher, eternal order that we should seek instead.'

'Like the sacred order reflected in the caste system in India?' asks Elemire Zolla.

'Precisely', Guenon replies, and at that moment Cristina Campo pulls us brusquely by the arm, leading us away. It seems that she does not want us to witness the most disquieting aspect of Perennialist discourse – when nostalgia for a pre-Modern past veers towards grotesquely hyper-conservative positions, like violent fantasies acting out a sense of frustration.

'Let us join those people instead', Cristina suggests, taking us forward along the corridor. We approach another group, much larger and livelier than the first, standing near a verdant patch of aquatic vegetation.

## 12.

A tall woman with a wavy blonde bob stands at the centre of the group. She carries herself with an air of royalty, though the tips of her fingers are stained with remnants of ink and paint. She is an artist, clearly, but Cristina tells us that it is not her art that has drawn the others around her. This is Olga Fröbe-Kapteyn, the daughter of a Dutch feminist and an inventor. For three decades, her house in the Swiss town of Ascona, near Monte Verità, sailed through the storms of the Twentieth Century like a flying castle, where the remnants of the Mediterranean tradition could find some respite from the horrors of the age. A galaxy of scholars, versed in the most arcane aspects of the history of the imagination, travelled from far and wide to join her yearly summit of *Eranos*, the 'banquet'. Now, in this subterranean refuge, they are once again with her, as they used to be when they were still alive. Death counts for nothing here, where time is just another plant sprouting from the mud. Carl Gustav Jung, the explorer of the archetypes of the human psyche, and Joseph Campbell, the geographer of the mythological imagination, stand by her sides. Her company also includes Toshihiko Izutsu, the Japanese scholar of Sufism and Taoism, Gershom Scholem, the historian of Jewish mysticism, Walter Otto, the German philologist enamoured with Greek Paganism, and many others. Their chattering voices interweave seamlessly, like the steps of a well-practiced company of dancers. Olga begins, describing an image: a Buddhist mandala, perhaps, or the rose window in a Christian church, or the snake in Hopi art. The others riff on this theme, each bringing examples from all kinds of artistic practice, including the plastic art of one's own dreams. No image is too obscure or too obscene to be passionately examined through the lenses of symbolism, philosophy, theology, literature and psychology. As they play on, a mineral gleam emanates from the dark green of the moss and leaves growing around them.

A moment of silence ensues while the speakers catch their breath. We remain silent too, as does Cristina at our side. Almost imperceptibly, a voice breaks the stillness – a member of the group who has remained quiet until now. A pair of thick square glasses frames his round face, and his hair is neatly parted on one side. His name is Henry Corbin, and out there, back in the Twentieth Century, he was one of the foremost scholars of Shia mysticism. He smiles politely, pointing out that the conversation has only touched the appearance of symbolic images, but not what they are or where they exist.

'But of course – Jung interjects – they are the archetypal features of the collective psyche, which live in the mind of every human being.'

'As they do in the mythology of each culture, albeit under different guises', reinforces Campbell.

'Yes, we meet them in our mind, but why confine them there?' objects Corbin. 'I believe – he continues – that symbols like the "cosmic mountain", which is the prototype of all sacred buildings, or the invisible cities that guide the quest of mythical heroes, truly exist somewhere beyond our mind.'

'How can we find them?' asks Olga excitedly.

'They are right here, with us, right now – Corbin replies – even though they are invisible to our normal state of consciousness. Reality is much wider than it appears. It has a material aspect, accessible to our regular sensorial perceptions and to the measurements of our rational mind. And it has an ineffable dimension, the dimension of the "Godhead", which is accessible only to the mystic; and even then, only faintly. But in between these two, in between language and silence, visibility and invisibility, there is another dimension: I call it *Mundus Imaginalis*, the world of the imagination. That is where symbols truly exist and truly live. They are a bridge and a barrier between the dimensions of Reality.'

'Like dreams connect and separate the different part of the psyche?' intervenes James Hillman, who so far has nodded to everything Jung said.

'Yes – Corbin responds – but I wouldn't call them dreams. "Angels" would be a better definition. When they are not low fantasies, or tricks concocted by social powers, the figures of our imagination are angelic presences that come to visit us from the *Mundus Imaginalis*.'

As he says so, a surge of light dissipates the twilight of the tunnel, and faint shapes suddenly appear moving between its curves. Are these the angels of whom Corbin is talking about? Among them, we recognize a few of the people we have met before, in the earlier stages of our Mediterranean journey. Was it perhaps always the *Mundus Imaginalis*, the ultimate destination of the protagonists of our story, who abandoned their world in search of that 'elsewhere' from which all possible worlds spring?

While we are entranced in contemplating the wonders evoked by Corbin, Cristina Campo gently touches our shoulder.

'We should move on – she says – there is another person I want you to meet.'

## 13.

We stop in front of a short man with a round forehead extended by baldness. His narrow eyes are surrounded by deep dark circles, bestowing a charismatic force to his severe stares. He is dressed formally in a shirt and a dark suit.

This is Roberto Calasso, says Cristina, one of the driving forces of *Adelphi*. Most of the authors we have just met had their works on the imagination published in his collection of 'unique' books.

Calasso imparts the slightest stretch to his thin lips. 'Who do I have the pleasure to meet?' he asks with brusque politeness.

'We come here from very far away – we respond a little taken aback – indeed our journey started millions of years ago, when the waters of the Atlantic Ocean first flooded the dry Mediterranean basin. We have travelled following the traces left by the champions of the Mediterranean Imagination: not those celebrated by history books as the founders of civilisations, but the exiles and the migrants who had to find a way out of the societies of their time. Our companions have been those who answered the question "what can be done, when nothing can be done?" by reinventing entirely the substance of the world. Finally, we have ended up down here, in this labyrinth.'

'I don't know who you met so far – says Calasso in his gravelly voice – but I must agree with them that society itself is the first catastrophe. It gives us the illusion of having mapped out the whole of reality and trapped its primordial forces within the cage of our conventions. It makes us forget the eternal, ineffable *Chaos* that stretches all around our linguistic fortifications. But *Chaos* cannot be dispelled, because it is the essence of what we are, of our awareness, of everything existing. The more we deny its existence, the more it returns to haunt us in devastating forms. Isn't it precisely what is happening out there?' he says, nodding upwards, to the dripping ceiling of the tunnel.

'We haven't been out there yet, in the Twenty-first Century – we respond – but if it is anything like the continuation of the Twentieth.'

'It is the continuation of an age of forgetfulness that started long ago – Calasso interjects – and that cyclically returns throughout history. You see, whenever a society neglects to maintain a relationship with the immeasurable, indistinct, "continuous" dimension of reality, sooner or later it begins to take its own conventions as absolute laws. And it enforces them as such, superstitiously and murderously. That is why I published and wrote so much on the "analogic" techniques that ensure the preservation of this relationship with Chaos: mythology, rituals, but above all, sacrifice.'

We shift on our feet uneasily on the ground. 'But certainly – we dare to object – sacrifice is a blood ritual that is best left to more archaic times.'

Calasso shakes his head. 'And then what happens? It is substituted by extermination. Anything that does not fit within a society's perception of reality is cleansed and exterminated. But sacrifice does the opposite: by ritualising destruction, loss, impermanence, it reminds us that there is an infinite elsewhere, beyond the limits of the visible, and it offers our awareness of this excess as a gift to this realm, which we can only call "divine". Without this sense of the sacred, society will always try to confirm its total dominion over reality by amputating itself of anything that might remind it of its own limitations: the impure, the non-conforming, the monsters. I believe that these include the people who have accompanied you through your journey.'

'Yes, they were certainly considered as such by – '

Suddenly, a loud crash, like the sound of falling rocks, breaks through the tunnels, covering our words. We jump towards the wall, instinctively taking shelter. Cristina and Calasso have not flinched. They stare at us impassively, a little amused by our reaction. They have nothing to fear, having already died to the physical world out there. Our eyes move around rapidly. We are still bound to the emotional life of matter.

Another rumbling shakes the floor beneath our feet, like the tremor that announces the crashing of an immense wave. Water begins to seep through the ceiling, soaking the earthen walls, pulling them down in rivulets of mud. The twilight fills with menacing glints, shimmering over the streams that are rapidly covering the ground. The soil beneath us becomes unstable, sticky, treacherous.

'Death reunites the separate parts to the eternal unity' continues Calasso with a sinister tone, but his voice fades behind us as we run desperately through the corridors.

## 14.

Lumps of earth start falling from the ceiling, doubling the darkness. We sink ankle-deep into the mud, no longer knowing the direction. We run like prey, colliding with the walls without feeling pain, stumbling and getting back up. The darkness is now almost total – except for a flicker of light, appearing and disappearing each time we fall. We chase it stubbornly, like the mirage of a lifeboat. Panic disintegrates our vision into a swirl of images, but our legs keep churning, pushing forward. We run as if in a dream, while the roaring waters and the booms of collapsing tunnels pile onto each other in a chorus of crashes.

Everything goes blank, and we find ourselves face down on the earth, exhausted. We keep perfectly still, incredulous that death might have really failed to catch us. An indefinite span of time passes while our panting recedes, and we slowly return to our senses.

It is bright. Brighter than we can bear, having just emerged from the earth. The mouth of the tunnel is behind us, obstructed by an avalanche of mud. Our fingers feel the dryness of the ground. An echo of waves still rings in our ears. Through the narrow opening of our eyelids, we catch flashes of a white beach, shrubs, a stormy sea. A fisherman's hut is nearby, topped with aerials flapping black plastic bags in the wind to scare off the seagulls. The salty air has the density to which we were used, when we were still out there, in the physical world. We are back. This is the Twenty-First Century.

Marine waste, seaweed, broken shells, filaments of fishing nets litter the beach. A powerful wave reaches as far as us, throwing something over our face which feels like a wet rag. We pull it away; it is a t-shirt, ripped and stained with blood. Someone is wailing with high, monotonous cries. We shield our eyes from the light, scanning the horizon. A few metres from the shore, an old man, perhaps the owner of the fisherman's hut, is standing in the water, submerged up to his chest. He is frantically turning this way and that, pushing against the wind to try to reach an object that floats inertly. When he finally grabs it, he pulls it towards himself with both hands, struggling to hold his balance among the currents. He sobs, in between curses and invocations. As he reaches the beach, we recognize his macabre load. A drowned woman, her head still wrapped in a hijab. He places her gently on the sand, then rushes back to recover something else from the water. He carries it back in his arms, small as the child is. Drowned. Squinting through the sunlight, we see that the expanse of the sea is covered with the debris of a shipwreck. Pieces of wood, clothes, shards of plastic. The round shapes of human bodies surface and disappear like the backs of sea creatures.

## 15.

When the coast guard arrives, a few survivors have also reached the beach. They scream the names of those who have not resurfaced, begging in broken English for someone to help them. The ambulances come jolting off the road down the cliffs onto the sand, nurses and doctors rushing out from their doors. The piercing sound of sirens announces the first police vehicles. The officers remain a few steps away from the rescue teams, perhaps aware that the labour of care and that of repression should never mix. Whenever an ambulance departs from the beach, however, a police car goes in its wake. We ask a nurse what is happening, and she tells us in a whisper that the survivors will be temporarily held in a hospital, then they will be transferred to the detention centre for illegal migrants – an overcrowded cage of concrete and steel, a few miles inland from the coast. There they will be interrogated, identified, their mugshots taken and there they will be held indefinitely while their request for asylum is being processed. Those considered to be economic migrants will be moved on to other centres, where they will be detained until the date of their deportation. Only the dead, encased within their coffins, will not be treated like criminals.

We watch another ambulance steer through the sandy dunes and disappear over the cliff onto the road. Behind us, the waves continue to hurl debris onto the sand, while the undertow keeps pulling it back, as if competing in a relentless game to be the first to reduce matter to its finest grain. The old man now walks slowly among the bodies, crouching from time to time to close their eyelids. Heavy banks of phosphorescent clouds are approaching from the horizon, driven by the wind, filling the sky. The storm at sea seems to be calling upon its sibling in the sky to wash away the products of its destruction. By the time the first thunder breaks, however, there is nothing left for the rain to wash away, apart from the scattered remnants of the sunken boat. The authorities have already removed from the beach the living and the dead, as if to hide the evidence of a crime in which they feel complicit.

We walk up the cliff, while a deep sense of powerlessness pervades and numbs us. We hug the margin of the road, while cars speed past us, honking; the sounds of the sea and storm grow fainter as they recede into the distance. The detention centre is somewhere ahead of us, at the end of this road.

## 16.

The road snakes between potholes and landslides, cutting through cultivated fields and clusters of half-finished houses, where the elderly gather under the large neon signs of the bars. We march on mechanically, pushing away the images of the shipwreck, the bodies lying on the beach, the survivors kneeling in the sand. The storm clouds have disappeared from the sky, and for a long expanse, nothing surrounds us but the steady hum of the cars whizzing past. Yet, as we walk alone towards the migrant detention centre, a slight change in the atmosphere gives us the feeling that some invisible presence has started to accompany us along the way.

Although we see no one around us, we feel pervaded by that sense of familiarity that we once experienced in the company of the itinerant Medieval translators. It is almost as if they were back with us, here, on the course of their eternal migrations. The dark rumblings of the Gnostics, with their nightmarish visions and infinite longing, too, seem to resound near us. When our feet hit the ground, we hear them thumping in unison with those of Cabeza de Vaca, the survivor of another shipwreck in another foreign land. Even the faint silhouette of Joseph Roth, bent on his walking stick, seems to appear at times as a shadow over the road. We would not be surprised if Dat al-Himma and Digenis Akritas were galloping among the cars.

As we trudge through the semi-urbanized countryside, we feel closer to us than ever the presence of a secret network of alliances against any attempt at imprisoning and subjugating existence. Voices from the past mix in our memory with the screams we have just heard on the beach, as if those who once chanted mythological stories to exorcize the fate of *lullu*, the human machine, were still the same who mourn the tragedies of our times.

Now, on the tracks of ambulances and police cars, we no longer ask ourselves what new dreams and fantasies might await us at the next stop of our journey. We are walking towards the detention centre simply because we carry within ourselves something that belongs among the survivors of today's shipwrecks, trapped there like ashes caught in a chimney. Town after town, along the scarred landscape of the contemporary Mediterranean, we carry with us the last spark of a tradition of which we have been, so far, merely the witnesses. We are bringing it where it will continue to grow: among the undocumented migrants who resist identification, among those who are foreigners to every land.

A bifurcation splits the road ahead of us. The cars follow the green road signs, flowing towards the entrance to the highway, but we turn to the narrow sideway that penetrates through the fields. In the distance, stark against the burnt yellow of the wheat, the white walls of the centre rise sharply. Barbed wire runs over their rim, and the rectangular rhythm of guard posts marks their confines. The sun shines over the bars of the gate and the plastered concrete.

We stop here, just a few steps from our destination, and sit on the gravel path of this dirt road. We breathe in the scent of this threshold between town and fields, where prison and agriculture, policing and farming turn into one another. Our breathing oscillates in the same rhythm that, in the beginning, birthed the child-god Amun from the waters of Nun and swung the spines of Apophis, the serpent of destruction. We inhale the warm Mediterranean air and exhale the spirit that inhabits it. Through our nostrils, the tradition of which we have become the vessels, the stories that were given to us, flow out and soar, then roll over the barbed wire, and slide inside the narrow windows of the detention centre. Just as the ancients believed that each element tends towards its natural place – the fire up towards the sun, the earth down by its weight – so the tradition of the Mediterranean imagination now moves beyond us, to make its nest among its rightful inheritors. In the heat of an overcrowded cell, where the future is a mirage or a threat, it sinks to grow again in the fertile soil of the homeless minds.

## 17.

Here, between the ominous quiet of the migrant detention centre and the echo of traffic, it is also time for us to part ways. I leave you sitting on the dust of this country road, while the day wanes towards evening and the shadows of the wheat ears lengthen over one another. I leave you here, free to choose your next step. Perhaps you will wait for the right moment to climb the walls and cut the bars of a cell, or perhaps you will turn back through the fields to take the highway, seeking the comfort of a modern city.

As the story nears its conclusion, the author should leave the readers and the characters to their shared intimacy. It is they – not the author – who have brought the story to this point, shouldering it together like water carriers. They have conspired to make imaginary worlds emerge from the page, mixing their breath to enliven the dead ink. Now that our journey has run aground on the shore of the present, it is up to you, readers and characters, to continue it together beyond the end of this book. All along, the author was only a light cast on the scene, the floorboards holding up the stage.

So, I rise to my feet, shaking dust and gravel off my trousers. I leave the detention centre to one side, the silhouette of the highway to the other and I walk ahead towards the darkening side of the sky. The evening advances quickly, blending more and more the undulating plantations with the rare shapes of trees. I don't dare to turn my head, remembering how every myth warns against looking back at the end of a story. I trust in the darkness, in its ability to deepen space and to transform every surface into an exit from the world.

And as I walk on, my thoughts reach to another evening, many decades ago, when I also waited for the darkness with trepidation. My family was living in an old apartment in Milan, and I had just started primary school. My room was chilly, I remember, and I shivered in my pyjamas as I tiptoed to the windowsill, looking expectantly out to the street. My mother walked in, young as she always is in my memory, and took me to bed, tucking my sheets tight and recommending me to keep my eyes well closed. It was the eve of the second day of November, a special night for us Sicilians. That night, the dead came to visit their living relatives to bring them sweets and little gifts. I insisted on keeping the window open to make sure that they would find their way into my room, where my bedside table stood perfectly empty, like an open hand. My mother turned off the light and I squeezed my eyes closed to hasten sleep. I was a little afraid of seeing the dead.

In the morning, feeble sunrays lit my bedside table. On its faux-wood surface, a cascade of marzipan chestnuts, quinces, sorb fruits, all painted in warm, glossy colours. In the middle, magnificent, stood the centrepiece: *il pupo di zucchero*, a sugar knight as tall as my head, with a silver shield and a red plume, on a horse rearing up in the greenest grass. His head was turned to one side, and he smiled, bringing the greetings of the dead. I looked at him transfixed, barely daring to touch his armour and lick my fingers stained with food colouring. I had been told that the dead hid a small piece of their soul inside sugar statuettes like this one, and that they were happy if I ate them because they would continue to live in me. I do not remember how long it took before I summoned the courage to bite into the knight, but I can still taste the overpowering sweetness of sugar mixing in my mouth with the bitter scent of almond oil. An incomprehensible taste, at once moreish and repulsive, through which the dead instilled themselves inside the living. I sat up in bed, munching conscientiously despite the mounting nausea. I spent the rest of the day in a state of heightened alert, waiting to sense the presence of the dead I had just ingested. They had trusted me, a child, with the crucial mission of carrying a speck of the otherworld into this one. But nothing happened. The day went on like any other, and by the time evening returned, I was left with the uneasy feeling of having failed their request.

So many years later, with this book, I have done my best to fulfil it.

# Notes

## Dedication

1 E. Montale, *La Storia*, my translation.

## Chapter 1

1 D.J. Stanley and F.C. Wezel (eds.), *Geological Evolution of the Mediterranean Basin*, New York and Berlin, Springer, 1985; D. Garcia-Castellanos et al., 'The Zanclean megaflood of the Mediterranean – Searching for Independent Evidence', *Earth-Science Reviews*, Vol. 201, 2020; P. L. Blanc, 'The Opening of the Plio-Quaternary Gibraltar Strait: Assessing the Size of a Cataclysm', *Geodinamica Acta*, Vol. 15, 2002, pp. 303–17.

2 A. Leroi-Gourhan, *Les religions de la préhistoire: Paléolithique*, Paris, Presses Universitaires de France, 2006. For a more positive (although still critical) view of the possibility of interpreting prehistoric imagination, see M. Eliade, 'In the Beginning . . . : Magico-Religious Behaviour of the Paleoanthropians', in *A History of Religious Ideas*, Vol. 1, Chicago, IL, The University of Chicago Press, 1981, pp. 3–28.

3 *Enuma Elish*, I, 1–9, in A. Heidel (ed. and trans.), *The Babylonian Genesis*, Chicago and London, The University of Chicago Press, 1963, p. 18.

4 Ibid., I, 58, p. 20.

5 Ibid., I, 140–144, pp. 23–4.

6 Ibid., II, 73, p. 27.

7 Ibid., II, 95, p. 28.

8   Ibid., II, 123–127, p. 29.

9   *Ibid.*, IV, 23–24, p. 37.

10  Heraclitus, *fr. 53*, in G. S. Kirk et al. (eds. and trans.), *The Presocratic Philosophers*, Cambridge, Cambridge University Press, 2005, p. 193.

11  *Enuma Elish*, IV, 63–64, in A. Heidel (ed. and trans.), *The Babylonian Genesis*, Chicago and London, The University of Chicago Press, 1963, p. 39.

12  Ibid., IV, 86–89, p. 40.

13  Ibid., VI, 32–33, p. 47.

14  Plutarch, *Consolatio ad Apollonium,* 115, in Plutarch, *Moralia*, Vol. II, edited and translated by F. C. Babbitt, Cambridge, MA, Harvard University Press, 1962, p. 179.

15  *Gilgamesh: The Standard Version*, XI, 176, in A. George (ed. and trans.), *The Epic of Gilgamesh*, London, Penguin, 2020, p. 91.

16  Ibid., XI, 23–27, p. 86.

17  Ibid., XI, 116, p. 89.

18  *Atrahasis*, III, IV, in S. Dalley (ed. and trans), *Myths from Mesopotamia*, Oxford, Oxford University Press, 2008, p. 33.

19  *Gilgamesh*, I, 164, in A. George (ed. and trans.), The Epic of Gilgamesh, London, Penguin, 2020, p. 3.

20  Ibid., I, 190–194, in A. George (ed. and trans.), The Epic of Gilgamesh, London, Penguin, 2020, p. 7.

21  Ibid., I, 201–202, in A. George (ed. and trans.), The Epic of Gilgamesh, London, Penguin, 2020, p. 8.

22  Ibid., II, 115, p. 16.

23  Ibid. I, 291, p. 11.

24  Ibid., VIII, 42–45, p. 63.

25  S. Freud, *Moses and Monotheism*, translated by K. Jones, London, Hogarth Press, 1939, pp. 29–85.

26  *Gilgamesh*, IX, Si 7–14, in A. George (ed. and trans.), The Epic of Gilgamesh, London, Penguin, 2020, p. 69.

27  Ibid., IX, 80–81, in A. George (ed. and trans.), The Epic of Gilgamesh, London, Penguin, 2020, p.71.

28  Ibid., X, 171–175, in A. George (ed. and trans.), The Epic of Gilgamesh, London, Penguin, 2020, p. 80.

29  'Gilgamesh at the End of the World', III, 3–5, in *Gilgamesh*, in A. George (ed. and trans.), The Epic of Gilgamesh, London, Penguin, 2020, p. 194.

30  *Gilgamesh*, XI, 323–325, in A. George (ed. and trans.), The Epic of Gilgamesh, London, Penguin, 2020, p. 96.

31  *Gilgamesh*, XI, 327–329, in A. George (ed. and trans.), *The Epic of Gilgamesh*, London, Penguin, 2020, p. 97.

32  'Gilgamesh and the Netherworld', 248–249 and 254, in *Gilgamesh*, in A. George (ed. and trans.), The Epic of Gilgamesh, London, Penguin, 2020, p. 142.

33  *Odyssey*, XI, 465–540.

34  The idea of a 'democratization' of Osiris, although widely accepted among historians, has recently been challenged – see M. Smith, 'Democratizing the Afterlife? Aspects of the Osirian Afterlife during the Transition from the Late Old Kingdom to the Middle Kingdom', in *Following Osiris: Perspectives on the Osirian Afterlife from Four Millennia*, Oxford, Oxford University Press, 2017, pp. 166–270.

35  Leo Tolstoy, *Anna Karenina*, translated by M. Schwartz, New Haven, CT, Yale University Press, p. 3.

36  S. Weil, *The Iliad or the Poem of Force*, translated by M. McCarthy, Wallingford, PA, Pendle Hill, 1991, p. 3.

37  Homer, *The Iliad*, Book XVI, 433–434 and 459–460, translated by R. Fagles, New York, NY, Penguin, 1991, p. 427.

38  R. Bespaloff, *On the Iliad*, translated by M. McCarthy, Princeton, NJ, Princeton University Press, 2019, pp. 47–8.

39  *The Qur'an*, 2:23, translated by M.A.S. A. Haleem, Oxford, Oxford University Press, 2005, p. 6.

40  Weil, *The Iliad or the Poem of Force*, p. 3.

## Chapter 2

1. Curtius Rufus, *The History of Alexander*, 8.1.22–8.2.7; Arrian, *The Anabasis of Alexander*, IV, 8; Plutarch, *Alexander's Life*, 50–1; Justin, *Epitome of the Philippic History of Pompeius Trogus*, XII, 6.

2. Plutarch, *Alexander's Life*, 8.2, 26.1.

3. Homer, *Iliad*, XXII, 346–55, translated by R. Fagles, London, Penguin, 1991, p. 551.

4. Curtius Rufus, *The History of Alexander*, 3.12.15-17; Diodorus Siculus, *Library of History*, 17.35.5–6; Arrian, *The Anabasis of Alexander*, 2.12.6–7.

5. Curtius Rufus, *The History of Alexander*, 8.5.5 ff.; Arrian, *The Anabasis of Alexander*, 4.9–14; Plutarch, *Alexander's Life*, 54–55.1.

6. Diodorus Siculus, *Library of History*, 17.49.2–51.4; Curtius Rufus, *The History of Alexander*, 4.7.5–32; Justin, *Epitome of the Philippic History of Pompeius Trogus*, 11.11.2–12; Plutarch, *Alexander's Life*, 26.6–27; Arrian, *The Anabasis of Alexander*, 3.3–4; Strabo, *Geografica*, 17.1.43.

7. C. Baudelaire, 'L'Albatros', in *Les Fleurs Du Mal*.

8. Herodotus, *The Histories*, III, 29–38; P. Briant, *From Cyrus to Alexander: A History of the Persian Empire*, Winona Lake, IN, Eisenbrauns, 2002, pp. 55–7.

9. Arrian, *The Anabasis of Alexander*, 5.25.1–5.29.2; Curtius Rufus, *The History of Alexander*, 9.2.1–9.3.19; Diodorus Siculus, *Library of History*, 17.94–5.2; Justin, *Epitome of the Philippic History of Pompeius Trogus*, 12.8.10–15; Plutarch, *Alexander's Life*, 62.1–4; Strabo, *Geographica*, 3.5.5 C.171, 15.1.32.

10. Arrian, *The Anabasis of Alexander*, 5.29.1–2; Curtius Rufus, *The History of Alexander*, 9.3.19; Diodorus Siculus, *Library of History*, 17.95.1–2; Justin, *Epitome of the Philippic History of Pompeius Trogus*, 12.8.16; Plutarch, *Alexander's Life*, 62.4.

11. Arrian, *Indica*; Arrian, *Periplus of the Euxine Sea*; Iambulus, *Islands of the Sun or The Adventures of Iambulus in the Southern Ocean*; Anonymous, *Periplus of the Erythraean Sea*; V. Bucciantini, 'From the Indus to the Pasitigris: Some Remarks on the Periplus of Nearchus in the Arrian's *Indikē*', in C. Antonetti and P. Biagi (eds), *With Alexander*

*in India and Central Asia: Moving East and Back to West*, Oxford, Oxbow Books, 2017, pp. 279–92.

12 Arrian, *The Anabasis of Alexander*, 6.21–22.3; Curtius Rufus, *The History of Alexander*, 9.10.5–11; Diodorus Siculus, *Library of History*, 17.104.3–105.5; Plutarch, *Alexander's Life*, 66.2.

13 Arrian, *The Anabasis of Alexander*, 6.23.1–26.3; Curtius Rufus, *The History of Alexander*, 9.10.11–18; Diodorus Siculus, *Library of History*, 17.105.6–8; Plutarch, *Alexander's Life*, 66.2–3.

14 Arrian, *The Anabasis of Alexander*, 7.4.4–8; Diodorus Siculus, *Library of History*, 17.107.6; Justin, *Epitome of the Philippic History of Pompeius Trogus*, 12.10.9; Plutarch, *Alexander's Life*, 70.1; *Moralia*, 329D-E.

15 Arrian, *The Anabasis of Alexander*, 7.14; Diodorus Siculus, *Library of History*, 17.110.7–8, 115; Justin, *Epitome of the Philippic History of Pompeius Trogus*, 12.12.11–12; Plutarch, *Alexander's Life*, 72; *Moralia*, 181D 29, 180D 14.

16 Arrian, *The Anabasis of Alexander*, 7.25–27; Curtius Rufus, *The History of Alexander*, 10.5.1–6; Diodorus Siculus, *Library of History*, 17.117; Plutarch, *Alexander's Life*, 75–6.

17 Arrian, *The Anabasis of Alexander*, 7.26.3; Curtius Rufus, *The History of Alexander*, 10.5.5; Diodorus Siculus, *Library of History*, 17.117.4; Justin, *Epitome of the Philippic History of Pompeius Trogus*, 12.15.8.

18 P. Wheatley and C. Dunn, 'Coinage as Propaganda: Alexander and his Successors', in J. Walsh and Elizabeth Baynham (eds), *Alexander the Great and Propaganda*, London/New York, Routledge, 2021, pp. 162–93.

19 A. Wojciechowska, *From Amyrtaeus to Ptolemy: Egypt in the Fourth Century BC*, Leipzig, Harrassowitz, 2016, pp. 52–72.

20 *The Alexander Romance*, 1.1–14.

21 *The Alexander Romance*, 2.31 (recensio γ).

22 *Alexander Romance* 2.39 (recensio).

23 On Dinocrates the architect, see Vitruvius, *On Architecture*, II, *Preface*, 1–4, Portsmouth, NH, Heinemann, 2002, pp. 72–5.

24 Arrian, *The Anabasis of Alexander*, 3.1.5–3.2.2; Plutarch, *Alexander's Life*, 26.2–6; Pseudo-Callisthenes, *The Greek Alexander Romance*, 1.32.

25  Plato, *Timaeus*, 22b

26  A. Momigliano, *Alien Wisdom: The Limits of Hellenization*, Cambridge, Cambridge University Press, 1990; J. Rodenbeck, 'Literary Alexandria', *The Massachusetts Review*, Vol. 42, No. 4, Winter 2001/2002, pp. 524–72; L. Russo, *La Rivoluzione Dimenticata: Il pensiero scientifico greco e la scienza moderna*, Milano, Feltrinelli, 2019.

27  D. Laertius, *Lives of Eminent Philosophers, Aristippus*, II, 65–104; Xenophon, *Memorabilia*, 2.1.7–14; R. Hard (ed.), *Diogenes the Cynic: Sayings and Anecdotes, Part 2: Aristippus and the Cyrenaics*, Oxford, Oxford University Press, 2012, pp. 123–57.

28  D. Laertius, *Lives of Eminent Philosophers, Diogenes*, VI, 20–81; R. Hard (ed.), Diogens the Cynic, *Sayings and Anecdotes*, Oxford, Oxford University Press, 2012.

29  D. Laertius, *Lives of Eminent Philosophers, Anthistenes*, VI, 1–19

30  Arrian, *The Anabasis of Alexander*, 7.2.1; D. Laertius, *Lives of Eminent Philosophers*, 6.32, 6.38, cf. 6.60, and 6.68; Plutarch, *Alexander's Life*, 14.1–3.

31  Arrian, *The Anabasis of Alexander* 7.2.2; Plutarch, *Alexander's Life*, 64–5; Pseudo-Callisthenes, *The Greek Alexander Romance*, 3.5 ff., 2.35A.

32  Palladius, *Epistola de Indicis Gentibus et de Bragmannibus*.

33  Plutarch, *Praecepta Gerendae Reipublicae*, 28, 6.

34  T. W. Rhys-Davids, *The Milinda Panha: The Questions of King Milinda*, Altenmünster, Jazzybee Verlag, 2017.

35  Arrian, *The Anabasis of Alexander*, 5.1–5.4; Curtius Rufus, *The History of Alexander*, 8.10.7–18; Justin, *Epitome of the Philippic History of Pompeius Trogus*, 12.7.6–8; Plutarch, *Alexander's Life*, 58.3–5; F. Maraini, *Where Four Worlds Meet*, London, Hamish Hamilton, 1965, pp. 242–71.

36  Nonnus of Panopolis, *Dionysiaca*, XIII–XLVIII.

37  Mentions of Alexander can be found in the anonymous texts *Namah-yi Tansar* (sixth century), *Karnamag-I Ardashir-I Babagan* (seventh century), *Ardavirafnamag* (nineth century), *Zand Akasih* (eleventh century).

38 Arrian, *The Anabasis of Alexander*, 3.18.11–12; Curtius Rufus, *The History of Alexander*, 5.7.1-11; Diodorus Siculus, *Library of History*, 17.72; Plutarch, *Alexander's Life*, 38; K. T. Van Bladel, *The Arabic Hermes: From Pagan Sage to Prophet of Science*, Oxford, Oxford University Press, 2009, pp. 33–5.

39 Ferdowsi, *Shahnameh: The Persian Book of Kings*, edited and translated by D. Davis, London/New York, Penguin, 2016, p. 567.

40 Ibid., 576.

41 *Quran*, Sura 18, *Al Kahf*, 'The Cave', 83–101.

42 *Iskandarnamah: A Persian Medieval Epic*, edited and translated by M. S. Southgate, New York, NY, Columbia University Press, 1978.

43 *Quran*, 18:31, 55:76, 76:21; Z. Abdollah, 'Color in Islamic Theosophy: An Analytical Reading of Four Scholars: Kubrā, Rāzī, Simnānī, and Kirmānī', *Journal of Islamic Philosophy*, Vol. 7, 2011, pp. 35–51.

44 *Iskandarnamah: A Persian Medieval Epic*, 54–58.

45 *Quran*, Sura 18, *Al Kahf*, 'The Cave', 60–82.

# Chapter 3

1 My translation from passages of the funerary inscriptions: CLE 120, CIL xi 4010, Capena, Italy; CLE 1495, CIL vi 26003, Rome, Italy; CIL iii 3980, ILS 5228. Pest, Hungary; CLE 2222, CIL viii 7277, Constantine, Algeria.

2 R. Namatianus, *De Reditu Suo* (Concerning His Return), I, 47–6; I, 61–6 and I, 119–24. My translation, compared with H. Isbell (ed. and trans.), *The Last Poets of Imperial Rome*, London, Penguin, 1971.

3 Ibid., 119–124.

4 Zosimus, *Historia Nova*, 4–5.

5 Saint Jerome, *Commentary on Ezekiel*, I, preface; III, preface. W. H. Fremantle's translation in P. Schaff (ed.), *Nicene and Post-Nicene Fathers*, 2, vol. 6, New York, Christian Literature Publishing Co., 1893, pp. 495–6.

6 Saint Augustine, *City of God*.

7 Namatianus, *De Reditu Suo*, 407–414.

8 Ibid., 439–46 and 515–26..

9 Eunapius, *Lives of the Philosophers*, 475.

10 Gregory of Nazianzus, *Julian the Emperor, Containing Gregory of Nazianzen's Two Invectives and Libanius's Monody with Julian's Extant Theosophical Works; Oration 5.23*, translated by C. W. King, London, Bohn's Classical Library, 1888, quoted in S. Elm, *Sons of Hellenism, Fathers of the Church: Emperor Julian, Gregory of Nazianzus, and the Vision of Rome*, Berkeley, University of California Press, 2012, p. 459.

11 Ammianus Marcellinus, *Res Gestae*, XV, 12.

12 Julian, *Letter to the Senate and the People of Athens*.

13 Julian, *Letter 51, To the Community of the Jews*, 398.

14 Julian, *Letter 36, On Christian Teachers*.

15 Salutius, *On the Gods and the World*, 4,8.

16 Salutius, *On the Gods and the World*, 3,3.

17 Plato, *Protagoras*, 352, c – translated by S. Lombardo and K. Bell, in J. M. Cooper, *Plato: Complete Works*, Indianapolis, Hackett, 1997.

18 Luke 23:34.

19 Damascius, *The Philosophical History*, 43A, translated by P. Athanassiadi, Athens, Apamea, 1999, p. 129.

20 Socrates Scholasticus, *Historia Ecclesiastica*, VII, 15, in *The History of the Church*, London, Awnsham and John Churchill, 1709, p. 376.

21 Ibid., 376.

22 Justinian, *Corpus Iuris Civilis*, vol. 2, I, 5.18.4, Berlin, 1954, p. 57.

23 Agathias, *The Histories*, 30.4–31.8, translated by J. D. Frendo, Berlin, Walter de Gruyter, 1975, pp. 65–7.

24 *Corpus Hermeticum, Asclepius*, 24–6, in B. P. Copenhaver (ed. and trans.), *Hermetica: The Greek Corpus Hermeticum and the Latin Asclepius*, Cambridge, Cambridge University Press, 2008, pp. 81–2.

25 *Corpus Hermeticum*, X, 24–25, in B. P. Copenhaver (ed. and trans.), *Hermetica: The Greek Corpus Hermeticutn and the Latin Asclepius*, Cambridge, Cambridge University Press, 2008, p. 36.

26 *Asclepius*, 6, in B. P. Copenhaver (ed. and trans.), *Hermetica: The Greek Corpus Hermeticutn and the Latin Asclepius*, Cambridge, Cambridge University Press, 2008, p. 69.

27 *Corpus Hermeticum*, X, 1, in B. P. Copenhaver (ed. and trans.), *Hermetica: The Greek Corpus Hermeticutn and the Latin Asclepius*, Cambridge, Cambridge University Press, 2008, p. 30.

28 *Corpus Hermeticum*, XII, 15–17, in B. P. Copenhaver (ed. and trans.), *Hermetica: The Greek Corpus Hermeticutn and the Latin Asclepius*, Cambridge, Cambridge University Press, 2008, pp. 46–7.

29 *Corpus Hermeticum*, I, in B. P. Copenhaver (ed. and trans.), *Hermetica: The Greek Corpus Hermeticutn and the Latin Asclepius*, Cambridge, Cambridge University Press, 2008, pp. 1–7.

30 Plotinus, *Enneads*, II, 9, 33, *Against the Gnostics*.

31 M. Meyer (ed.), *The Nag Hammadi Scriptures*, New York, NY, Harper One, 2008. All subsequent quotes from the Nag Hammadi Codices (NHC) are taken from M. Meyer's edition.

32 Yaldabaoth's exclamations of arrogance are a Gnostic reinterpretation of the Biblical passages in *Isaiah* 45:6 and *Exodus* 20:5.

33 The first part of the Gnostic cosmogony, as I presented it in this paragraph, can be found in the treatises *The Apocryphon of John* (NHC II, 1); *On the Origin of the World* (NHC II, 5).

34 My retelling of this section of the Gnostic myth is based on the treatises *The Apocryphon of John* (NHC II, 1); *The Hypostasis of the Archons* (NHC II, 4); *On the Origin of the World* (NHC II, 5).

35 My retelling of this section of the Gnostic myth is based on the treatises *The Apocryphon of John* (NHC II, 1); *On the Origin of the World* (NHC II, 5); *The Holy Book of the Great Invisible Spirit* (NHC III, 2); *The First Revelation of James* (NHC V, 3); *The Revelation of Adam*, (NHC V, 5); *The Second Discourse of the Great Seth* (NHC VII, 2). An account of the apocatastasis at the end of the world can be found in *The Treatise on Resurrection* (NHC I, 4); *The Tripartite Tractate* (NHC I, 5); and in Irenaeus' assessment of Valentinism, in *Against Heresies*, I, 6–7.

36 *The Gospel of Philip*, NHC II, 3, 67: 9.

37 See Epiphanius of Salamis, *Panarion*, 26, 4–5 and 9.

38 Epiphanes, *On Righteousness*, in Clement of Alexandria, *Stromateis*, III, 6–9, in J. Ferguson (ed. and trans.), *Clement of Alexandria: Stromateis Books One to Three*, Washington, D.C., The Catholic University of America Press, 2005, pp. 259–62.

39 *On the Origin of the World*, NHC II, 5, 125–26.

40 The tenth-century bibliographer Muhammad Ibn Ishaq Al-Nadim, in his *Kitāb al-Fihrist* (The Book Catalogue), IX, 1, 328, attests that the angel who transmitted the revelation to him was called *al-Tawn*, which in Nabatean means 'comrade' – see B. Dodge (ed. and trans.), *The Fihrist of Al-Nadim*, Vol. 1, New York and London, Columbia University Press, 1970, p. 774.

41 Mani, *Shabuhragan*, quoted in Al-Biruni, *al-Athar al-Baqiyah 'an al-Qurun al-Khaliyya*, VIII, 10; in C. E. Sachau (ed. and trans.), *Albirnuni's the Chronology of Ancient Nations*, London, William H. Allen and Co., 1879, p. 190.

42 John 15:18-19, in the translation of *The New Oxford Annotated Bible*.

43 My translation from the Italian translation of the Manichaean text *Omelia della Morte di Mani*, III, 47:25, in A. Gnoli, *Il Manicheismo: Volume 1, Mani e il Manicheismo*, Milano, Arnoldo Mondadori, 2003, p. 174.

44 Marco Polo, *The Description of the World*, Vol. 1, ed. and trans. by A. C. Moule and P. Pelliot, London, George Routledge and Sons Limited, 1938, pp. 349–50. (This part of Marco Polo's story can be found only in section 156 of a Latin manuscript dated to *c.* 1470 stored in Toledo, Biblioteca Catedral, marks 49,20; while it is not present in other editions of *Il Milione*).

# Chapter 4

1 D. B. Hull (ed. and trans.), *Digenis Akritas: The Two Blood Border Lord*, IV, 27–28, 36, Athens, OH, Ohio University Press, 1972, p. 34.

2 The story of Digenis Akritas can be found in Denison B. Hull (ed. and trans.), *Digenis Akritas: The Two Blood Border Lord*, IV, 27–28, 36, Athens, OH, Ohio University Press, 1972, p. 34. The story of Digenis Akritas' death is recounted in several Greek folksongs, some of which

were collected by Nikolaos Politis, as found in N. Politis, *Canciones del pueblo griego: selección*, Ediciones de la Universidad de Castilla-La Mancha, 2006. The story of Amira Dhat al-Himma can be found in M. Magidow (ed. and trans.), *The Tale of Princess Fatima, Warrior Woman: The Arabic Epic of Dhat al-Himma*, London/New York, Penguin, 2021.

3 Al-Tabari, *The Early Abbasi Empire*, translated by J. A. William, 2 vols., Vol. 1: *The Reign of Abu Ja'far al Mansur AD 754–775*, Cambridge, Cambridge University Press, 1998, p. 145.

4 F. Micheau, '*Baghdad, An Imperial Foundation*', in N. Yoffee (ed.), *The Cambridge World History*, vol. 3: *Early Cities in Comparative Perspective, 4000 BCE-1200 CE*, Cambridge, Cambridge University Press, 2015, p. 404.

5 As recounted in Einhard, *Annales Regni Francorum Inde Ab A. 741, Usque Ad A. 829, Qui Dicuntur Annales Laurissenses Maiores Et Einhardi*, Forgotten Books, 2018, and in Einhard and Notker the Stammerer, *Two Lives of Charlemagne*, London/New York, Penguin, 2008.

6 Ibn Al-Nadim, *Fihrist*, 243.3–8, translated by F. Rosenthal, *Classical Heritage*, Zurich, Artemis, 1965, pp. 48–9, quoted with modifications in D. Guptas, *Greek Thought, Arabic Culture*, London, Routledge, 1998, p. 98.

7 A. Komnene, *The Alexiad*, translated by E. R. A. Sewter, London/New York, Penguin, 2009.

8 Ibid., Book X, p. 275 (rendered in the English translation as 'mass movement', but equally translatable as 'mass migration').

9 Ibid., Book X, p. 275.

10 Ibid., Book X, p. 283.

11 U. Ibn Munqidh, *The Book of Contemplation: Islam and the Crusades*, edited and translated by P. M. Cobb, London/New York, Penguin, 2008; several instances throughout the book.

12 Ibid., pp. 145–6.

13 This legend, present in various versions in Christian and Muslim sources, is reported in R. Fletcher, *Moorish Spain*, Berkeley and Los Angeles, CA, University of California Press, 2006, p. 15.

14  Moshe ben Maimon, *A Letter of Maimonides about Conversion and Martyrdom*, translated and edited by R. Szpiech, in N. Hurvitz, C. Sahner, et al. (eds), *Conversion to Islam in the Premodern Age*, Oakland, CA, University of California Press, 2020, pp. 217–19.

15  D. di Cesare, *Marranos: The Other of the Other*, Cambridge, Polity, 2020, pp. 67–8.

16  *Exodus* 2:22, 'Zipporah gave birth to a son, and Moses named him Gershom, saying, "I have become a foreigner in a foreign land"'.

17  G. F. Pico, *Giovanni Pico della Mirandola: His Life by his Nephew Giovanni Francesco Pico*, translated by Sir T. Moore, London, David Nutt, 1890, p. 7.

18  Ibid., p. 8.

19  G. Pico della Mirandola, *Oration on the Dignity of Man: A New Translation and Commentary*, edited and translated by F. Borghesi et al., Cambridge, Cambridge University Press, 2012, p. 109.

20  Sophocles, *Antigone*, 332, in E. Hall (ed.), *Sophocles: Antigone, Oedipus the King, and Electra*, translated by H. D. F. Kitto, Oxford, Oxford University Press, 2008.

21  G. Pico della Mirandola, *Oration on the Dignity of Man*, pp. 115–17.

# Chapter 5

1  A. Nunez Cabeza de Vaca, *Castaways: the narrative of Alvar Nunez Cabeza de Vaca*, translated by F. M. Lopez-Morillas, Berkeley, CA, University of California Press, 1993, pp. 41–2.

2  Ibid., p. 46.

3  Ibid., p. 55.

4  Ibid., pp. 113–15.

5  B. de las Casas, *A Short Account of the Destruction of the Indies*, translated by N. Griffin, London, Penguin, 1992.

6  S. Bono, *Schiavi: Una storia mediterranea (XVI-XIX secolo)*, Bologna, il Mulino, 2016, pp. 71–5.

7   Ibid., p. 26.

8   Ibid., pp. 17–20.

9   E. de Aranda, *Il Riscatto: relazione sulla schiavitù di un gentiluomo ad Algeri*, translated by A. Pellegrino Ceccarelli, Milano, Serra e Riva, 1981, p. 27 – my translation from the Italian edition.

10  Pope Pius II's, born Enea Silvio Piccolomini, sent a letter to Mehmet II in 1460, quoted in Eugenio Garin, *Ritratto di Enea Silvio Piccolomini*, in *Ritratti di Umanisti*, Firenze, Sansoni, 1967, p. 32 – my translation from the Italian edition.

11  M. Lenci, *Corsari: guerra, schiavi, rinnegati nel Mediterraneo*, Roma, Carocci, 2007, pp. 23–4 and 149. S. Bono, *Guerre Corsare nel Mediterraneo: una storia di incursioni, arrembaggi, razzie*, Bologna, Il Mulino, 2019, pp. 128.

12  Quoted in A. Barbero, *Solimano il Magnifico*, Roma-Bari, Laterza, 2010, p. 9.

13  Ibid., p. 9.

14  E. de Aranda, *Il Riscatto: relazione sulla schiavitù di un gentiluomo ad Algeri*, translated by A. Pellegrino Ceccarelli, Milano, Serra e Riva, 1981, pp. 76–7 – my translation from the Italian edition.

15  L. F. Marsigli, *La schiavitu' del generale Marsigli sotto i Tartari e i Turchi da lui stesso narrata*, edited by E. Lovarini, Bologna, Zanichelli, 1931, pp. 89–91.

16  F. Sassetti, 'Lettera da Lisbona (10 ottobre 1578) al fiorentino Baccio Valori', in I. Luzzana Caraci and M. Pozzi (eds), *Scopritori e Viaggiatori del Cinquecento e Seicento*, Milano, Ricciardini, 1991, p. 887.

17  G. Fiume, *Il Santo Moro: i processi di canonizzazione di Benedetto da Palermo (1594–1807)*, Milano, Franco Angeli, 2008. V. Morabito, 'San Benedetto il Moro da Palermo, protettore degli africani di Siviglia, della penisola iberica e d'America latina', in B. Ares Queija and B. Stella (eds), *Negros, Mulatos y Zambaigos: derroteros africanos en los mundos ibericos*, Sevilla, Escuela de Estudios Hispano-Americanos de Sevilla, 2000.

18  M. de Cervantes, *The Bagnios of Algiers and The Great Sultana: Two Plays of Captivity*, translated by B. Fuchs and A. J. Ilika, Philadelphia, PA, University of Pennsylvania Press, 2009. M. A. Garces, *Cervantes*

*in Algiers: A Captive's Tale*, Nashville, TN, Vanderbilt University Press, 2005.

19 J. L. Africanus (Al-Hasan Ibn Muhammad al Wazzan), *The Cosmography and Geography of Africa*, London, Penguin, 2023. N. Zemon Davis, *Trickster Travels: A Sixteenth-century Muslim between Worlds*, London, Faber & Faber, 2008.

20 Pietro Gori, 'Addio a Lugano', in Istituto Ernesto de Martino (eds), *Avanti Popolo: due secoli di canti popolari e di protesta civile*, Milano, Ricordi, 1998, p. 42. My translation from the original Italian.

21 A. B. Çorlu, 'Anarchists and Anarchism in the Ottoman Empire, 1850–1917', in S. Karahasanoglu (ed.), *History From Below: A Tribute in Memory of Donald Quataert*, Istanbul, Istanbul Bilgi University Press, 2016, pp. 553–83.

22 Başbakanlık Osmanlı Arşivleri, *Yıldız Perakende Evrakı Adliye ve Mezahib Nezareti Maruzatı* (Y.PRK.AZN) 21/28 (24 R 1318/21 August 1901), quoted in Ibid.

23 A. Grassi, *Chartre Turque, ou Organisation Religieuse, civile et militare de l'empire Ottoman*, Paris, Mongies, 1825, vol. I, p. 35. Quoted in M. Isabella, 'Mediterranean Liberals?: Italian Revolutionaries and the Making of a Colonial Sea, ca. 1800-30', in M. Isabella and K. Zanou (eds), *Mediterranean Diasporas: Politics and Ideas in the Long 19th Century*, London, Bloomsbury, 2016, pp. 86–7.

24 Linny Babagor (i.e. Giorgio Libri-Bagnano), *Réponse d'un Turc à la Note surla Grèce, de M. le vicomte de Chateaubriand, membre de la Societé en faveur des Grecs*, Bruxelles, Mayet, 1825, pp. 33 and 15–18. Quoted in M. Isabella and K. Zanou (eds), *Mediterranean Diasporas: Politics and Ideas in the Long 19th Century*, London, Bloomsbury, 2016, pp. 87–8.

25 I. Eberhardt, *The Oblivion Seekers*, translated by P. Bowles, London, Peter Owen, 2010, p. 74.

26 G. De Rada, 'Testamento Politico', in *Opera Omnia*, vol. IX, *Opere filosofiche e politiche*, Soveria Mannelli, Rubbettino, 2009, pp. 167–78. Quoted in M. Isabella and K. Zanou (eds), *Mediterranean Diasporas: Politics and Ideas in the Long 19th Century*, London, Bloomsbury, 2016, p. 177.

27 A. Puto and M. Isabella, 'From Southern Italy to Istanbul: trajectories of Albanian nationalism in the writings of Girolamo de Rada and

Shemseddin Sami Frasheri, ca. 1843-1903', in M. Isabella and K. Zanou(eds), *Mediterranean Diasporas: Politics and Ideas in the Long 19th Century*, London, Bloomsbury, 2016, pp. 178–83.

28  I. Andric, *The Bridge on the Drina*, translated by L. F. Edwards, London, Allen & Unwin, 1921, p. 266.

29  G. Chevallier, *La Peur*, Paris, Le Dilettante, 2008 – my translation from the Italian edition, G. Chevallier, *La Paura*, translated by L. Carra, Milano, Adelphi, 2011, pp. 212–13, 243, 245.

30  G. D'Annunzio, 'Lettera a Ludovico Toeplitz', 8 March 1920, in L. Toeplitz, *Ciak A Chi Tocca*, Milano, Edizioni Milano Nuova, 1964, p. 57. My translation from the Italian original.

31  G. D'Annunzio, 'Italia e Vita', 24 October 2019, in *La Penultima Ventura: scritti e discorsi fiumani*, edited by R. de Felice, Milano, Mondadori, 1974, pp. 155–6. My translation from the Italian original.

32  G. D'Annunzio, 'Lettera a Randolfo Vella', *Umanità Nuova*, 9 June 1920, quoted in R. de Felice, *D'Annunzio Politico: 1918–1938*, Roma-Bari, Laterza, 1978, pp. 61–2. My translation from the Italian original.

33  G. D'Annunzio, 'Lettera a Giuseppe Giulietti', 6 January 1920, in F. Gerra, *L'Impresa di Fiume, 1: Fiume d'Italia*, Milano, Longanesi, 1975, p. 232. My translation from the Italian original.

34  L. Kochnitzky, *La Quinta Stagione: o i Centauri di Fiume*, translated by A. Luchini, Bologna, Zanichelli, 1922, p. 164. My translation from the Italian edition.

35  G. Comisso, *Le Mie Stagioni*, Milano, Longanesi, 1963, p. 65.

36  H. Bey, *T.A.Z.: The Temporary Autonomous Zone, Ontological Anarchism, Poetic Terrorism*, Second edition, Brooklyn, NY, Autonomedia, 2003, p. 124.

# Chapter 6

1  A. Polgar, 'Böse Bubenzeitung', quoted in *Prager Tagblatt*, 8 February 1921, p. 3. "'Die Lage in Österreich ist hoffnungslos, aber nicht ernst.'" – my translation.

2   R. Musil, *The Man Without Qualities*, Vol. 1, translated by S. Wilkins, London, Picador, 2017, p. 30.

3   Adapted from S. Mortgensen, *Fuga e Fine di Joseph Roth*, Milano, Adelphi, 2001, p. 250 – my adaptation and translation from the Italian edition. The politician is Pierre Laval.

4   Letter to Paula Grübel, 1916, in J. Roth, *A Life in Letters*, translated and edited by M. Hofmann, New York, NY, W. W. Norton, 2012.

5   Letter to Bernard von Brentano, 26 September 1926, in J. Roth, *A Life in Letters*, translated and edited by M. Hofmann, New York, NY, W. W. Norton, 2012, p. 85.

6   J. Roth, *The Radetzky March*, part 3, ch. 16, London, David Campbell Publishers, 1996, p. 228.

7   J. Roth, *The Radetzky March*, part 2, ch. 11, London, David Campbell Publishers, 1996, pp. 161–2.

8   Mortgensen, *Fuga e Fine di Joseph Roth*, p. 283 – my translation from the Italian edition.

9   H. von Hofmannsthal, 'On Mutability', in *The Whole Difference: Selected Writings of Hugo von Honfmannsthal*, edited and translated by J. D. McClatchy, Princeton, NJ, Princeton University Press, 2008, p. 27.

10  Musil, *The Man Without Qualities*, p. 12.

11  G. Morselli, *Contro-Passato Prossimo*, 'Intermezzo Critico', Milano, Adelphi, 2016, pp. 118 and 123. My translation.

12  Thucydides, *History of the Peloponnesian War*, 5.89.

13  R. Bazlen, *Scritti: Il capitano di lungo corso – note senza testo – lettere editoriali – lettere a Montale*, edited by R. Calasso, Milano, Adelphi, 1984, p. 264.

14  Salutius, *On the Gods and the World*, 4,8.

# Bibliography and Further Reading

## 1 – Mortals

### The Messinian Age and the Zanclean Flood

P. L. Blanc, 'The Opening of the Plio-Quaternary Gibraltar Strait: Assessing the Size of a Cataclysm', *Geodinamica Acta*, Vol. 15, 2002, pp. 303–317.

D. Garcia-Castellanos, Aaron Micallef, Ferran Estrada, Angelo Camerlenghi, Gemma Ercilla and Raúl Periáñez, José María Abril, 'The Zanclean Megaflood of the Mediterranean – Searching for Independent Evidence', *Earth-Science Reviews*, Vol. 201, 2020, 103061.

D. J. Stanley and F. C. Wezel (eds.), *Geological Evolution of the Mediterranean Basin*, New York and Berlin, Springer, 1985.

### Prehistoric imagination

M. Eliade, 'In the Beginning . . . : Magico-Religious Behaviour of the Paleoanthropians', in *A History of Religious Ideas*, Vol. 1, Chicago, IL, The University of Chicago Press, 1981, pp. 3–28.

A. Leroi-Gourhan, *Les religions de la préhistoire: Paléolithique*, Paris, Presses Universitaires de France, 2006.

D. Lewis-Williams, *The Mind in the Cave: Consciousness and the Origins of Art*, London and New york, Thames & Hudson, 2004.

G. Rigal, *Le Temps Sacré des Cavernes*, Paris, Corti, 2016.

## Babylonian Cosmology

S. Dalley (ed. and trans.), *Myths from Mesopotamia: Creation, the Flood, Gilgamesh, and Others*, Oxford, Oxford University Press, 2008.

A. Heidel (ed. and trans.), *The Babylonian Genesis*, Chicago and London, The University of Chicago Press, 1963.

W. G. Lambert, *Babylonian Creation Myths*, Winona Lake, IN, Eisenbrauns, 2013.

J. Pritchard (ed. and trans.), *Ancient Near Eastern Texts Relating to the Old Testament*, Princeton, NJ, Princeton University Press, 1969.

## Gilgamesh and Utnapishtim

R. Calasso, *The Tablet of Destinies*, translated by T. Parks, New York, NY, Farrar Straus and Giroux, 2022.

A. George (ed. and trans.), *The Epic of Gilgamesh*, London, Penguin, 2020.

A. Heidel, *The Gilgamesh Epic and Old Testament Parallels*, Chicago, IL, The University of Chicago Press, 1963.

## Egyptian Cosmology

J. Assmann, *From Akhenaten to Moses: Ancient Egypt and Religious Change*, Cairo, The American University in Cairo Press, 2014.

E. Hornung, *Conceptions of God in Ancient Egypt: The One and the Many*, translated by J. Baines, Ithaca, NY, Cornell University Press, 1996.

A. Piankoff (trans.) and N. Rambova (ed.), *Mythological Papyri*, Bollingen Series XL 3, New York, NY, Pantheon Books, 1957.

G. Pinch, *Egyptian Mythology: A Guide to the Gods, Goddesses, and Traditions of Ancient Egypt*, Oxford, Oxford University Press, 2004.

## Osiris and Resurrection

B. Mojsov, *Osiris: Death and Afterlife of a God*, Oxford, Blackwell, 2005.

M. Smith, *Following Osiris: Perspectives on the Osirian Afterlife from Four Millennia*, Oxford, Oxford University Press, 2017.

E. A. Wallis Budge, *Osiris and the Egyptian Resurrection*, Two Volumes in One, London, Philip Lee Warner; Eastford, CT, Martino Fine Books, 2019.

### The Iliad and the problem of Force

R. Bespaloff, *On the Iliad*, translated by M. McCarthy, Princeton, NJ, Princeton University Press, 2019.
S. Weil, *The Iliad or the Poem of Force*, translated by M. McCarthy, Wallingford, PA, Pendle Hill, 1991.

## 2 – Foreigners

### The Macedonian Empire

J. Roisman and I. Worthington (eds.), *A Companion to Ancient Macedonia*, Chichester, Wiley-Blackwell, 2010.
I. Worthington, *By the Spear: Philip II, Alexander the Great, and the Rise and Fall of the Macedonian Empire*, Oxford, Oxford University Press, 2014.

### The Persian Achaemenid Empire

Herodotus, *The Histories*, c. 430 BC.
P. Briant, *From Cyrus to Alexander: A History of the Persian Empire*, Winona Lake, Eisenbrauns, 2002.
M. A. Dandamaev, *A Political History of the Achaemenid Empire*, Leiden, Brill, 1989.
A. Kuhrt, *The Persian Empire: A Corpus of Sources from the Achaemenid Period*, London/New York, Routledge, 2010.
J. Morgan, *Greek Perspectives on the Achaemenid Empire: Persia Through the Looking Glass*, Edinburgh, Edinburgh University Press, 2016.
Xenophon, *Cyropaedia*, 370 BC.

### The Diadochoi

J. Romm, *Ghost on the Throne: The Death of Alexander the Great and the Bloody Fight for His Empire*, London, Vintage, 2012.
R. Waterfield, *Dividing the Spoils: The War for Alexander the Great's Empire*, Oxford, Oxford University Press, 2012.

## The Alexander Romance

W. Kroll, *Historia Alexandri Magni*, Berlin, Weidmann, 1926.

P. Matthey, 'The Once and Future King of Egypt. Apocalyptic Literature in Egypt and the Construction of the Alexander Romance', in L. Arcari (ed.), *Beyond Conflicts: Cultural and Religious Cohabitations in Alexandria and Egypt between the 1st and the 6th Century CE*. Tübingen, Mohr Siebeck, 2017, pp. 47–72..

M. Stock (ed.), *Alexander the Great in the Middle Ages: Transcultural Perspectives*, London, University of Toronto Press, 2016.

R. Stoneman, *Alexander the Great: A Life in Legend*, London, Yale University Press, 2010.

R. Stoneman, 'Introduzione', in *Il Romanzo di Alessandro*, Vol. 1, Milano, Arnoldo Mondadori, 2007.

R. Stoneman (ed. and trans.), *The Greek Alexander Romance*, London, Penguin, 1991.

## The Spring of Eternal Youth

*The Alexander Romance*, 2.39 (recensio β).

*The Epic of Gilgamesh*, Tablet XII.

Herodotus, *The Histories*, III, 23.

J. Mandeville, *The Travels of Sir John Mandeville*, London/New York, Penguin, 2005, p. 123.

A. Szalc, 'In Search of Water of Life: The Alexander Romance and Indian Mythology', in R. Stoneman, K. Erickson and, I. Netton (eds), *The Alexander Romance in Persia and the East*, Eelde, Barkhuis, 2012, pp. 327–38.

E. Washburn Hopkins, 'The Fountain of Youth', *Journal of the American Oriental Society*, Vol. 26, 1905, pp. 1–67.

## Alexandria-by-Egypt

L. Canfora, *The Vanished Library*, Oakland, CA, University of California Press, 1990.

W. V. Harris and G. Ruffini, *Ancient Alexandria between Egypt and Greece*, Leiden, Brill, 2004.

A. Hirst and M. Silk (eds.), *Alexandria, Real and Imagined*, Milton Park, Taylor & Francis, 2004.

J. G. Manning, *The Last Pharaohs: Egypt Under the Ptolemies*, Princeton, NJ, Princeton University Press, 2012.

J. McKenzie, *The Architecture of Alexandria and Egypt, C. 300 B.C. to A.D. 700*, New Haven/London, Yale University Press, 2007.

## Syncretic Religion in Hellenistic Egypt

A. Chastel, 'Signum Harpocraticum', in *Il Gesto nell'Arte*, Roma/Bari, Laterza, 2007, pp. 67–95.

S. Pfeiffer, 'The God Serapis, his Cult and the Beginnings of the Ruler Cult in Ptolemaic Egypt', in P. McKechnie and P. Guillaume (eds), *Ptolemy II Philadelphus and his World*, Leiden, Brill, 2017, pp. 387–480.

Plutarch, *De Iside et Osiris,* in *Moralia*, 351C–384C.

J. Stambaugh, *Sarapis under the Early Ptolemies*, Leiden, Brill, 1972.

R. Stiehl, 'The Origin of the Cult of Sarapis', *History of Religions*, Vol. 3, no. 1, 1963, pp. 21–33.

## Cleopatra VII

Cassius Dio, *The Roman History*, 42–51.

M. Chauveau, *Cleopatra: Beyond the Myth*, Ithaca, NY, Cornell University Press, 2002.

Cicero, *Letters to Atticus*, 374, 377.

M. Grant, *From Alexander to Cleopatra*, London, Weidenfeld & Nicolson, 1982.

P. Green, *Alexander to Actium: The Historical Evolution of the Hellenistic Age*, Berkeley, CA, University of California Press, 1993.

Horace, *Odes and Epodes*, I, 37.

Plutarch, *Life of Antony*, 1988.

## Cyrenaic Philosophy

U. Zilioli, *The Cyrenaics*, Oxon and New York, Routledge, 2014.

## Diogenes and Cynic Philosophy

G. Boas, *Primitivism and Related Ideas in the Middle Ages*, Baltimore, MD, Johns Hopkins University Press, 1997, pp. 87–126.

W. Desmond, *Cynics*, Oakland, CA, University of California Press, 2008.

W. Desmond, *The Greek Praise of Poverty: Origins of Ancient Cynicism*, Notre Dame, IN, University of Notre Dame Press, 2006.

F. G. Downing, *Cynics and Christian Origins*, London, T&T Clark, 1992.
R. Hard (ed.), *Diogens the Cynic, Sayings and Anecdotes*, Oxford, Oxford University Press, 2012.
D. Laertius, *Lives of Eminent Philosophers, Diogenes*, VI.

## Pyrrho and Ancient Sceptic Philosophy

J. Annas and J. Barnes, *The Modes of Scepticism: Ancient Texts and Modern Interpretations*, Cambridge, Cambridge University Press, 1985.
C. I. Beck with, *Greek Buddha: Pyrrho's Encounter with Early Buddhism in Central Asia*, Princeton, NJ, Princeton University Press, 2015.
R. Bett, *Pyrrho, His Antecedents, and His Legacy*, Oxford, Oxford University Press, 2000.
Cicero, *On Academic Scepticism*.
A. Kuzminski, *Pyrrhonism: How the Ancient Greeks Reinvented Buddhism*, Lanham, MD, Lexington Books, 2010.
Sextus Empiricus, *Outlines of Pyrrhonism*.
R. Stoneman, 'Naked Philosophers: The Brahmans in the Alexander Historians and the Alexander Romance', *The Journal of Hellenic Studies*, Vol. 115, 1995, pp. 99–114.

## The Greeks in India

P. J. Kosmin, *The Land of the Elephant Kings: Space, Territory, and Ideology in the Seleucid Empire*, Cambridge, MA, Harvard University Press, 2014.
R. Mairs (ed.), *The Graeco-Bactrian and Indo-Greek World*, London/New York, Routledge, 2020.
R. Mairs, *The Hellenistic Far East: Archaeology, Language, and Identity in Greek Central Asia*, Oakland, CA, University of California Press, 2016.
A. K. Narain, *The Indo-Greeks: Revisited and Supplemented*, Delhi, B.R. Publishing Corporation, 2003.
S. Sherwin-White and A. Kuhrt, *From Samarkhand to Sardis: A New Approach to the Seleucid Empire*, Oakland, CA, University of California Press, 1993.
R. Stoneman, *The Greek Experience of India: from Alexander to the Indo-Greeks*, Princeton, NJ, Princeton University Press, 2021.

W. W. Tarn, *The Greeks in Bactria and India,* Cambridge, Cambridge University Press, 1966.

## Mahayana Buddhism

A. Heirman and S. P. Bumbacher (eds.), *The Spread of Buddhism*, Leiden, Brill, 2007.

P. Williams, *Mahayana Buddhism: The Doctrinal Foundations*, London/New York, Routledge, 2008.

H. Zimmer, *Philosophies of India*, Princeton/Oxford, Princeton University Press, 1951, pp. 507–34.

## Gandharan Art and the Image of the Buddha

A. K. Coomaraswamy, *Elements of Buddhist Iconography,* Cambridge, MA, Harvard University Press, 1935.

A. K. Coomaraswamy, 'The Indian Origin of the Buddha Image', *Journal of the American Oriental Society*, Vol. 46, 1926, pp. 165–70.

A. K. Coomaraswamy, 'The Origin of the Buddha Image', *The Art Bulletin*, Vol. 9, No. 4, June 1927, pp. 287–329.

R. DeCaroli, *Image Problems: The Origin and Development of the Buddha's Image in Early South Asia*, Seattle, WA, University of Washington Press, 2015.

M. S. Falser, 'The Graeco-Buddhist Style of Gandhara – a "Storia Ideologica", Or: How a Discourse Makes a Global History of Art', *The Journal of Art Historiography*, Vol. 13, 2015, pp. 1–53.

A. Kouremenos, Sujatha Chandrasekaran and Roberto Rossi (eds.), *From Pella to Gandhara: Hybridisation and Identity in the Art and Architecture of the Hellenistic East*, Oxford, BAR Publishing, 2011.

W. Rienjang and P. Stewart (eds.), *Gandharan Art in its Buddhist Context*, Oxford, Archaeopress, 2023.

## The Persian Reception of The Alexander Romance

Ferdowsi, *Shahnameh: The Persian Book of Kings*, edited and translated by D. Davis, London/New York, Penguin, 2016.

H. Manteghi, *Alexander the Great in the Persian Tradition History, Myth and Legend in Medieval Iran*, London, I.B. Tauris, 2018.

M. S. Southgate (ed. and trans.), *Iskandarnamah*, New York, NY, Columbia University Press, 1978.
R. Stoneman, K. Erickson and I. Netton (eds), *The Alexander Romance in Persia and the East*, Eelde, Barkhuis, 2018.
E. Venetis, 'The Iskandarnama: An Analysis of an Anonymous Medieval Persian Prose Romance', PhD thesis, Edinburgh, University of Edinburgh, 2006, pp. 92–95.

## The Muslim Reception of The Alexander Romance

Al-Dinarawi, Abu Hanifah, *Kitab al-akhbar al-tiwal*, Leiden, 1888.
Al-Mas'udi, Abu al-Hasn 'Ali, *Kitab al-tanbih wa-al-ishraf*, Beirut, 1965.
Al-Tabari, Abu Ja'far Muhammad, *Tarikh al-rusul wa-al-muluk*, edited by J. Barth, 15 vols., Beirut, 1962–65.
Al-Tarsusi, Abu Tahir Muhammad, *Darabnamah-yi Tarsusi*, edited by Z. Safa, 2 vols., Persian Text Series, nos. 23, 36, Tehran, 1965–68.
Jami, Abd al-Rahman, 'Khiradnamah-yi Iskandari', in M. Madrasi Gilan (ed.), *Masnavi-yi haft awrang*, Tehran, 1958.
Nizami, Nizam al-Din Ilyas, *Sharafnamah*, edited by V. Dastgirdi, Tehran, 1937.
Nizami, Nizam al-Din Ilyas, *Iqbalnamah ya Khiradnamah*, edited by V. Dastgirdi, Tehran, 1956.
R. Stoneman, 'Alexander the Great in the Arabic Tradition', in S. Panayotakis, Maaike Zimmerman and Wytse Keulen (eds), *The Ancient Novel and Beyond*, Leiden, Brill, 2003, pp. 1–21.
D. Zuwiyya, 'The Alexander Romance in The Arabic Tradition', in D. Zuwiyya (ed.), *A Companion to Alexander Literature in the Middle Ages*, Leiden, Brill, pp. 73–112.

## The Syncretic al-Khidr

*Quran*, Sura 18, *Al Kahf*, 'the Cave', lines 60–82. (The same sura that contains the story of 'He of the two horns')
Al-Bukhari, *Sahih al-Bukhari*, 1:63, 1:65-66, 1:90-93, 4:406, 6:211-215, 6:220-224.
A. Augustinovic, *"El Khadr" and the Prophet Elijah, Jerusalem*, Jerusalem, Franciscan Printing Press, 1972.
A. K. Coomaraswamy, 'Khwaja Khadir and the Fountain of Life in the Tradition of Persian and Mughal Art', in *"What is Civilisation" and Other Essays*, Cambridge, Golgosova Press, 1989, pp. 157–67.

H. Corbin, *Alone with the Alone: Creative Imagination in the Ṣūfism of Ibn ʿArabī*, Princeton, NJ, Princeton University Press, 1998, pp. 32–101.

W. Dalrymple, *From the Holy Mountain: A Journey Among Christians of the Middle East*, New York, NY, Henry Holt, 1997, pp. 339–399.

H. T. Halmat, *Where the Two Seas Meet: Al-khidr and Moses-the Qurʾanic Story of Al-khidr and Moses in Sufi Commentaries as a Model for Spiritual Guidance*, Louisville, KY, Fons Vitae, 2013.

J. Latif, 'The Green Man: What Reading Khidr as Trickster Evinces about the Canon', *Ilahiyat Studies*, Vol. 11, No. 1, 2020, pp. 9–46.

H. Yusuf, 'Buddha in the Qurʾan?' in R. S. Kazemi and H. Yusuf (eds), *Common Ground Between Islam & Buddhism*, Louisville, KY, Fons Vitae, 2010, pp. 113–36.

# 3 – Cosmonauts

## Late Antiquity

P. Browne, *The Body and Society: Men, Women, and Sexual Renunciation in Early Christianity*, New York, NY, Columbia University Press, 2008.

P. Brown, *The World of Late Antiquity*, London, Thames & Hudson, 2004.

A. Cameron, *The Mediterranean World in Late Antiquity: AD 395-700*, London and New York, Routledge, 2011.

H. Isbell (ed and trans.), *The Last Poets of Imperial Rome*, London, Penguin, 1971.

Justinian, *Corpus Iuris Civilis*, vol. 2, I, 5.18.4, Berlin, 1954, p. 57.

S. Mazzarino, *La Fine del Mondo Antico*, Torino, Bollati Boringhieri, 2008.

Saint Augustine, *City of God*, translated by H. Bettenson, London and New York, Penguin, 2003.

## Julian and The Late Pagan Milieu

P. Athanassiadi, *Julian: An Intellectual Biography*, Abingdon-on-Thames, Routledge, 2014.

A. Cameron, *The Last Pagans of Rome*, Oxford, Oxford University Press, 2010.

Celsus, *On the True Doctrine*, edited and translated by R. J. Hoffman, Oxford, Oxford University Press, 1987.

Gregory of Nazianzus, *Julian the Emperor, Containing Gregory of Nazianzen's Two Invectives and Libanius's Monody with Julian's Extant Theosophical Works; Oration 5.23*, translated by C. W. King, London, Bohn's Classical Library, 1888,

Julian, *Complete Works in 3 Vols.*, Cambridge, MA, Harvard University Press, 1989.

Porphyry, *Against the Christians*, edited and translated by R. J. Hoffman, Amherst, NY, Prometheus, 1994.

Salutius, 'On the Gods and the World', in T. Taylor (ed. and trans.), *Sallust on the Gods and the World: and the Pythagoric Sentences of Demophilus and Five Hymns by Proclus*, London, Edward Jeffrey, 1793.

S. Elm, *Sons of Hellenism, Fathers of the Church: Emperor Julian, Gregory of Nazianzus, and the Vision of Rome*, Berkeley, University of California Press, 2012, p. 459.

A. Momigliano (ed.), *The Conflict Between Paganism and Christianity in the Fourth Century*, Oxford, Oxford University Press, 1963.

H. U. Wiemer and S. Rebenich (eds.), *A Companion to Julian the Apostate*, Leiden, Brill, 2020

For a modern revival of the late Pagan outlook, see W. Otto, *Teofania*, translated by G. Moretti, Milano, Adelphi, 2021.

## Ancient Philosophy as a Way of Life

P. Hadot, *Philosophy as a Way of Life*, Chichester, Wiley-Blackwell, 1995.

P. Hadot, *What is Ancient Philosophy?*, translated by M. Chase, Cambridge, MA, Harvard University Press, 2002.

For the same theme in Christianity, see *John*, 14:6; *Matthew* 7:13-14; *Acts*, 9.2.

## Neoplatonism

Addey, *Divination and Theurgy in Neoplatonism: Oracles of the Gods*, Abingdon-on-Thames, Routledge, 2019.

Agathias, *The Histories*, 30.4–31.8, translated by J. D. Frendo, Berlin, Walter de Gruyter, 1975, pp. 65–7.

L. E. Goodman (ed.), *Neoplatonism and Jewish Thought*, Albany, NY, SUNY, 1992.

P. M. Gregorios (ed.), *Neoplatonism and Indian Philosophy*, Albany, NY, SUNY, 2017.

Iamblichus, *On the Mysteries*, translated by E. C. Clarke and J. M. Dillon, Atlanta, GA, Society of Biblical Literature, 2003.

P. Morewedge (ed.), *Neoplatonism and Islamic Thought*, Albany, NY, SUNY, 1992.

D. Nikulin, *Neoplatonism in Late Antiquity*, Oxford, Oxford University Press, 2019.

D. J. O'Meara (ed.), *Neoplatonism and Christian Thought*, Albany, NY, SUNY, 1981.

Plotinus, *The Enneads*, translated by L.P. Gerson, Cambridge, Cambridge University Press, 2019.

Porphyry, *On the Cave of the Nymphs in the Odyssey*, translated by T. Taylor, Lamp of Trismegistus, 2021.

Proclus, *The Elements of Theology*, edited and translated by E. R. Dodds, Oxford, Oxzford University Press, 1995.

Pseudo Dionysius, *The Complete Works*, edited and translated by C. Luibheid, New York, NY, Paulist Press, 1987.

G. Reale, *Toward a New Interpretation of Plato*, translated by J. R. Catan and R. Davies, Washington, DC, The Catholic University of America Press, 1996.

R. T. Wallis and J. Bregman (eds.), *Neoplatonism and Gnosticism*, Albany, NY, SUNY, 1992.

## Hypatia

Damascius, *The Philosophical History*, 43A, translated by P. Athanassiadi, Athens, Apamea, 1999, p. 129.

M. Dzielska, *Hypatia of Alexandria*, Cambridge, MA, Harvard University Press, 1995.

Socrates Scholasticus, 'Historia Ecclesiastica, VII, 15', in *The History of the Church*, London, Awnsham and John Churchill, 1709, p. 376.

E. J. Watts, *Hypatia: The Life and Legend of an Ancient Philosopher*, Oxford, Oxford University Press, 2017.

## Hermes Trismegistus

B. P. Copenhaver (ed. and trans.), *Hermetica: The Greek Corpus Hermeticutn and the Latin Asclepius*, Cambridge, Cambridge University Press, 2008.

A.-J. Festugière. *La Révélation d'Hermès Trismégiste*, Vol. 4, *Le Dieu Inconnu*, Paris, Librairie Lecoffre, 1954.

G. Fowden, *The Egyptian Hermes: A historical Approach to the Late Ancient Mind*, Princeton, NJ, Princeton University Press, 1986.

## Mythical Androgyny

L. Birsson (ed. and trans.), *Sexual Ambivalence: Androgyny and Hermaphroditism in Graeco-Roman Antiquity*, Berkeley, CA, University of California Press, 2002

W. Doniger O'Flaherty, *Women, Androgynes and Other Mythical Beasts*, Chicago, IL, University of Chicago Press, 1980.

Z. Zhou, *Androgyny in Late Ming and Early Qing Literature*, Honolulu, HI, University of Hawaii Press, 2003

E. Zolla, *The Androgyne: Reconciliation of Male and Female*, New York, NY, Crossroad, 1981.

## Gnosticism

D. M. Burns, *Apocalypse of the Alien God: Platonism and the Exile of Sethian Gnosticism*, Philadelphia, PA, University of Pennsylvania Press, 2014.

Epiphanes, 'On Righteousness, in Clement of Alexandria, *Stromateis*, III, 6-9', in J. Ferguson (ed. and trans.), *Clement of Alexandria: Stromateis Books One to Three*, Washington, D.C., The Catholic University of America Press, 2005, pp. 259–62.

G. Filoramo, *A History of Gnosticism*, Cambridge, MA, Blackwell, 1990.

H. Jonas, *The Gnostic Religion: The Message of the Alien God and the Beginnings of Christianity*, Boston, Beacon, 2001.

M. Meyer (ed. and trans.), *The Nag Hammadi Scriptures*, New York, NY, Harper One, 2008.

H. C. Puech, *En Quete de la Gnose*, Paris, Gallimard, 1979.

K. Rudolph, *Gnosis: The Nature and History of Gnosticism*, translated by R. McLachlan Wilson, San Francisco, CA, Harper & Row, 1987.

M. A. Williams. *Rethinking Gnosticism: An Argument for Dismantling a Dubious Category*, Princeton, NJ, Princeton University Press, 1999.

## Anti-Gnostic Christian literature

Epiphanius of Salamis, *The Panarion of Epiphanius of Salamis*, translated by F. Williams, Leiden/New York, NY, Brill, 1987.

Hyppolitus of Rome, *Philosophumena: or, The Refutation of All Heresies*, translated by F. Legge, 2 vols., New York, NY, MacMillan, 1921.

Irenaeus of Lyons, *Against Heresies*, translated by A. Roberts and J. Donaldson, Jackson, MI, Ex Fontibus, 2020.

## Mani and Manichaeism

I. Gardner (ed. and trans.), *The Kephalaia of the Teacher: The Edited Coptic Manichaean Texts in English Translation with Commentary*, Leiden, Brill, 1995.

I. Gardner, *The Founder of Manichaeism: Rethinking the Life of Mani*, Cambridge, Cambridge University Press, 2020.

A. Gnoli, *Il Manicheismo*, 3 Vols., Milano, Arnoldo Mondadori, 2003–2008.

S. N. C. Lieu, *Manichaeism in Central Asia and China*, Leiden, Brill, 1998.

S. N. C. Lieu, *Manichaeism in Mesopotamia and the Roman East*, Leiden, Brill, 1997.

J. Ries, *Mani et Manicheisme*, Paris, Beauchesne, 1964.

Y. Stoyanov, *The Other God: Dualist Religion from Antiquity to the Cathar Heresy*, New Haven, CT, Yale University Press, 2000.

M. Tardieu, *Manichaeism*, Chicago, IL, University of Illinois Press, 2008.

R. C. Zaehner, *Zurvan: A Zoroastrian Dilemma*, Oxford, Clarendon Press, 1955.

## The Afterlife of Manichaeism

M. Barber, *The Cathars: Dualist Heretics in Languedoc in the High Middle Ages*, London and New York, Routledge, 2013

D. Obolensky, *The Bogomils: A Study in Balkan Neo-Manichaeism*, Cambridge, Cambridge University Press, 2008.

# 4 – Translators

## Digenis Akritas and the Byzantine border epic

D. B. Hull (ed. and trans.), *Digenis Akritas: The Two Blood Border Lord*, IV, 27–28, 36, Athens, OH, Ohio University Press, 1972.

C. Jouanno, 'Shared Spaces: 1 Digenis Akritis, the Two-Blood Border Lord', in C. Cupane and B. Krönung (eds), *Fictional Storytelling in the Medieval Eastern Mediterranean and Beyond*, Leiden/Boston, Brill, 2016, pp. 260–84.

V. Mitevski, 'The Akritic Hero in Byzantine and Macedonian Epic Poetry', *Colloquia Humanistica*, Vol. 7, 2018.

N. Politis, *Canciones del pueblo griego: selección*, Ediciones de la Universidad de Castilla-La Mancha, 2006.

## Amira Dat Al-Himma and the Arabic border epic

*The Cycle of Omar and His Sons*, in M. C. Lyons (ed. and trans.), *The Arabian Nights: Tales of 1001 Nights*, 3 vols., London/New York, Penguin, 2010.

M. Magidow (ed. and trans.), *The Tale of Princess Fatima, Warrior Woman: The Arabic Epic of Dhat al-Himma*, London/New York, Penguin, 2021.

C. Ott, 'Shared Spaces: 2 Cross-border Warriors in the Arabian Folk Epic', in C. Cupane and B. Krönung (eds), *Fictional Storytelling in the Medieval Eastern Mediterranean and Beyond*, Leiden/Boston, Brill, 2016, pp. 285–311.

## Baghdad and the Arabic Translation Movement

P. Adamson, *Al-Kindi*, Oxford, Oxford University Press, 2007.

J. Al-Khalili, *The House of Wisdom: How Arabic Science Saved Ancient Knowledge and Gave Us the Renaissance*, London/New York, Penguin, 2012.

Al-Tabari, *The Early Abbasi Empire*, trans. J. A. William, 2 vols., Cambridge, Cambridge University Press, 1998.

D. Guptas, *Greek Thought, Arabic Culture: The Graeco-Arabic Translation Movement in Baghdad and Early Society (2nd–4th / 8th–10th centuries)*, London, Routledge, 1998.

M. G. S. Hodgson, *The Venture of Islam: The Classical Age of Islam*, 3 vols.: Vol. 1, Chicago/London, The University of Chicago Press, 1977.

F. Rosenthal, *The Classical Heritage in Islam*, translated by E. Marmorstein and J. Marmorstein, London, Routledge, 1975.

G. Saliba, *Islamic Science and the Making of the European Renaissance*, Cambridge, MA, The MIT Press, 2007.

N. Yoffee (ed.), *The Cambridge World History, vol. 3: Early Cities in Comparative Perspective, 4000 BCE–1200 CE*, Cambridge, Cambridge University Press, 2015.

## The First Crusade

U. Ibn Munqidh, *The Book of Contemplation: Islam and the Crusades*, edited and translated by P. M. Cobb, London/New York, Penguin, 2008.
A. Komnene, *The Alexiad*, translated by E. R. A. Sewter, London/New York, Penguin, 2009.
A. Maalouf, *The Crusades Through Arab Eyes*, London, Saqi, 2006
C. Tyerman (ed. and trans.), *Chronicles of the First Crusade*, London/New York, Penguin, 2011.

## Constantinus Africanus and the Arabic-to-Latin Translation Movement

H. Bloch, *Monte Cassino in the Middle Ages*, Cambridge, MA, Harvard University Press, 1988.
C. Burnett, *Arabic into Latin in the Middle Ages: The Translators and their Intellectual and Social Context*, London, Routledge, 2009.
C. Burnett and D. Jacquart, *Constantine the African And 'Ali Ibn Al-'Abbas Al-Magusi: The Pantegni and Related Texts*, Leiden, Brill, 1994.

## Andalusia and Toledo

M. R. Cohen, *Under Crescent and Cross: The Jews in the Middle Ages*, Princeton, NJ, Princeton, 1994.
E. Fidalgo Francisco, *Alfonso X el Sabio: cronista y protagonista de su tiempo*, La Rioja, Fundación San Millán de la Cogolla, 2021.
R. Fletcher, *Moorish Spain*, Berkeley and Los Angeles, CA, University of California Press, 2006.
H. Kennedy, *Muslim Spain and Portugal: A Political History of al-Andalus*, London, Routledge, 1996.
M. R. Menocal, *The Literature of al-Andalus*, Cambridge, Cambridge University Press, 2000.

M. R. Menocal, *The Ornament of The World: How Muslims, Jews, and Christians Created a Culture of Tolerance in Medieval Spain*, Boston, MA, Little, Brown, 2003.

A. Vanoli, *La Reconquista*, Bologna, Il Mulino, 2009.

## Ibn Rushd (Averroes)

Averroes (Ibn Rushd) of Cordoba, *Long Commentary on the De Anima of Aristotle*, translated by R. C. Taylor, New Haven, CT, Yale University Press, 2009).

Averroes, *On the Harmony of Religion and Philosophy*, translated by G. F. Hourani, London, Gibb Memorial Trust, 2012.

P. Adamson and M. di Giovanni, *Interpreting Averroes: Critical Essays*, Cambridge, Cambridge University Press, 2018).

H. A. Davidson, *Alfarabi, Avicenna and Averroes on Intellect*, Oxford, Oxford University Press, 1992.

## Moses Ben Maimon (Maimonides)

M. Maimonides, *The Guide of the Perplexed*, 2 vols., translated by S. Pines, Chicago, The University of Chicago Press, 1974.

Moshe ben Maimon, 'A Letter of Maimonides about Conversion and Martyrdom', translated and edited by R. Szpiech, in N. Hurvitz, C. Sahner, Uriel Simonsohn and Luke Yarbrough (eds), *Conversion to Islam in the Premodern Age*, Oakland, CA, University of California Press, 2020, pp. 217–19.

J. Kraemer, *Perspectives on Maimonides: Philosophical and Historical Studies*, Oxford, Oxford University Press, 1991.

## Marranos and Moriscos

David M. Gitlitz, *Secrecy and Deceit. The Religion of the Crypto-Jews*, Albuquerque, NM, University of New Mexico Press, 2002.

D. di Cesare, *Marranos: The Other of the Other*, Cambridge, Polity, 2020.

F. Heymann, *Morte o battesimo. Una storia di marrani*, edited by J. H. Schoeps, Firenze, Giuntina, 2007.

M. E. Perry, *The Handless Maiden: Moriscos and the Politics of Religion in Early Modern Spain*, Princeton, NJ, Princeton University Press, 2013.

C. Roth, *A History of the Marranos*, New York, NY, Sepher-Hermon Press, 1992.

Y. H. Yerushalmi, *From Spanish Court to Italian Ghetto: Isaac Cardoso: A Study in Seventeenth Century Marranism and Jewish Apologetics*, New York, NY, Columbia University Press, 1971.

## The Kabbalah and Jewish Mysticism

G. Busi, *La Qabbalah*, Bari, Laterza, 2016.

G. Busi (ed.), *Zohar: Il libro dello splendore*, translated by A. L. Callow, Torino, Einaudi, 2016.

M. Idel, *Kabbalah: New Perspectives*, New Haven, CT, Yale University Press, 1990.

G. Scholem, *Major Trends in Jewish Mysticism*, New York, NY, Schocken Books, 1995.

## Giovanni Pico della Mirandola and Humanism in the Italian Renaissance

G. Busi and R. Ebgi, *Giovanni Pico della Mirandola. Mito, magia, Qabbalah*, Torino, Einaudi, 2014.

M. Cacciari, *La Mente Inquieta*, Torino, Einaudi, 2019.

H. de Lubac, *Pico della Mirandola. L'alba incompiuta del Rinascimento*, Milano, Jaca Book, 2016.

A. Foa, *Gli Ebrei in Italia: I primi 2000 anni*, Bari, Laterza, 2022.

M. Fumagalli Beonio Brocchieri, *Pico della Mirandola*, Bari, Laterza, 2011.

E. Garin, *Giovanni Pico della Mirandola: Vita e dottrine*, Istituto Nazionale di Studi sul Rinascimento, Roma/Firenze, 2011.

E. Garin, *L'Umanesimo Italiano*, Bari, Laterza, 1994.

G. F. Pico, *Giovanni Pico della Mirandola: His Life by his Nephew Giovanni Francesco Pico*, translated by Sir T. Moore, London, David Nutt, 1890.

G. Pico della Mirandola, *On the Dignity of Man, On Being and the One, Heptaplus*, translated by C. G. Wallis, Paul J. W. Miller and Douglas Carmichael, Indianapolis/Cambridge, Hackett, 1998.

## 5 – Traitors

## Americas

B. de las Casas, *A Short Account of the Destruction of the Indies*, translated by N. Griffin, London, Penguin, 1992.

A. Nunez Cabeza de Vaca, *Castaways: The Narrative of Alvar Nunez Cabeza de Vaca*, translated by F. M. Lopez-Morillas, Berkeley, CA, University of California Press, 1993.

## Mediterranean Corsairs

B. & L. Bennassar, *Les Chretiens d'Allah*, Paris, Editions Perrin, 1989.

S. Bono, *Guerre Corsare nel Mediterraneo: una storia di incursioni, arrembaggi, razzie*, Bologna, Il Mulino, 2019.

M. Lenci, *Corsari: guerra, schiavi, rinnegati nel Mediterraneo*, Roma, Carocci, 2007.

## Mediterranean Slavery

S. Bono, *Schiavi: una storia mediterranea (XVI-XIX secolo)*, Bologna, il Mulino, 2016.

F. Caronni, *Ragguaglio del Viaggio in Barberia*, edited by S. Bono, Milano, San Paolo, 1993.

E. de Aranda, *Il Riscatto: relazione sulla schiavitù di un gentiluomo ad Algeri*, translated by A. Pellegrino Ceccarelli, Milano, Serra e Riva, 1981.

M. de Cervantes, *The Bagnios of Algiers and The Great Sultana: Two Plays of Captivity*, translated by B. Fuchs and A. J. Ilika, Philadelphia, PA, University of Pennsylvania Press, 2009.

M. A. Garces, *Cervantes in Algiers: A Captive's Tale*, Nashville, TN, Vanderbilt University Press, 2005.

L. F. Marsigli, *La schiavitu' del generale Marsigli sotto i Tartari e i Turchi da lui stesso narrata*, edited by E. Lovarini, Bologna, Zanichelli, 1931.

I. Luzzana Caraci and M. Pozzi, *Scopritori e Viaggiatori del Cinquecento e Seicento*, Milano, Ricciardini, 1991.

O. of Timisoara, *Prisoner of the Infidels: The memoir of an Ottoman Muslim in Seventeenth-Century Europe*, edited and translated by G. Casale, Oakland, CA, University of California Press, 2021.

## St. Benedetto il Moro

G. Fiume, *Il Santo Moro: i processi di canonizzazione di Benedetto da Palermo (1594–1807)*, Milano, Franco Angeli, 2008.

V. Morabito, "San Benedetto il Moro da Palermo, protettore degli africani di Siviglia, della penisola iberica e d'America latina", in B. Ares Queija and B. Stella (eds), *Negros, Mulatos y Zambaigos: derroteros africanos en los mundos ibericos*, Sevilla, Escuela de Estudios Hispano-Americanos de Sevilla, 2000.

## Leo Africanus

J. L. Africanus (Al-Hasan Ibn Muhammad al Wazzan), *The Cosmography and Geography of Africa*, London, Penguin, 2023.

N. Zemon Davis, *Trickster Travels: A Sixteenth-Century Muslim between Worlds*, London, Faber & Faber, 2008.

## Fortuna

Seminario Mnemosyne (ed.), 'Fortuna during the Renaissance: A Reading of Plate 48 of Aby Warburg's Bilderatlas Mnemosyne', *La Rivista di Engramma*, n. 137, agosto 2016, pp. 23–58.

## Vivaldi and Tiepolo

R. Calasso, *Tiepolo Pink*, London, Penguin, 2020.

R. Gjerdingen, *Music in the Galant Style*, Oxford, Oxford University Press, 2019.

M. Levey, *Painting in Eighteenth Century Venice*, New Haven, CT, Yale University Press, 1994.

M. Talbot, *Vivaldi*, Oxford, Oxford University Press, 2000.

## The Ottoman Empire

A. Barbero, *Solimano il Magnifico*, Roma-Bari, Laterza, 2010.

C. Finkel, *Osman's Dream: The History of the Ottoman Empire*, New York, NY, Basic Books, 2007.

D. Goffman, *The Ottoman Empire and Early Modern Europe*, Cambridge, Cambridge University Press, 2002.

H. Inalcik, *The Ottoman Empire: 1300–1600*, London, W&N, 2000.

N. Itzkowitz, *Ottoman Empire and Islamic Tradition*, Chicago, IL, The University of Chicago Press, 1980.

M. Levey, *The World of Ottoman Art*, London, Thames and Hudson, 1975.

S. McMeekin, *The Ottoman Endgame: War, Revolution and the Making of the Modern Middle East, 1908–1923*, London/New York, Penguin, 2016.

D. Quataert, *The Ottoman Empire, 1700–1922*, Cambridge, Cambridge University Press, 2005.

## The Ottomanists

G. De Rada, 'Testamento Politico', in *Opera Omnia, vol. IX, Opere filosofiche e politiche*, Soveria Mannelli, Rubbettino, 2009.

A. Grassi, *Chartre Turque, ou Organisation Religieuse, civile et militare de l'empire Ottoman*, Paris, Mongies, 1825.

Linny Babagor (i.e. Giorgio Libri-Bagnano), *Réponse d'un Turc à la Note sur la Grèce, de M. le vicomte de Chateaubriand, membre de la Societé en faveur des Grecs*, Bruxelles, Mayet, 1825.

## The Balkans

I. Andric, *The Bridge over the Drina*, translated by L. F. Edwards, London, Allen & Unwin, 1921.

M. Crnjanski, *Migrazioni*, 2 vols., Milano, Adelphi, 1998-2011.

M. Glenny, *The Balkans, 1804–2012: Nationalism, War and the Great Powers*, London, Granta, 2017.

M. Mazower, *Salonica, City of Ghosts: Christians, Muslims and Jews*, New York, NY, Harper Perennial, 2005.

## The Bektashi Sufi order

R. Elsie, *The Albanian Bektashi: History and Culture of a Dervish Order in the Balkans*, London, I. B. Tauris, 2019.

H. Kucuk, *The Role of the Bektashis in Turkey's National Struggle*, Leiden, Brill, 2002.

B. Rexheb, *Islamic Mysticism and the Bektashi Path*, translated by H. Abiva, Chicago, IL, Babagan Books, 2016.

## Modern Mediterranean Diasporas

J. A. Clancy-Smith, *Mediterraneans: North Africa and Europe in an Age of Migration, c. 1800–1900*, Oakland, CA, University of California Press, 2010.

M. Isabella and K. Zanou, *Mediterranean Diasporas: Politics and Ideas in the Long 19th Century*, London, Bloomsbury, 2016.

## Anarchist diaspora

A. B. Çorlu, 'Anarchists and Anarchism in the Ottoman Empire, 1850–1917', in S. Karahasanoglu (ed.), *History From Below: A Tribute in Memory of Donald Quataert*, Istanbul, Istanbul Bilgi University Press, 2016.

I. Eberhardt, *The Oblivion Seekers*, translated by P. Bowles, London, Peter Owen, 2010.

Pietro Gori, 'Addio a Lugano', in Istituto Ernesto de Martino (eds), *Avanti Popolo: due secoli di canti popolari e di protesta civile*, Milano, Ricordi, 1998.

## WWI

L. F. Celine, *Journey to the End of the Night*, translated by R. Manheim, London, Alma Classics, 2012.

G. Chevallier, *Fear*, translated by J. Berger, London, Serpent's Tail, 2012.

## Fiume and D'Annunzio

H. Bey, *T.A.Z.: The Temporary Autonomous Zone, Ontological Anarchism, Poetic Terrorism*, Second edition, Brooklyn, NY, Autonomedia, 2003.

G. Comisso, *Le Mie Stagioni*, Milano, Longanesi, 1963.

G. D'Annunzio, *La Penultima Ventura: scritti e discorsi fiumani*, edited by R. de Felice, Milano, Mondadori, 1974.

R. de Felice, *D'Annunzio Politico: 1918–1938*, Roma-Bari, Laterza, 1978.

F. Gerra, *L'Impresa di Fiume, 1: Fiume d'Italia*, Milano, Longanesi, 1975.

L. Kochnitzky, *La Quinta Stagione: o i centauri di Fiume*, translated by A. Luchini, Bologna, Zanichelli, 1922.

C. Salaris, *Alla Festa della Rivoluzione: Artisti e libertari con D'Annunzio a Fiume*, Bologna, Il Mulino, 2002.

L. Toeplitz, *Ciak A Chi Tocca*, Milano, Edizioni Milano Nuova, 1964.

6 – Migrants

## Joseph Roth

J. Roth, *A Life in Letters*, translated and edited by M. Hofmann, New York, NY, W. W. Norton, 2012.

J. Roth, *Job: The Story of a Simple Man*, London, Granta, 2022.

J. Roth, *The Radetzky March*, London, David Campbell Publishers, 1996.

J. Roth, *The White Cities: Reports from France 1925–1939*, London, Granta, 2013.

S. Mortgensen, *Fuga e Fine di Joseph Roth*, Milano, Adelphi, 2001.

K. Pim, *Endless Flight: The life of Joseph Roth*, London, Granta, 2022.

## Late Austro-Hungarian Literature

M. Cacciari, *Dallo Steinhof: Prospettive viennesi del primo Novecento*, Milano, Adelphi, 2005.

A. Lernet-Holenia, *Die Standarte*, Berlin, Fischer, 2016.

C. Magris, *Il Mito Asburgico Nella Letteratura Austriaca Moderna*, Torino, Einaudi, 2009.

R. Musil, *The Man Without Qualities*, 2 vols., translated by S. Wilkins, London, Picador, 2017.

M. Perloff, *Edge of Irony: Modernism in the Shadow of the Habsburg Empire*, Chicago, IL, The University of Chicago Press, 2016

L. Perutz, *By Night Under the Stone Bridge*, translated by E. Mosbacher, London, HarperCollins, 1991.

H. von Hofmannsthal, *The Whole Difference: Selected writings of Hugo von Honfmannsthal*, edited and translated by J. D. McClatchy, Princeton, Princeton University Press, 2008.

F. Werfel, *Twilight of A World*, translated by H. T. Lowe-Porter, New York, NY, Viking, 1937.

S. Zweig, *The World of Yesterday: Memoirs of a European*, translated by A. Bell, London, Pushkin, 2024.

## Guido Morselli

G. Morselli, *Contro-Passato Prossimo*, Milano, Adelphi, 2016.

## Adelphi

R. Bazlen. *Scritti: Il capitano di lungo corso – note senza testo – lettere editoriali – lettere a Montale*, edited by R. Calasso, Milano, Adelphi, 1984.
R. Calasso, *L'Impronta dell'Editore*, Milano, Adelphi, 2013.
A. Ferrando, *Adelphi: Le origini di una casa editrice (1938–1994)*, Roma, Carocci, 2023.

## Cristina Campo

C. Campo, *Sotto Falso Nome*, Milano, Adelphi, 1998.
C. Campo, *The Unforgivable: And Other Writings*, New York, Ny, New York Review of Books, 2024.
C. De Stefano, *Belinda E Il Mostro: Vita segreta di Cristina Campo*, Milano, Adelphi, 2002.

## The Perennialists

A. K. Coomaraswamy, *Christian and Oriental Philosophy of Art*, Mineola, NY, Dover, 1956.
A. K. Coomaraswamy, *Figures of Speech or Figures of Thought?: The Traditional View of Art*, Bloomington, IN, World Wisdom, 2007.
R. Guenon, *The Multiple States of the Being*, Hillsdale, NY, Sophia Perennis, 2004.
R. Guenon, *The Reign of Quantity and the Signs of the Times*, Hillsdale, NY, Sophia Perennis, 2004.
M. Lings, *The Underlying Religion: An Introduction to the Perennial Philosophy*, Bloomington, IN, World Wisdom, 2007.
F. Schuon, *Esoterism: As Principle and as Way*, translated by W. Stoddart, Bedfont, Perennial Books, 1990.
F. Schuon, *The Transcendent Unity of Religions*, Wheaton, IL, Quest Books, 2011.
E. Zolla, *Che Cos'è La Tradizione*, Milano, Adelphi, 1998.
E. Zolla, *Verità Segrete Esposte in Evidenza: Sincretismo e fantasia, contemplazione ed esotericità*, Venezia, Marsilio, 1990.

## Eranos

J. Campbell (ed.), *Papers from the Eranos Yearbooks*, 5 vols., Princeton, NJ, Princeton University Press, 1982–2017.
J. Campbell, *The Hero with a Thousand Faces*, Novato, CA, New World Library, 2012.
J. Campbell, *The Masks of God*, 4 vols., Novato, CA, New World Library, 2021–2024.
H. Corbin, *Mundus Imaginalis: Or the Imaginary and the Imaginal*, translated by R. Horine, Ipswich, Golgonooza Press, 1976.
H. Corbin, *Spiritual Body and Celestial Earth: From Mazdean Iran to Shiite Iran*, Princeton, NJ, Princeton University Press, 1992.
J. Hillman, *Archetypal Psychology*, Thompson, CT, Spring Publications, 2021.
C. G. Jung, *The Archetypes and the Collective Unconscious*, translated by R. F. C. Hull, Abingdon-on-Thames, Routledge, 1991.
H. T. Hakl, *Eranos: An Alternative Intellectual History of the Twentieth Century*, translated by C. McIntosh, Abingdon-on-Thames, Routledge, 2013.
S. M. Wasserstrom, *Religion After Religion: Gershom Scholem, Mircea Eliade, & Henry Corbin at Eranos*, Princeton, NJ, Princeton University Press, 1999.

## Roberto Calasso

R. Calasso, *La Letteratura e gli Dei*, Milano, Adelphi, 2001.
R. Calasso, *La Rovina di Kasch*, Milano, Adelphi, 1994.
R. Calasso, *L'Ardore*, Milano, Adelphi, 2016.
R. Calasso, *La Tavoletta dei Destini*, Milano, Adelphi, 2020.
R. Calasso, *L'Innominabile Attuale*, Milano, Adelphi, 2020.
E. Sbrojavacca, *Letteratura Assoluta: Le opere e il pensiero di Roberto Calasso*, Milano, Feltrinelli, 2021.

## Contemporary Mediterranean Migrations

L. Casarini, *La Cospirazione del Bene*, Milano, Feltrinelli, 2024.
A. Dal Lago, *Non-persone: L'esclusione dei migranti in una società globale*, Milano, Feltrinelli, 2002.
A. Sciurba, *Campi di Forza: Percorsi confinati di migranti in Europa*, Verona, Ombre Corte, 2009.

# Index

*The 900 Thesis* 222

Abbasid dynasty 185–6, 189, 191
Abdullah, Asan bin 264
Abel 159
Achaemenid dynasty 77
Achilles 25, 55, 73, 80, 180
Acropolis of Athens 109
Adam 64, 112, 156–60, 167, 224
*Adelphi* 302, 304–6, 309, 315
Aedesius 129
Aesop's fables 83–4
Ahriman 166
Akhenaten, pharaoh 48–9
Akritas, Digenis 180–3, 322, 336
al-Amin 187–8
Alaric, rebellious generals 124–5
Albanian communities 267–8
Alemanno, Yohanan 226
Alemannus, Hermannus 209
*The Alexander Romance* 83–90, 97–9, 102, 113
Alexander the Great 7, 66, 70–7, 133, 282
   and Diogenes 98, 99
   meeting the naked sage 101, 102
   public collective wedding 79
   Sekandar 74
Alfonso X *el sabio*, kingdom of 209–10
Alfred of Sareshel 209
Alì, Uluç, *see* Galeni, Giovan Dionigi
al-Kindi 190–1
Allah 112–14, 179, 184, 223

Al-Ma'mun 187–9, 191
Amarna, city of 48
Ammon, the greatest among the gods 75, 93
*Ananke*, the force of Necessity 59
androgyny
   *Anthropoi* (humans) 149
   Third Envoy 167
Anglo-American imperialism 274
*Anschluss* 286–7
Anthropos 149
Antioch, city of 130, 184
Apis 77, 93
Apophis 19–20, 41–2, 47, 56–7, 323
Aquinas, Saint *Thomas* 208
Arcesilaus 103
archangels 155–60
Archimedes 95
Archons 154, 155, 166–7, 174
*arete* 60–1, 97
Argentoratum, town of 133
Aristarchus of Samothrace 96
Aristippus the Elder 97
Aristophanes of Byzantium 96
Aristotle 82, 100, 110–11, 184, 188–9, 208, 216, 219
Asclepius 80, 223
Aten 48–9
Atum 20, 23, 36–7, 41, 133
Augustine, Saint 125
Averroes, *see* Ibn Rushd
Avignon 290

Babylon, city of 81, 90, 99, 164–5

Baghdad, the city founded by
        God   178, 185–9
Balkans   171, 193, 251, 266–7, 271–2
Barbarossa, Hayreddin   251
Barbary coast of North
        Africa   250, 307
battle of Adrianople   102
battle of Ksar el Kebir   232
battle of Lepanto   249, 257
battle of the Granicus   71
battle of Tours   177
*Bayt al-Hikma*   189
Bazlen, Roberto   304
Bektashi Sufi   268
Benedetto il Moro, Saint   254
Benivieni, Girolamo   222, 227–8
Bey, Hakim   281
Bible   35, 96, 151, 173, 213
Black African slaves   253–4
Blood Christmas of Fiume   280
*Bodhisattvas*   107–8
Bogomil sect in Bulgaria   171
Borges, Jorge Luis   306
Brahmins   102, 105
Bronze Age
    afterlife, democratisation of   56
    Apophis and Amun   19–20
    Apsu and Mummu   21–2
    artistic transfiguration of a mortal
        life   62–3
    Atum, creator god of the
        Egyptians   22–4
    cosmic conflict in in Mediterranean
        cosmologies   22–3
    cosmic law of *tuche*   29
    cosmogonic inventiveness   65
    creation myths   42
    creation of humans   35
    discovery of death   44
    divinity and artistic perfection   62
    earliest development of
        Mediterranean imagination
        (*see* Mediterranean)
    Egyptian imagination
        curse of mortality   28
        fratricide   26
    eternal aspect of time   48
    fatalism   65
    First Intermediate Period   58
    hope and hopelessness   58
    human destiny   35
    lack of written records   16
    *maat*   57
    Mediterranean Catholicism   65
    Mesopotamian language   26
    mortality   46, 58, 64
    mountain range from Iberia to
        Morocco   13
    myths   17–19
    Palaeolithic and Neolithic
        tribes   16–17
    Perfect Moment   24
    person's soul   49
    polytheism   49
    principles of good and evil   19
    retirement   54
    sermons of heretical preachers   64
    shared humanity   44
    Shu and Tefnut   23–4
    Sky and the Earth, creation   32
    suffering   42–3
    Tablet of Destiny   59
    Tiamat, the primal waters   20
    war between generations   24–
        6, 30–1
    Waters of Death   50
Buber, Martin   293
Buddha   105–8, 165, 173
Buddhism
    *dharma*   105
    eightfold path   106
    mandala   313
    stupas   104
al-Burtuqali, Sultan Muhammad   225

Caesar, Julius   119, 132

Cain  159
Cairo, city of  177
Calasso, Roberto  304, 315–18
Callimachus of Cyrene  96
Cambyses II  77
Campo, Cristina  306–7, 309–12, 315
Canetti, Elias  293
cannibalism  235
capitalism  274
Capraia and Gorgona, islands of  126–7
Carthage, city of  196
Castillo, Alonso del  236, 239
Catholicism  65, 291–2
*chaos* of reality  7, 10, 213, 306
Charlemagne  177, 187
Chinese Turkestan  172
Chnodomar, King  133
Christ  82, 151, 158–61, 169–73, 179, 192, 235–6
Christian Armenian minority  270
Christian Gnostics  152
Christianity  58, 63, 96, 128, 134–5, 140, 152, 163–4, 179–82, 198, 205, 210, 220, 221, 246, 255–6, 268, 274
Christian 'reconquest' of Spain  8
Cleitus  70–3
colonization  228, 265
Columbus, Christopher  228
Confucius  173
Constantinople  120, 134, 178, 181, 182, 193, 255
Constantinus (known as Africanus)  196, 197
Constantius, Julius  129
Constantius II  129, 131
contemporary age
    Adelphi  302, 304–6, 309, 315
    Austro-Hungarian writers and intellectuals  293–6
    esotericism  311
    gatherings and groups  310

Great War  298
Holocaust  281, 293, 302
Internationalist socialism  299
Jewish (*see* Jew(ish))
Late Modernity  307–9
liberation struggle  308
Mediterranean imagination (*see* Mediterranean)
migrant detention centre  321, 323
*Mundus Imaginalis*  314–15
nostalgia  296–7
Roth (*see* Roth, Joseph)
Second World War  302
*Contro-Passato Prossimo* (*Near Counter-Past*)  300
Coomaraswamy, Ananda  310
Corbin, Henry  154, 313, 314
cosmogonies, Egyptian and Mesopotamian  10, 28
*The Cosmography and Geography of Africa*  256
*cosmos*  4, 6, 10, 17, 20–1, 47–50, 56–62, 64–5, 146, 147, 213, 306
creation myths  42
Crusaders  192–4
Crusades  8, 178, 192–7
Ctesibius  95
    science of pneumatics  95
Ctesiphon, city of  171
cult of the nation  264
cultural homogeneity  267
Cyrenaics  97
Cyrene, city of  96

Damascius  141–2
D'Annunzio, Gabriele  273–81
Dara, Persian emperor  111
Darab (Darius)  111
Darius  68, 72–3, 80, 109, 111
Dat al-Himma  322
Daud, Abraham ibn  208–9

de Ambris, Alceste 275
de Aranda, Emanuel 244, 253
de la Barca, Calderon 256
de las Casas, Bartolome 240
de León, Moses 210
del Medigo, Elia 219–20, 293
Democritus, the theorist of
    atomism 102
de Narvaez, Panfilo 233–4, 240
de Rada, Girolamo 267
de Sauvetât, Francis Raymond 207
de Torres, Luis 228
de Vaca, Alvar Nunez Cabeza 235–40, 321
D'Ghies, Hassuna 265
Dhu al-Qarnayn 112
Dinocrates, city to 91
Diogenes 98–101
Dionysus 93, 106–8
Dorantes, Andrés 236, 239

Ea, the god of wisdom 21, 24–5, 35, 38
Eberhardt, Isabelle 266
Ecbatana, city of 80
Egyptian Horus the Child 94
*Einaudi* 303–4
Emir 179–80, 310–11
*En Sof*, God's infinity 211
esotericism 311
Estevanico 236, 239
Euclid 189
Euphrates River 38, 44, 185
Eve 64, 157–62, 167, 324
existence, concept of 211
Eye 23, 36–7, 40–1, 51, 149, 158, 208, 223, 306

*falsafa*, philosophy 190
fascists
    anti 281, 304
    dictatorship 302
    era 280

Party 273, 281
    terrorism 303
Fatima 181–2
Fatimid dynasty 177, 192
Ferdinand, Archduke Franz 268
Ferdowsi, Abul-Qasem 110, 111
*feuilletons* 289
Fifteenth century to Seventeenth
    century 231–2
Fiume, town of 272–82
    revolution 275–8
Fiumicino, port of 123, 128
Flemish Rudolf of Bruges 209
Fourth century BC to Sixth century
    AD 119–20
*Francis of Assisi*, Saint 178
Frasheri, Shemseddin Sami 268
French Mediterranean 290
French Revolution 261
Freud, Sigmund 293
Fröbe-Kapteyn, Olga 312
Fuzhou, city of 172

Galen 184, 189, 196
Galeni, Giovan Dionigi 249
Gallus 129–31
Gandhara 108
    *Bodhisattvas* 108
    Gandharan statues of the
        Buddha 108
Geminiani, Francesco 259
*Genesis* 35, 213, 227
genocide 228
Gerard of Cremona 209
Gilgamesh 40, 44–7, 50–5
*gnosis* (knowledge) 153, 161
Gnosticism 7, 152–4, 159–63, 215, 282, 307, 321
    anti-Gnostic polemic 152
God's infinity, the *En Sof* 211
Gog and Magog 84, 112
Golden Age of Chronos 22
Grassi, Alfio 265

Greek Eros   94
Greek nymph   138
Greek Paganism   313
Greek philosophers   105
Greek *pilosophoi*   102
Greeks, ancient
   Arabic translations of the classics of   200
   medical treatises, Arabic translation of   194
   myths of human condition   38
   pagans   189
Greek translation of the Hebrew Bible   96
Greek war council   25
Guénon, René   310–11
*gujastak*   74, 109
*gymnosophoi* (naked sages)   102

Habsburg Empire   266, 272
Harpocrates   94, 308
Hathor, goddess of love and Lady of Drunkenness   41
healers   237, 238
Heaven   35, 46, 92, 113, 155–7, 162, 186
Hecate, goddess   125
Heliopolis, city of   40
Hellenism   66, 69, 75, 110, 118
   Alexander (*see* Alexander the Great)
   *The Alexander Romance*   83–92
   Buddhism   106
   cosmopolitism   98
   good and evil, distinctions   116
   Great Vehicle (*Mahayana*), Buddhism   107
   Hellenistic Alexandria   96
   Indian sages   103–4
   Indo-Greeks   104
   Muslim Alexander   113
   Persian Alexander   111
   Ptolemaic dynasty   97
   Ptolemaics   96–7
   Ptolemy   93–4
   Queen Cleopatra VII   97
   storytellers of *Iskandarnamah*   115
   war for partition of Alexander's empire   82
   Zoroastrian faith   110
Hephaestion   72, 80
Heraclitus   26
Hermeticists   8, 174
Hijrah of the Prophet Muhammad   179
al-Himma, Amira Dhat   181, 337
hippopotami of Cyprus   15
Hispaniola, island of   228
Hofmannsthal   293, 305
Holocaust   281, 293, 302
Holy Roman Empire   193
Homer   55, 60–1, 72–3, 96, 135, 180, 193
homosexuality   278
Horus, falcon-headed   32–3, 37, 41, 48, 57, 94, 141, 223, 318
*hu* (naming) of the Egyptians   25
human destiny   35
human pharaohs   41
Hunayn family   190
al Hurra, Sayyida   251
hybrid race of human-fairies   113
Hypatia   140–1

Iberian Peninsula   171, 198, 214, 255
Ibn Bajja   199
Ibn Gabirol   199
Ibn Hazm   199
Ibn Rushd   199–200, 219
Ibn Tufayl   199
*Iliad*   25, 59, 61–2, 72, 80
Indian sages   102–3
infinite *chaos* of reality   10
Isis   26–7, 32–3, 36–7
*Iskandarnamah*   113, 115

Islam/Islamic
  conquests  184
  converting to  247, 250, 256, 265
  era  184
  establishment of the Muslim
    faith  112
  intelligentsia/ intellectual
    revolution  188–9
  Islamic Middle Ages  113
  and Judaism  260
  mystical tradition  117
  notion of *Tawhid*  190
  principle of the absolute
    unity  191
  rise through the Crusades  8
  role of Christian translators  185
  rulers  171
  Sunni and Shia  268
  transcendence of God  191
Islamic Middle Ages  113
Italian Christian Democratic
    Party  303
Izutsu, Toshihiko  313

Janissaries  247, 251, 268
Jerome, Saint  125
Jesus Christ  169, 179, 192
Jew(ish)  49, 96, 143, 164, 184,
    186, 193, 197–8, 202,
    208–10, 216–17, 226–7, 290,
    303, 313
  assimilated Jewish families  293
  *conversos*  216
  exile in Mesopotamia  35
  *Marranos*  211
  mysticism  313
  prophets  112
  sages  112
  Temple in Jerusalem  134
  translators  96
Joseph, Franz  286–7
Judaism  163–4, 205, 210, 221,
    260, 291

Julian  129–30
  expedition to Mesopotamia  135
  micro-court  130
  military training  132
  reasons for his rebellion  134
  reform of education  134
  school of the Priscus of
    Thesprotia  131
  victory of Alamanni.  133
Jung, Carl Gustav  312

Kaaba in Mecca  110
Kabbalah  210, 212, 220
Kabbalists/Kabbalism  211–12, 220
Kafka, Franz  293, 306
Kakania  286
Khan, Genghis  172
Khidr
  adventure in the Land of
    Darkness  113
  Alexander's army  114
  archetype of the perfect master  117
  erratic behaviour  116
Khosrow I, Persian king  142
*Kitab Kamil as-sina'a at-tibbiya*  197
Komnene, Anna  193
Komnenos, Alexius I  193
*kosmopolites*  98
Kraus, Karl  293
Krauss  306
Kublai  172

Land of Darkness  113–14, 116
Land of Wonders  88–9, 113
Lao Tzu  173
Late Antiquity  7
  Bible  151
  Christ  151
  Christian monks  127
  divine Fullness (*Pleroma*)  155
  female body as Eve, Zoe and
    Sophia  162
  foreign divinities  138

Gnostics, God-haters   152
God-haters   151–3
God's Essence   146
hieroglyphic language   143
Julian (*see* Julian)
Pagan (*see* Pagans)
Platonic Academy in Athens   142
pure light and pure darkness
    principles   166
Sassanian kings   171–2
Latinised Bolshevism   274
Leo, Leonardo   210
Leo Africanus   256
Leo X, Pope   256
Lernet-Holenia   294, 297
libraries of Toledo   208
Libri-Bagnano, Giorgio   265
Livorno, city of   250
Locatelli, Pietro   259
*logos* (discourse) of the Greeks   25,
    101, 103, 149
Lord of Darkness   166–7
Lorenzo the Magnificent   222, 226–7
*Lullu*   34–5, 38, 54, 322
Luria's cosmic story   215

*maat*, the harmony of the cosmic
    order   41, 57–8
Maffeo   172–3
Magi   105
*Mahayana* Buddhism   109–10
Mahler, Gustav   293
Maimonides   199, 202–3
Manasseri, Benedetto   254
Manichaeism   164–5, 168, 172
    cosmology   165
    Manichaeans of Fuzhou   171
    Mani's death   171
    message of non-violent struggle
        against the darkness   172
    reform of the Aramaic
        alphabet   169
    religion   169

war against darkness.   168
Manicheans   6, 173
Al-Mansur, caliph   185
Marco Polo   172
Marduk   24, 28, 30–3
*Marranos* (converted Jews)   204, 211
materiality   2
Maximus   130, 132
Mecca, city of   184
Mediterranean
    Catholicism   65
    Christianity   63
    civilizations   5
    cosmologies   22
    eastern Mediterranean
        coast   183–4
    French   261
    gods   126, 137–8
    imagination   5–6, 9–10, 15, 23,
        48–50, 55, 58, 62, 65, 75,
        118, 144, 152, 163, 174, 189,
        201, 210, 213, 241, 266, 271,
        279, 282, 294, 301–2, 308,
        214, 323
    intellectuals   207, 209
    languages   251
    Late Ancient   154, 161
    Late Antiquity   153
    Modern   242, 255
    mythological Alexander   105
    mythologies   26
    new clandestine groups   262
    Pagans (*see* Pagans)
    pan-Mediterranean   199, 272
    people   5, 16, 93–4, 203
    piracy, golden age of   250–1, 258
    radical displacement   28
    revolutionaries   261–2
    slave trade   250, 253, 258
    Southern European and Ottoman
        shores   260
    stories about the birth of
        humanity   43

syncretism 166
translators of the Middle
    Ages 213, 219, 229
Mehmed II, Ottoman Sultan 246
Menander 105
metaphysics 3, 189
Middle Ages
    Abbasid dynasty 191
    Akritas, Digenis (see
        Akritas, Digenis)
    Almoravids 202
    Amira Dhat al-Himma (see al-
        Himma, Amira Dhat)
    Arabic translation of ancient Greek
        medical treatises 194
    Aristotle's apparition to al-
        Ma'mun 188
    Baghdad 187
    'barbarian' invaders 198
    Christian
        communities of *Dar al
            Islam* 192
        and Islamic philosophy 190
        kingdoms, expansion of 206
        translators 184, 187
    conversion or expulsion of non-
        Christian subjects 228
    Crusades 187, 195–6
    *dhimmi* Christian translators 187
    European Christians and the
        Muslims, encounter 196
    existence, concept of 211
    *falsafa*, philosophy. 190
    God as a Trinity 191
    Greek Galenic medicine 196
    Holy Roman Empire 193
    Ibn Rushd 200
    Islamic era 184
    Kabbalists/Kabbalism 213, 221
    Luria's cosmic story 215–16
    *Moriscos* and *Marranos* 204
    networks of intercontinental
        commerce 207

*Oration on the Dignity of the
    Human* 222
Ottoman (*see* Ottoman Empire)
Pagan knowledge via non-Muslim
    translators 190
practice of dissimulation 203
principle of unity within
    multiplicity 201
Reconquista 204
Spain, Christian kingdoms of 204
Syriac 184, 189
Umayyad caliphal dynasty 199
migrants, *see also* contemporary age
    cosmic 161
    economic 5, 320
    Greek 104
    illegal 320
    intuition of 3
    poetic inventions 7
    and time 2
    undocumented 322
*Mihna* 191
*milieu* of *Adelphi* 309
*Milinda Panha* (Buddhist text) 106
Miqlas 186
Mirandola, Giovanni Pico
    della 218, 228
Mithra 130, 166
Mithridates, Flavius 220
mob violence 140
modernity
    adventure of Alvar Nunez Cabeza
        de Vaca 235
    banking system 257
    Blood Christmas of Fiume 280
    corsairs 258
    counterculture 281
    cult of the nation 264
    early Modern Mediterranean 255
    Enlightenment 258
    equality 275
    exploitation 276
    Fiume's revolution 277

*Fortuna*, effect of 245
French Revolution 261, 264
healers 237, 238
Italian anarchists 264
Janissaries 268
Latinised Bolshevism 274
liberalism, monarchy and aristocracy, combination of 263
Mediterranean piracy 248
*Motifs a' la turca* (Turkish style) 260
Ottoman
  anti-Ottoman revolt of the Greeks 265
  Empire 257
  miniatures 260
  practice of the *devshirme* 247
pan-Mediterranean project 272
pirates 248
*qadar* 245
racism 253
rise of nationalism 266
scientific reorganization 271
sexual exploitation 249
shipbuilding techniques 255
slavery (*see* slavery)
states of the Maghreb 255
Sunni and Shia Islam 268
*taifa* of Algiers 201
women, active as corsairs 251
Muhammed 173
monastery
  Franciscan 254
  of Monte Cassino 196
Moncada, Guglielmo Raimondo 220
monotheism 48, 134, 163
  Akhenaten's 48
  of the Jewish people 49
  rise of 134
  trio of 163
*Moriscos* 204
Moro, Saint Benedetto il 254

Morselli, Guido 300–1
mortals 28, 36, 150, *see also* Bronze Age
Moses 116–17
muftis and ulamas 265
*Mundus Imaginalis* (Corbin) 314–15
Munqidh, Usama ibn 194
Musil, Robert 286
Muslim faith 112
mysticism 205, 223, 311, 313

Nagasena 105
Nag Hammadi, town of 153–4
Namatianus, Rutilius 122, 135
Nectanebo, Pharaoh 86–8, 93
Nephthys 26
Nephtys 26, 36
Nietzsche, Friedrich 303–4
Nile valley 92, 86
nominalism 300
Northern European Christianity 63
nostalgia 137, 250, 296–7, 301, 306, 312

Odysseus 25, 55
Ohrmazd 166, 174
Olympian gods 79, 104
Olympias 81, 87
*On Righteousness* (Epiphanes) 163
*On the Gods and the World* 137
*Oration on the Dignity of the Human* (Giovanni) 222,
Osiris 26–7, 32, 36–7, 41, 47–8, 56–7, 93, 126, 128, 174
Otto, Walter 313
Ottoman Empire 229, 231, 241, 253, 257–8, 263–5, 267, 269, *see also* modernity

Pagans 126, 137–8, 142, 152–3, 163, 217, 245, 307
  ancient Greek 189
  anti-pagan violence 141

    of antiquity   5
    of Late Antiquity   150
    Late Pagan intelligentsia   140
    libertine' Gnostics   162
    life in   144
    Manichaeism   164
    Mediterranean   142
    Mongols   172
    mythic stories and laws of
        mathematics   138
    mythological tropes   148
    Nag Hammadi   153
    Neoplatonism   132, 138
    Ohrmazd   166, 174
    pre-Christian   198
    prophets   127
    revolution   128–9
palace
    of Babylon   90, 99
    of Ctesiphon   186
Palermo, city of   254
Palladius of Galatia   102
Pandrosion   141
pan-Mediterranean project   199, 272
Papal intellectuals in Rome   225–6
papyri, Nag Hammadi   154
Pasolini, Pier Paolo   307–8
pastoral poetry   96
Patroclus   59, 80
Pergamon, city of   129
Pergolesi, Giovanni   259
Persepolis, city of   109
Perutz, Leo   293, 297, 305
Peter, Saint   256
Philip II   86
Piazzetta, Giovan Battista   260
Pico family   218, 228
pirates   98, 248, 250
    adventures   8, 271
    Christian   250
    economics   281–2
    states of the Barbary Coast   307
    Uscocchi   279

Pius II, Pope   246
Plato   10, 68, 189
Platonic Academy in Athens   82, 103, 142
Platonism   103, 132, 138
Pleroma   155–9
Plotinus   139, 152, 189
Poimandres   149
Popper, Karl   293
Porphyry   184, 189
Porpora, Nicola   259
*preces* (prayers)   38
predestination, idea of   61, 63
primal waters   20
Priscus of Thesprotia   131
prophet Elijah or the angel
        Samael   116
Pseudo-Dionysius the
        Areopagite   185
Ptolemaic dynasty   97
Ptolemaics   96–7
Ptolemy   92, 95, 189
    construction of a monumental
        temple to Serapis   93
    creation of the Museion and of its
        Library   95–6
    king of Egypt   90
    the Saviour   92
    secrecy   94
Ptolemy II Philadelphus   96
Pyrrho's teachings   103–4

Qaf   113
al-Qarnayn, Dhu   112
queer theory   225
Quran   62, 112, 115, 209, , 191, 201, 265

Ra, the god of the Sun   37, 40–2, 47
racism   253–4, 262
*The Radetzky March*   290
al-Rahman *al-Dakhil*, Abd   199
al-Rashid, caliph Harun   186–8

Rathenau, Walther  298
rationalism  191, 223
rational languages  10
Reconquista  204
Renaissance  6, 63, 216–17, 221–2, 228, 290
renegades  8, 244, 246, 251, 255, 263, 307
Revolutionary Dictatorship  282
revolutionary socialism  277
Rhodius, Apollonius  96
Ricci, Sebastiano  260
Roman 'Byzantine' Empire  178, 184
Romanesque style  207
Romanticism, age of  76
Rome, city of  120, 122
Roth, Joseph  285, 288, 290–3, 301, 305, 322
Roxelana, story of  247–8

Salerno, city of  196–7
Salutius, Saturninus Secundus  137–40
sarcophagus  27
Sassanian
   empire  186
   kings  171
Sassanid dynasty  165
Savonarola, Girolamo  227–8
   sermons  228
sceptics  103
Schnitzler, Arthur  293
Schoenberg, Arnold  293
Scholasticus, Socrates  141
Scholem, Gershom  313
Schuon, Frithjof  310–11
scientific racism  262
scorpion-men  50–1
second millennium BC to fourth century BC  67–8
*Sefirah*  212
Sekandar  74, 109, 111
*Sekandar gujastak*, 'Alexander the accursed'  109

Sephardi  214
*Septuaginta*  96
Serapis  93–4
Seth  26–8, 33, 36–7, 159–60
Seventeenth century to Twentieth century  283–4
*Shahnameh* (Ferdowsi)  110
shamanism, Turkish  268
Shapur I  170
*A Short Account of the Destruction of the Indies* (de las Casas)  240
Shu, the god of air  20, 23–4, 36, 41
Sixth century to Fifteenth century  177–8
Sixtus IV, Pope  220
slavery
   Black African slaves  253–4
   in the early Modern Mediterranean  255
   economy of  244
   memoir of  255
   ontologically slaves, status as  243
   slave trade  250, 253, 258
   transatlantic trade of enslaved African people  243
Socrates  141
Sophia  154–61
storytelling  84, 256
stupas  104–5
Sufism/Sufi  117, 199, 266, 310, 313
Süleyman, sultan  248
summit of *Eranos*  312
Sunni and Shia Islam  268
Svevo, Italo  304
syncretism  9, 95, 98, 140, 166, 202, 311

*taifa*  251–2
Taoism  172, 313
*Tawhid*, Islamic notion of  190
Tefnut, goddess of moisture and rain  20, 23, 36

temples
   Egyptian   77, 87, 92
   Hindu divinities   104
   sacrifices   125
Teresa of Avila, Saint   205
thaumaturge Rabbi, cult of   289
Theocritus   96
Theodorus, known as 'The Atheist'   97
Thoth, the Ibis-headed god of wisdom   142–3
*Thousand and One Night*   186
Tiamat   20–1, 24–5, 28, 31–2, 34
Tiepolo, Giovanni Battista   260
Tigris River   164, 185
Timbuktu, city of   255
Toledo, city of   206, 208
Toledo School of Translators   207–8
tomb of Achilles   73
totalitarianism   281, 299
town of Argentoratum   133
town of Ascona   312
town of Fiume   272–3
town of Medina   184
town of Mirandola   218
town of Nag Hammadi   153
transformations   7, 48, 106, 299
   existential   240
   of the grand narratives   96
   law of   246
   social   64
treatises of Porphyry   184
Tree of Knowledge   158
triad of Dionysus, Demeter and Zeus   93
Trieste, city of   304
Trismegistus, Hermes   144–50, 223
Tutankhamun   48

Ukrainian steppes   288
Umayyad caliphal dynasty   199, 201
Urban II, Pope   178, 192
Uruk, city of   44–6, 53–4

Uscocchi of Fiume   279
Utnapishtim, island of   38–40, 50–1

Valentinus   152
Vandals   198
Veracini, Francesco   259
*verbum* (word) of the Christians   25
Visigoths   120, 123–4, 198–9
Vivaldi, Antonio   259
von Hofmannsthal, Hugo   293, 306

Wahram I   170
Waters of Death   40, 50–1, 53
al-Wazzan, al-Hasan ibn Muhammad   193
Western barbarians   193–4
Western Roman Empire   7, 120, 127, 198
Wilde, Oscar   277
winemaking, art of   107
Wittgenstein, Ludwig   293
women
   active as corsairs   251
   dancing women in miniatures   260
   transexual, as strongest warriors   237
worshippers of the One   8
Wu Zeitan, Empress   172

Yaldabaoth   154, 156
*Yonas* (Ionians)   104

Ziyad, Tariq ibn   199
Zoe   157–9, 162
*Zohar*   210, 220
Zolla, Elemire   310–11
Zoroastrian holy scriptures   109
Zoroastrianism   73, 82, 109, 113, 117, 153, 164, 166, 170, 184, 222
Zurvan   166–7
Zweig, Stefan   293, 297, 305